HISTORIC
BRITAIN

**POCKET
GOOD
GUIDES**

GOOD · GUIDES ·

POCKET GOOD GUIDES HISTORIC BRITAIN

EDITED BY ALISDAIR AIRD
DEPUTY EDITOR FIONA STAPLEY
ASSOCIATE EDITORS: ELIZABETH ADLINGTON, KAREN FICK

EBURY PRESS

First published in Great Britain in 2003
Ebury Press
Random House
20 Vauxhall Bridge Road
London SW1 2SA

10 9 8 7 6 5 4 3 2 1

Random House Australia (Pty) Limited
20 Alfred Street, Milsons Point
Sydney
New South Wales 2061, Australia

Random House New Zealand Limited
18 Poland Road, Glenfield, Auckland 10
New Zealand

Random House South Africa (Pty) Limited
Endulini, 5A Jubilee Road
Parktown 2193
South Africa

Random House UK Limited Reg. No. 954009

www.randomhouse.co.uk

A CIP catalogue record for this book is available from the British Library

ISBN 0091889057

Papers used by Ebury Press are natural, recyclable products made from wood grown in sustainable forests

Typeset by Textype, Cambridge
Cover design by Nim Design
Front cover image © ImageBank
Printed and bound in Denmark by Nørhaven Paperback A/S, Viborg

Introduction

The best of Britain's great past

Responsible for a top-selling list of successes including the annual *Good Britain Guide* and *Good Pub Guide,* the Good Guides Team has now put together the very best of Britain's historic attractions. From a comprehensive database of up-to-date information, the team have painstakingly picked out the most enjoyable outings – whether you're looking to explore some of Britain's lesser-known gems for yourselves, wanting to keep a young family entertained for the day, or simply wondering where to take visitors.

As well as more traditional historic places from haunted castles to steam train rides and stunning stately homes, this book also includes a wealth of unexpected treasures. Reliable recommendations for handy places to eat are backed by over 45,000 recent confidential reports from readers and the team's own anonymous inspections.

From the 900 places to stay in the current *Good Britain Guide* we have hand-picked the cream of places with real historic appeal and distinction, from cosily heavy-beamed ancient inns to the oldest moated house in England, and Scotland's oldest inhabited castle. Naturally, such history doesn't come cheaply, so if you're not actually staying in these places you might want to pop in just for a coffee and a peek around.

To contact the Pocket Good Guides team,
please write to

Historic Britain
Freepost TN1 569
Wadhurst
E. Sussex
TN5 7BR

or check out
www.goodguides.co.uk

Contents

Using this book

The regions and the maps

We have split Great Britain into four regions (see Contents). Each region is covered in the double-page maps at the end of the book. Within each region, our recommended outings are numbered. These numbers are shown on the maps. The place names shown on the map are just to give you an idea of which cities the various outings are closest to.

Historic places to stay in

Each section ends with our recommendation of hotels, inns and other places to stay such as farmhouses, listed alphabetically by county then by town or village.

The price we show is the total for two people sharing a double or twin-bedded room with its own bathroom, for one night in high season. It includes full English breakfast (unless only continental is available, in which case we say so), VAT and any automatic service charge that we know about. So the price is the total price for a room for two people. We say if dinner is included in this. We also say if bedrooms do not have their own bathrooms.

An asterisk beside the price means that the establishment concerned assured us that that price would hold until the end of summer 2003. Many establishments were unable to give us this assurance; it would be prudent to allow for an increase of around 5% by then.

A few hotels will do a bargain break price at weekends even if you're staying for just one night. If so, that's the price we give, and we show this with a **w** beside the price. Many more hotels have very good value short break prices, especially out of season, if you stay a minimum of at least two nights; if you plan to stay in one area rather than tour around, it's well worth asking if there's a special price for short breaks when you book. Many more hotels than previously now offer short-notice bargains which don't appear on their tariffs if they are underbooked on a particular night, so as to fill their rooms even at a discount. So, especially if you are not booking in advance, ask what price they can quote you for that particular night.

Special events

Our web site, www.goodguides.co.uk, includes an easily searched calendar of several thousand special events, country-wide, often involving historic buildings and sometimes vivid reconstructions of historic events. All you need to do is pick a day, and you can see what's happening where. The web site also includes some detailed recommended day-out tours.

European Heritage Open Days are well worth knowing about. On these, many notable buildings which are normally closed will be open to the public. English National Heritage Weekend will be 13–14 September, and around 2,000 properties will be open ranging from intriguing follies to all sorts of official and office buildings, plus there are special events and guided walks. As we went to press individual details were undecided so for more information ring (020) 7930 0914 or look at their web site: www.civictrust.org.uk. The Welsh Civic Trust run open weekends through the three last weekends of September; ring (029) 20 484606 for details. The Scottish equivalent, Doors Open Days, takes in over 700 properties and will run most weekends in September; ring (0141) 221 1466. During London Open House Weekend, 20–21 September, there will be free admission to over 500 buildings; anything from City Hall to private residences. For more details write to London Open House, PO Box 25361, London, NW5 1GY, or call (020) 7267 2070.

Prices and other factual details

Information about opening times and so forth is for 2003. In a very few cases establishments were uncertain about these when the *Guide* went to press; if so, we say in the text. (And of course there's always the risk of changed plans and unexpected closures.) When we say 'cl Nov-Mar' we mean closed from the beginning of November to the end of March, inclusive; however, when we say 'cl Nov–Easter' we mean that the establishment reopens for Easter.

Where establishments were able to guarantee a price for 2003, we have marked this with an asterisk. In many cases establishments could not rule out an unscheduled price increase, and in these cases – ie, no asterisk against the price – it's probably prudent to allow for a small increase by the summer of 2003.

The heritage organisations

NT after price details means that the property is owned by the National Trust, and that for members of the Trust admission is free. There is a similar arrangement for properties owned by the National Trust for Scotland (NTS); the two Trusts have a reciprocal arrangement, so that members of one may visit the properties of the other free. Membership is therefore well worth while if you are likely to visit more than a very few properties in the year – quite apart from its benefit to the Trusts' valuable work. NT membership is £32.50 a year (£60 family membership); details from National Trust, PO Box 39, Bromley, Kent BR1 3XL, (020) 8315 1111. NTS membership is £32 (£53 family); details from National Trust for Scotland, 28 Charlotte Sq, Edinburgh EH2 4ET, (0131) 243 9300.

The Friends of Historic Houses Association has NT-style membership offering free entry to around 280 historic houses and gardens in private ownership throughout Britain. Membership is £28 a year (£40 for joint membership), so you only have to go to four or five houses and you've got your money back. Details from

Historic Houses Association, Heritage House, PO Box 21, Baldock, Herts SG7 5SH, (01462) 896688.

EH stands for English Heritage, HS for Historic Scotland, and Cadw for the organisation in charge of Welsh historic buildings. All three organisations have a similar membership scheme, giving free entry to those of their properties which charge for admission.

Disabled access

We always ask establishments if they can deal well with disabled people. We mention disabled access if a cautious view of their answers suggests that this is reasonable, though to be on the safe side anyone with a serious mobility problem would be well advised to ask ahead (many establishments tell us that this helps them to make any special arrangements needed). There may well be at least some access even when we or the establishment concerned have not felt it safe to make a blanket recommendation – again, well worth checking ahead. There are of course many places where we can't easily make this sort of assessment – particularly the less formal 'attractions' such as bird reserves, waterside walks, viewpoints. In such cases (which should be obvious from the context) the absence of any statement about disabled access doesn't mean that a visit is out of the question, it simply means we have no information about that aspect. We're always grateful to hear of readers' own experiences. An important incidental point: many places told us that they would give free admission to a wheelchair user and companion.

South-East England & The Midlands

Including Leicestershire, Rutland, Warwickshire and the West Midlands, Northamptonshire, Cambridgeshire, Norfolk, Suffolk, Essex, Hertfordshire, Bedfordshire, Buckinghamshire, Oxfordshire, Berkshire, Wiltshire, Isle of Wight, Hampshire, Surrey, Sussex, Kent, and London.

1. Civil War destruction — and Ivanhoe

Ashby-de-la-Zouch Castle (Ashby-de-la-Zouch) The Norman core and its 15th-c extension were largely destroyed in the Civil War, but the ruins are impressive (inc an underground passage, now illuminated), and the adjoining fields were the setting for Sir Walter Scott's *Ivanhoe*. Snacks, shop, limited disabled access; cl 24–26 Dec, 1 Jan, and Mon, Tues Nov–Mar; (01530) 413343; £3; EH. There's a little **museum** with local history displays (cl 1–2 and Oct–Easter (01530) 560090, free admission if you've been to the castle first, otherwise 50p), next to the Tourist Information Centre on North St. The Thirsty Millers (Mill Lane Mews) has fresh local food — and a reputed tunnel to the castle.

2. Where the Tudors won the Wars of the Roses

Bosworth Battlefield (Market Bosworth) Site of the deciding action in the War of the Roses, when Henry VII's 1485 victory over Richard III led to the Tudors' seizing the English throne. The visitor centre has explanatory films and exhibitions, as well as a detailed trail through the country park, following the sites of the fighting (now thought to be ever so slightly out). Meals, snacks, shop, disabled access; cl Mon–Sat Nov–Dec, all Jan–Feb, Mon–Fri in Mar; (01455) 290429; £3 entry, plus £1 for parking. The Royal Arms at nearby Sutton Cheney has good food. Market Bosworth village itself is interesting to walk through, and the Black Horse (by the Market Pl alms houses) has good value food.

3. Historic motorbikes and a grand old house

Stanford Hall and Motorcycle Museum (Swinford) 5,000 books line the library of this handsome 17th-c house, an elegant place that still keeps a cosy lived-in atmosphere. Highlights are the painted ceiling in the ballroom, the portraits that accompany the winding grand staircase, and a good costume collection. The excellent motorcycle museum (open pms most Suns and bank hol Mon; £1 extra) is in the grounds, which also have a lovely 14th-c church with splendid stained glass, walled rose garden, Sun craft centre, and a replica of the country's first successful flying machine – well, it flew, but crashed fatally. Snacks, shop, limited disabled access; open pm only wknds, bank hol Mon Easter–Sept; (01788) 860250; house and grounds £4.50, grounds only £2.50. The Chequers (Swinford High St) is useful for lunch.

4. What George Eliot had to live up to

Arbury Hall (Arbury, off B4102 just S of Nuneaton) Splendid-looking mansion, the original Elizabethan house elaborately spruced up in the 19th c to make it one of the best examples of the Gothic Revival style. The writer George Eliot was born on the estate, and her *Mr Gilfil's Love Story* describes some of the rooms – not unreasonably comparing the dining room to a cathedral. Some work by Wren in the stables, and the gardens are a pleasure. Snacks, shop, limited disabled access; open pm Sun and Mon of bank hol wknds Easter–Sept; (024) 763 82804; *£6.50, *£4.50 gardens only.

5. Intriguing tales in a moated manor

Baddesley Clinton House (Baddesley Clinton) Romantic 15th-c moated manor house, mostly unchanged since the 17th c. Interesting portraits, priest's holes, chapel and garden with pretty walks. The family history is intriguing. Meals, snacks, shop, some disabled access; cl am, and Mon (exc bank hols), Tues and mid-Dec to mid-Feb (house cl Nov–Dec too; shop and restaurant open till Christmas); (01564) 783294; £5.80 (timed ticket system); NT. The nearby **church** has a lovely E window, and the canalside Navigation at Lapworth and prettily set Cock Horse at Rowington do decent food.

6. Historic houses hidden in Birmingham – and Tolkien's watermill

Aston Hall (Aston, 2m NE of Birmingham centre) Strikingly grand Jacobean mansion with panelled long gallery, balustraded staircase and magnificent plaster friezes and ceilings. Snacks, shop, disabled access to ground floor; cl am, all Mon, and Nov–Apr; (0121) 327 0062; free (and more satisfying than a good many houses you'd have to pay for). A few minutes' walk away on Witton Lane, a **transport museum** in a former tram depot is usually open wknds and bank hols; snacks, shop, disabled access; (0121) 322 2298; £1.

Blakesley Hall (Blakesley Rd, Yardley, 6m E of centre) This timber-framed 16th/17th-c farmer's house, furnished according to an inventory of 1684, now has a new visitor centre (with a café and exhibitions), and a replanted 17th-c herb garden. Shop, disabled access to ground floor and garden; cl am, all day Mon and Nov–Mar; (0121) 464 2193; free.

Sarehole Mill (Hall Green, 3m SE of centre) Working 18th-c watermill, with displays explaining the milling process, and on Victorian farming; Tolkien often came here as a child. Cl am, Mon (exc bank hols) and Nov–Apr; (0121) 777 6612; free. Other local sites that influenced Tolkien are listed on a leaflet available at Tourist Information Centres, and a Tolkien Trail, following where the writer lived as a child, went to school, and might have dreamed up various characters, has been devised to catch interest generated by the *Lord of the Rings* films.

Selly Manor Museum (Maple Rd, A441 4m S) When the Cadbury family moved their factory out of the city centre in 1879, part of their plans for this new garden suburb involved uprooting timber-framed manor houses from elsewhere and re-erecting them here; two survive as this museum, with herb garden, crafts and various exhibitions. Shop, disabled access to ground floor only; cl Mon Apr–Sept, plus wknds in winter, and 2 wks at Christmas; (0121) 472 0199; £2.

Soho House (Soho Avenue, off A41 NW of centre) Elegant former home of Matthew Boulton, famous for his development of the steam engine with James Watt, and possibly the first centrally heated house in England since Roman times. Furnished in 18th-c style with Boulton-related displays. Snacks, shop, disabled access; cl am Sun, and all day Mon (exc bank hols); (0121) 554 9122; £3.

7. Black Country a century ago, come to life

Black Country Living Museum (Tipton Rd, 1m N of Dudley centre) Good value, well thought out, open-air museum (with much under cover), giving a good feel of how things used to be in the Black Country, the heavily industrialised and proudly individual areas in the W part of the Birmingham conurbation. It's an authentically reconstructed turn-of-the-century village, complete with cottages, chapel, chemist, baker, pub, and trips into limestone caverns (summer only) or even down a mine, as well as black and white comedies from Laurel and Hardy or Harold Lloyd in the old cinema, school lessons in the school room, and an old-fashioned working fairground just outside the village (extra charges for rides). Staff in period costumes illustrate traditional crafts and test-drive old vehicles, and there are plenty of extra activities for children during school holidays. Meals and snacks (and space for picnics), shop, mostly disabled access; cl Mon and Tues Nov–Feb, and several days over Christmas, best to phone; (0121) 557 9643; £8.25.

Not far off, the Dudley Canal Trust do **boat trips** along part of a unique network of canal tunnels and limestone mines. Trips Mar–Nov, and some days in Dec – best to ring for times; (01384) 236275; £3.35.

8. A welcoming and nicely uncommercialised historic house

Packwood House (Packwood, off A34) Friendly old house with origins as a 16th-c farmhouse, carefully restored and not at all commercialised; interesting panelling, furniture and needlework, and in the garden unusual yew trees clipped to represent the Sermon on the Mount; look out for the 18th-c bee boles built into the S face of the garden terrace wall. Snacks, shop, some disabled access; cl Mon (exc bank hols), Tues and Nov–Mar; (01564) 782024; £5.20, £2.60 garden only ; NT. The Boot at Lapworth (B4439) is a fairly handy canalside dining pub.

9. Shakespeare's town

Visitors who look at Stratford-upon-Avon just as a town can be disappointed, but if you have a grounding in Shakespeare's plays the interesting buildings seem that bit more interesting – and not so outnumbered by the workaday ones, the high-priced antiques shops and the gift shops. The gardens by the River Avon make a memorable setting for the Royal Shakespeare Theatre. If you're looking forward to a good production at the theatre that evening, or, better still, able to run through much of the verse in your head, then you'll love Stratford. But if you've always thought Shakespeare overrated, then you'll think the same about Stratford, too. The pub with the most thespian connections is the Mucky Duck (Southern Way); the Arden Hotel has the closest bar to the Memorial Theatre, with good snacks. Useful places for lunch include the quaint old Garrick (High St), Brasserie (Henley St), Vintner Wine Bar (Sheep St) and Slug & Lettuce (Guild St/Union St). Tea in the smart Shakespeare Hotel (Chapel St) is relaxing, and the White Swan Hotel (Rother St) has a pre-Shakespeare mural of Tobias, the angel and the fish. With lively recreations and lots of bizarre facts, **Falstaffs Experience** on Sheep St is well worth a visit; cl 25–26 Dec and 1 Jan; (01789) 298070; £3.50.

Holy Trinity church (Waterside) 15th-c, where Shakespeare was baptised and buried; cl Sun am and for other services; £1 to enter the chancel where the grave is.

New Place/Nash's House (Chapel St) Shakespeare died here in 1616; the house was destroyed in the 18th c, but the Elizabethan knot garden remains, and the adjacent house, former home of the writer's granddaughter, has a good collection of furniture and local history. Disabled access to ground floor and gardens only; cl 23–26 Dec; (01789) 292325; £3.50.

Royal Shakespeare Theatre (Waterside) Shakespeare's plays are of course still performed here by the Royal Shakespeare Company. You can book guided tours of the Royal Shakespeare Theatre and their other theatre, the Swan (usually at 1.30, 5.30, and after evening performances; best to phone as they quickly get booked up); the gallery has temporary exhibitions. Meals, snacks, shop, disabled access for plays but not tours; phone for opening times as they depend on performances; (01789) 403405; £2 for gallery, theatre tours £4. The RSC productions themselves are performed in repertory, so if you're in the area for a few days it's quite possible to see several. Advance booking is recommended – (01789) 403403 – though some tickets are kept back for each performance and sold on the day from 9.30am; don't leave it much later, they go pretty fast. A two-hour guided walk around Shakespeare's Stratford leaves the RSC Thurs, Sat and every day during the Easter hol, plus Sun July–Sept; (01789) 403405; £6.

Shakespeare's Birthplace (Henley St) Though there's no guarantee the playwright really was born here, there are interesting period features, and good interpretative displays. Shop, disabled access to ground floor; cl 23–26 Dec; (01789) 204016; £6.50. If you want to see all the Shakespearian houses it makes sense to buy a joint ticket; this costs £12, and covers this, New Place, Hall's Croft, and the Shottery and Wilmcote sites. You can also buy tickets covering just the three in-town sites for £8.50. A tour bus with commentary links the sites but costs another £7.50; (01789) 294466.

10. Britain's most lively castle

Warwick Castle (Castle Hill, Warwick) This lively place is one of the country's most splendid castles, with plenty for all ages, especially in summer; you can spend a happy day exploring every corner, though half a day is probably enough for most families. The influence of the Tussauds group, who own the site, shows in the flair for presentation, and of course the castle's waxwork inhabitants, done in careful and convincing life-size detail. Live castle-dwellers add to the fun: perhaps the jocular wandering rat-catcher, or an instructive bowman. The rooms are excellently preserved, and their fine furnishings and art well worth braving the crowds for; the armoury really kindles interest, instead of being a dry-as-dust collection. The marvellous grounds were designed by Capability Brown, and as well as the delightful gardens, have pleasant strolls along the banks of the River Avon; the views from the parklands are dramatic. They've recently restored the Mill and Engine House, which in Victorian times provided the castle with electricity. Good café, shop, disabled access to grounds only; cl 25 Dec; (0870) 442 2000; £13, £10.75 in winter.

The town itself is well worth a look around. Though many older buildings survived a major fire in 1694, today's centre is dominated by elegant Queen Anne rebuilding. Some of the oldest structures are to be found around Mill St, which is very attractive to stroll along; there are a good few antiques and other interesting shops. There is a Farmers' Market on the 3rd Fri of each month. The Tilted Wig (Market Pl – neat bedrooms too) and Zetland Arms (Church St) do good lunches; the Saxon Mill (Guy's Cliffe) is a prettily placed waterside family dining pub, and the Warwick Arms Hotel does good value teas.

11. Two contrasting gems on the edge of Wolverhampton

Moseley Old Hall (Featherstone, off A460/A449 4m N, just over Staffs border) Tudor house famed as a hiding place for Charles II after the Battle of Worcester. The façade has altered since, but the furnishings and atmosphere in its panelled rooms don't seem to have changed much, and there's a 17th-c knot garden. Readers particularly enjoy the guided tours. Teas, shop, limited disabled access; cl am, also Mon and Tues (exc bank hols), Thurs and Fri, and all Nov–late Mar (exc tours Sun 9 Nov to mid-Dec); (01902) 782808; £4.20; NT.

Wightwick Manor (just off A454, 3m W of centre) Only a century old, but beautifully and unusually designed by followers of William Morris, and a fine testimonial to the enduring qualities of his design principles. Flamboyant tiles, fittings, furnishings and glass, and lots of Pre-Raphaelite art. Also period garden with yew hedges and topiary. Snacks, shop, some disabled access; open pm Thurs, Sat and bank hol wknds Mar–Dec, garden also open Weds; (01902) 761108; £5.60, £2.50 garden only; NT. The Fieldhouse Inn is a useful food pub just below the car park.

12. The Spencer family home

Althorp The home of the Spencer family since 1508, remodelled several times, especially in the 17th and 18th c, with a splendid collection of furnishings and porcelain, paintings by Rubens, Van Dyck and Lely. The staff are particularly pleasant and helpful. It is of course the resting place of Diana, Princess of Wales. You can't see the grave itself (it's on an islet in the Oval Lake in a small arboretum just NE of the house), but you can view the lake, and the former stable block is now a museum/memorial filled with her personal possessions, favourite clothes inc bridal gown, and audio-visual displays. Snacks, shop, good disabled access in many parts; open daily July, Aug and Sept (cl 31 Aug) but advance booking recommended; (0870) 167 9000; £10.50. The attractive **church** is on the edge of the park; its graveyard has fine views. On the far side of the estate there's public access to a sandy-floored area of wildlife-filled pine woods and heathland known as Harlestone Firs, pleasant for walking. The village of Great Brington is charming, and the Fox & Hounds here has decent food, and lots of character.

13. A favourite manor house

Canons Ashby House (B4525, Canons Ashby) Exceptional little manor house, more northern-looking than Midlands, beautifully restored with Elizabethan wall paintings and glorious Jacobean plasterwork. The formal gardens have also been carefully restored over the last 20 years, and now closely reflect the layout of the early 18th c. A reasonably sized park has a hilltop 12th/14th-c priory church. Cottage garden tearoom, shop; open pm Sat–Weds Apr–Oct; (01327) 860044; £5.20; NT. The Royal Oak at Eydon is handy for lunch.

14. A pair of most eccentric buildings

Lyveden New Bield (nr Oundle, out towards Brigstock) This ruined Elizabethan garden lodge was abandoned in 1605 after the owner, Sir Thomas Tresham, died in debt. Intriguing and unusual, it was intended to celebrate the Passion of Christ, and is shaped like a Greek cross. The moated Elizabethan garden (thought to be one of Britain's oldest) now includes a young orchard which has been replanted with period varieties following the details of a letter written by Sir Thomas from prison. Snacks, shop; cl Mon (exc bank hols), and Tues; (01832) 205358; *£2.50; NT. It's a half-mile walk from the car park, but has disabled parking next to the house.

Triangular Lodge (1m W of Rushton) One of England's most unusual buildings, this 16th-c oddity was also designed and built by Sir Thomas, and lived in by his rabbit-breeder. Purposely intriguing and infuriating, it's covered in the symbolism of Tresham's Roman Catholic beliefs – notably three levels, three walls, three windows, three triangular gables and a three-sided chimney, to represent the Holy Trinity. Shop, limited disabled access; cl Nov–Mar; (01536) 710761; £1.95; EH. In the attractive village, opposite the cricket green, the Thornhill Arms has good value food inc OAP bargains.

15. Cambridge, power-house of medieval learning

Quieter than Oxford (which the colleges here were founded to escape), the centre of Cambridge is dominated by ancient and graceful university buildings, and you get a real sense of centuries of study. It still has the character of a small, old-fashioned market town; Cambridge's hi-tech light industry is kept firmly on the outskirts. Between the colleges and university buildings are numerous less imposing but attractive old buildings, often grouped together quite picturesquely. The architecture has a striking diversity (continuous development of the colleges means that most have much-loved or maligned modern blocks), though it isn't always shown off at its best, thanks to layers of muck and grime that rather spoil some of the libraries and faculty buildings. Happily, one of the most delightful parts of town, **The Backs**, where the river snakes through the colleges, always looks charming, with its delightful lawns, trees, college gardens, punts gliding past the weeping willows and grazing cattle opposite King's. Don't try to drive around town; there isn't really any parking, and apart from the pedestrianised centre there's a frustrating tangle of congested one-way streets. Head for one of the big out-of-town car parks and use the excellent park and ride system. If you don't plan to take a car at all, it's worth noting that the railway station is far from central, although there is a frequent bus service into the historic centre. For a first-time visit, the Tour Bus (about an hour) is a good introduction. Walking tours set off from the Tourist Information Centre (Wheeler St) four times a day in summer (£7.25 inc entrance to King's Chapel, last tour £6.25 inc entrance to St John's – best to book in advance; (01223) 457574). Cyclists will enjoy the towpaths here; nettle-free, and safe if you have children with you. Quite a few shops are that bit different and worth popping into. In term-time, there are countless events; any college notice-board will show what's on. West Road concert hall has outstanding acoustics, while a concert in one of the smaller college chapels can be a charmingly intimate experience.

The **colleges** look private, but you can usually wander into the courtyards (access limited at exam time, and expect to be charged by many during the summer). Be warned, though, college porters will get extremely agitated if you even look at the grass let alone accidentally step on it. Several of the dining halls and chapels are worth seeking out. The largest, finest and richest college is Trinity, where the imposing Great Court is usually open to the public, and the Wren Library (open wkdys 12–2pm) in Nevilles Court is definitely worth a visit. King's is probably the best known, with its magnificent chapel, and is pleasant to walk through. Gonville & Caius (pronounced 'keys') is small and slightly snooty, but very pretty. Queen's has a half-timbered courtyard and an eye-catchingly gaudy painted hall, as well as the famous Mathematical Bridge. Peterhouse is the oldest, founded in 1284; the buildings carry their years very gracefully, although these days its deer park is devoid of deer. Opposite, Pembroke's chapel is one of Wren's first buildings. St John's has the very photographed Bridge of Sighs. Jesus, a bit off the main beat, is huge and grandly impressive, and

Emmanuel has notable gardens. Clare and Trinity Hall are smaller yet charming colleges, next to each other by The Backs.

King's College Chapel The annual Festival of Nine Lessons and Carols has made the interior and something of the atmosphere familiar to most visitors, but you're still not fully prepared for the grandeur and scale of the fan-vaulted ceiling, or the miraculously preserved 16th-c stained glass. The overall effect is marred slightly by the unique dark oak screen added by Henry VIII, but the chapel's other famous feature – Rubens's *Adoration of the Magi* – is quite breathtaking. In term-time try to attend choral evensong (5.30pm Mon–Sat, Sun 10.30am and 3.30pm). Shop, disabled access; cl most of Sun during term-time, Advent, Easter Sun and 24 Dec–3 Jan – phone to check other times; (01223) 331212; £3.50.

Of the many churches here, it's worth noting **St Bene'ts**, one of the city's oldest, the popular **Holy Sepulchre** or Round Church (which has brass-rubbing), and **Great St Mary's** with its fine roof and good city views from the tower.

16. Oliver Cromwell's town

Ely is a busy little market town with good shops and some lovely old buildings; it well repays a leisurely stroll. A Passport to Ely ticket allows you to visit the cathedral, stained-glass museum and Oliver Cromwell's House, as well as an interesting museum in the old gaol (Market St), for £9. The Prince Albert (Silver St, nr cathedral) has a nice garden, and the Lamb (Brook St) is useful for lunch, too.

Ely Cathedral One of England's most striking, its distinctive towers dominating the skyline for miles; especially good views coming in on the Soham rd. Complete by the late 12th c, it was restored in a surprisingly sympathetic manner mainly in the mid-19th c. The façade, covered in blind arcading, is fantastic, but most remarkable perhaps is the Octagonal Tower, over 400 tons suspended in space without any visible means of support; it looks especially impressive from inside. The Lady Chapel has the widest medieval vault in the country, and the walls are carved with hundreds of tiny statues which were all brutally beheaded in the Reformation – look out for the controversial new life-sized statue of the Virgin Mary (some say it looks like the TV presenter Charlie Dimmock in a wet T-shirt). The splendid Norman nave seems even longer than it really is because it's so narrow. Also not to be missed are a couple of elaborately sculpted medieval doors. It's worth trying to catch the evensong here, 5.30pm daily exc Weds (Sun at 3.45pm). Meals, snacks, shop, disabled access; (01353) 667735; £4.

Oliver Cromwell's House (St Mary's St) Next to the unexpectedly grand Church of St Mary, this fine old house was the home of Oliver Cromwell and his family from 1636 until shortly before he became Lord Protector. Period furnished rooms, useful videos (one on the draining of the Fens), and information centre in the downstairs front room. Shop; usually cl 25–26 Dec, 1 Jan, best to check; (01353) 662062; £3.50.

17. Where prehistoric marsh people lived by a lake

Flag Fen Bronze Age Excavation (Fengate, 2m E of Peterborough) Fascinating and well organised prehistoric site. Remains of a wooden platform which crossed a shallow lake have been unearthed; from it Bronze Age settlers appear to have thrown all sorts of deliberately broken bronze objects as part of a ritual – some of the best finds (inc England's oldest wheel) are in the very good adjacent museum, and they've recently opened a new environmentally friendly Heritage Centre. In summer you should be able to watch archaeologists painstakingly uncovering more secrets, while reconstructed Bronze and Iron Age roundhouses help put the discoveries in context; peaceful lakeside walk and primitive breeds of sheep and pigs. Snacks, new shop, mostly disabled access; cl 24 Dec–2 Jan; (01733) 313414; £4.00, EH.

18. House and gardens full of treasures

Anglesey Abbey, Gardens and Lode Hill (Lode) All that remains of the original priory is a medieval undercroft, but the handsome 17th-c house has an engaging collection of clocks and eclectic range of furniture and paintings; it's definitely worth pausing at Constable's view of the Thames and the landscapes by Claude. The bookshelves in the library are made from Rennie's Waterloo Bridge. The lovely gardens were laid out from 1926 by the first Lord Fairhaven; a restored **watermill** still produces flour. Varied events and activities, inc highly regarded open-air theatre and jazz. Meals, snacks, shop, some disabled access; house open pm Weds–Sun and bank hols Apr–Oct, daily Jul–Aug (when it's open till 8 on Thurs), grounds open daily. Meals, shop and plant centre; (01223) 811200; *£6.40, *£4 grounds only (discount voucher not available on bank hols or special events days); NT. The Quy Mill at Stow cum Quy does enjoyable lunches.

19. Peterborough Cathedral

One of the most dramatic in the country, its extraordinary west front a medieval masterpiece, with a trio of huge arches. Despite the damage inflicted by Cromwell, the richly Romanesque interior has preserved its original fabric to a remarkable degree; especially worth a look are the elaborately vaulted retro-choir and the fine early 13th-c painted wooden nave ceiling; an exhibition in the north aisle tells more about its history. Till Easter 2003 there may be restricted access to some parts, while smoke damage from a fire in 2001 is made good. Meals, snacks, shop, some disabled access; cl 25–26 Dec and am Sun (except for services); (01733) 345064; donations.

The town around it has preserved much of its long history and fine old buildings, though it expanded hugely in the mid-1970s and is now a thriving industrial town (with a good pedestrianised shopping centre). Handily, a network of cycleways, footpaths and bridleways link tourist attractions and nature reserves with residential areas. Charters (by Town Bridge) is an enjoyable floating pub/restaurant in a converted barge.

Longthorpe Tower (Thorpe Rd, W of centre) 13th/14th-c fortified house with rare wall paintings (open pm wknds and bank hols Apr–Oct; £1.70, best to phone; EH.

St Margaret's church (Fletton) On the southern edge of Peterborough, this has some exceptionally fine little Anglo-Saxon sculptures.

20. Cambridgeshire farming life, in a Norman abbey

Denny Abbey & Farmland Museum (Waterbeach, off A10) 12th-c Benedictine abbey with some impressive Norman remains and a 14th-c nuns' refectory. The museum focuses on farming and the county's rural history, with reconstructions of a village shop, kitchen and dairy, and there's a 1940s cottage; various workshops and events. Snacks and picnic area, shop, disabled access (limited in the abbey and cottage), and they'll lend you a wheelchair; open pm Apr–Oct; (01223) 860489; £3.60; EH. The Travellers Rest at Chittering has decent food.

21. Lots to see and do on a great estate

Wimpole Hall and Home Farm (Wimpole, off A603) The varied attractions at this huge estate can easily fill most of a day. Children like the working stock farm best, its thatched and timbered buildings designed by Sir John Soane when it was at the forefront of agricultural innovation. A restored barn houses machinery and tools from those days, and there are plenty of farm animals (with younger ones to pet and feed) inc various rare breeds; separate play areas for older and younger children. The mainly 18th-c house is one of the most striking mansions in East Anglia. Behind its imposing and harmonious Georgian façade is a lovely trompe l'oeil chapel ceiling, and rooms by James Gibbs and Sir John Soane. Perfect for a relaxing stroll, the gardens are good for spring daffodils, and vegetables grow in the restored walled garden. Best of all perhaps are the 360 acres of parkland, home to the National Walnut Collection, and designed by several different notable landscapers inc Capability Brown and Repton; the remains of a medieval village are under the pasture. Good programme of concerts and events in the hall or grounds. Meals, snacks, shops, some disabled access (not to house). Hall open pm Tues–Thurs and wknds mid-Mar to early Nov, plus bank hol and Fri pm in Aug. Farm open same times plus mornings, wknds in winter, and Fri in July and Aug; (01223) 207257; £9.50 hall, farm and garden (£6.40 hall, £4.90 farm, £2.60 gardens); NT. The surrounding park is open all year, with walkers welcomed free of charge to the extensive paths and tracks through its farmland and woodland, past a folly and up to a surprisingly elevated ridge path. The handsome Hardwicke Arms has decent food.

22. Traditional brewing, and the birth of the National Trust

Elgoods Brewery Museum and Gardens (North Brink, Wisbech) Watch traditional brewing methods in practice at this handsome 200-year-old brewery on the banks of the River Nene. Behind, four acres of gardens include a hot-house, lake and lawns leading to a maze. Snacks, shop, disabled access to gardens only; usually open pm Weds–Fri, Sun and bank hols May–Sept, brewery tours 2pm; (01945) 583160; £6 brewery hall, £2.50 gardens only.

Peckover House (North Brink) Lovely early 18th-c house with rococo decoration, restored Victorian library, and a two-acre Victorian garden with a pond, herbaceous borders, rose gardens, summer houses and glasshouses – where orange trees are still fruiting after 300 years. Meals and snacks when house open, shop, disabled access in garden; house and garden open pm Weds, wknds and bank hol Mon (plus Thurs May–Aug), garden open pm Sat–Thurs Apr–end Oct; (01945) 583463; £4, £2.50 garden only; NT.

Octavia Hill Birthplace Museum (South Brink) Commemorating the life and work of lesser known Victorian housing reformer Octavia Hill, five rooms in this Georgian house document her influence in modern life (her vigorous public campaigns to save recreational open space led to the foundation of the National Trust). The highlight is probably the re-created slum dwelling of 1861, though there are also some interesting tales about Octavia's eccentric family (until she was 13 her father kept Jeremy Bentham's skeleton in the corner of one room). Open pm wknds, Weds and bank hol Mon end Mar–Oct, or by appointment; (01945) 476358; £2.

23. Two thousand years of village life

Lots of interesting historical things to see around the village of Cockley Cley (pronounced to rhyme with 'sly'). There's a **museum** in a 17th-c cottage, nature reserve, carriage collection, and 7th-c Saxon church, but most unusual is the **Iceni Village**, built as and where it was believed to have existed 2,000 years ago. Snacks, shop, disabled access; open Apr–Oct; (01760) 724588; £4 covers all attractions. The Twenty Churchwardens is good for lunch.

24. Norwich and its treasured past

Busy but civilised, the old centre has quite a concentration of attractive streets and buildings, with all sorts of surprises in the narrow streets and lanes that still follow its medieval layout. One such surprise is the **Forum**, a sleek horseshoe-shaped, glass-covered building between Bethel St and Theatre St; as well as one of Britain's most advanced public libraries, this has Origins, a good heritage centre with interactive displays on local history, several cafés, and a new Tourist Information Centre; cl 25 Dec; (01603) 727290; £4.95. Elm Hill is especially handsome, and there are plenty of antiques shops and so forth. Even the more commercial/industrial centre N of the River Wensum has fine patches (such as Colegate), and the main shopping areas are closed to traffic. Fortunately the visually disappointing university is hidden away out on the W edge, though in term-time its students do bring a good bit of life into the centre. Norwich is the home of Colmans Mustard, and the Mustard Shop (Royal Arcade) has some varieties you may not have come across before. There's a lively spring arts festival (first half of May). The ancient Adam & Eve (Bishopgate) is good for lunch, the Gardeners Arms (Timber Hill – also known as the Murderers) is interesting, and two pleasant riverside pubs are the Gibraltar Gardens (Heigham St) and Ribs of Beef (Wensum St).

Norwich Cathedral The modern city is firmly shut out by the great medieval gateways of the close. Basically Norman/ Romanesque, the church has some fine features from later periods – the flying buttresses for example, and the late 15th-c vaulted roof, spire and west window with Victorian glass. The Norman cloisters are the largest in the country, rebuilt after a serious riot between city and cathedral in 1272, and remarkable for the 400 bosses carved with scenes of medieval life; there are hundreds more in the cathedral itself (you can see close-up pictures of the ones on the roof on touch-screen computers). Meals, snacks and shop (not Sun), disabled access; (01603) 218321; suggested donation £3. Free guided tours leave the Welcome Desk at 10.45am and 2.15pm Mon–Sat Jun–Sept, with additional tours in July–Aug, but there's often someone available who will be happy to show you around; they have children's activities too. The extensive precincts make an awe-inspiring impression: medieval alleys and secluded gardens, with all sorts of varied buildings from the cottages of Hooks Walk through the finer houses in the Upper Close to the buildings of Norwich School. The best view of the cathedral is from the river by Pulls Ferry; it's not easy to see from other parts of the town.

Norwich Castle & Museum (Castle Meadow) This impressive four-square Norman fortress dominates the city from the hill. Built as a Royal palace, it now houses an art gallery and museum. As well as displays of art (with particular emphasis on the Norwich school), silverware (for which the town was famous), and ceramics (inc a huge collection of teapots), a gallery traces the history of Boudica and the Iceni–Roman conflict, while another has displays on Egyptian mummies; there are regular exhibitions from the Tate. Hands-on exhibits, interactives and a model give an idea what life was like in Norman times. Snacks, shop, disabled access, cl am Sun, and 23–26 Dec; (01603) 493625; *£4.70.

Assembly House (Theatre St) Across the road from the new library, this is one of the only so-called Assembly Houses that actually still houses assemblies. In its time it's been much more, too: founded as a hospice in 1248, it has served as a priests' college, family home, 18th-c cards house, girls' school and wartime camouflage school. Although the chapel was completely destroyed in 1548 and, more recently, a fire ravaged the building in 1995, all the 18th-c buildings have now been restored, and a brick-vaulted medieval cellar still lies beneath the restaurant. Meals, snacks, shop, disabled access; cl Sun; (01603) 626402; free.

Boat trips From the River Wensum you can clearly see how some of the city's older buildings were designed for water-borne traffic, rather than road transport.

25. Needlework by Mary, Queen of Scots – and much more

Oxburgh Hall (Oxborough) Henry VIII stayed in this pretty moated manor house in 1487, which shows hangings worked by Mary, Queen of Scots. Most of the house was thoroughly refurbished during Victorian times, but the gatehouse remains as an awe-inspiring example of 15th-c building work, 24 metres (80 ft) high. The garden has a colourfully restored French parterre, and there are pleasant woodland walks. Meals, snacks, shop, disabled access to ground floor only; cl Thurs and Fri, and early Nov–Mar, garden also open some wknds Mar, house cl am (exc bank hols), best to check; (01366) 328258; £5.50, £2.80 garden only; NT. The Bedingfeld Arms opposite has decent food.

26. The Royal Family's country home

Sandringham House (Sandringham) Many people come to this part of the county for its connection with the Royal Family. The house and 20,000-acre estate was bought by Queen Victoria for her son Edward in 1862, and has become famous as the family's Christmas residence; the 19th-c building is filled with their portraits and those of their continental counterparts, and has various gifts presented to the family over the years. Unlike at their other homes, you can see most of the rooms they actually use, so there's a much more intimate feel than you'd get at Windsor or Buckingham Palace, and the staff are particularly pleasant; expect queues though. The grounds and surrounding country park are lovely, with lakes, streamside flowers, handsome trees, sweeping lawns, and the colourful North Garden (the late Queen Mother's favourite); also nature trails, adventure playground, and the parish Church of St Mary Magdalene. Lovely rhododendrons in the woods May–Jun. Meals, snacks, shop, very good disabled access (a train runs between the grounds' entrance and the house); open Easter–Oct, exc during summer Royal visit (mid-July to early Aug); (01553) 772675; £6.50, £5.50 grounds and museum only. There's free access to **Sandringham Country Park** with its majestic trees and glades, a notable parkland walking area (readers recommend coming when the daffodils are in season). The Feathers towards Dersingham is useful for lunch.

27. Bury St Edmunds

This busy shopping town has a good deal of character, with quite a few attractive Georgian and earlier houses, and several antiques shops. The **cathedral** gained that status only in 1913; parts are 15th-c, but the hammer-beamed ceiling is 19th-c, and work on building the tower continues. The tiny nearby Nutshell (the Traverse, Abbeygate St) is as much a quaint piece of history as a pub, with lots of interest inside; the Queens Head (Churchgate St) has good food. Another fine old church, **St Mary's** (Crown St), contains the tomb of Mary Tudor. Walking tours usually leave the tourist information centre at 2.30 every day Jun–Sept; (01284) 764667; £2.50. The Linden Tree (Out Northgate St), Old Cannon (Cannon St) and Cupola House (Traverse) are other useful food places.

28. In Constable's footsteps

Bridge Cottage, Flatford (East Bergholt) 17th-c cottage nr the mill immortalised by Constable, with a good interpretative centre for his paintings. Good teas, shop, disabled access; cl Mon and Tues (exc May–Sept), wkdys Jan–Feb, and Christmas–New Year, limited opening times in winter so best to phone; (01206) 298260; free; NT. Guided walks through areas that inspired his work leave here several times a day Apr–Sept, but fill up quickly (£2). You can hire rowing boats for trips along the River Stour. The mill itself and its famous partner, **Willy Lott's Cottage**, are both owned by the NT and leased by them to the Field Studies Council. You can see inside only by taking part in one of their many courses, such as art and photography, or popular wildlife-watching wknds; (01206) 298283. The church with its uncompleted tower has a unique 16th-c timber-framed bell cage, and the Kings Head (with a haywain out in front) has good value food. From the village the walk along the water-meadows by the Stour is East Anglia's most famous walk – picturesque views immortalised by Constable, and well worth while. This ties in with the more elevated Essex Way to make a very worthwhile circular walk, from Dedham to Lawford church, then via Manningtree Station (extraordinarily good station buffet) to join the Stour itself.

29. Clare – a very special village

One of the area's finest timber-and-plaster villages, with a huge and beautiful **church**, the sketchy ruins of a **castle** on an Iron Age earthwork above the River Stour, some remains of a 13th-c Augustinian priory, and little modern intrusion; nature trails around the castle. There's a three-storey antiques warehouse (Maltings Lane); and the Bell and the Swan (which does not allow children) have decent food. The A1092 to Long Melford, with a back road on to Lavenham, links this trio of lovely villages, and passes Cavendish, also pretty, with an attractive medieval church, and good value food at the 16th-c Bull. The back roads N of here are also pleasant drives, with plenty of colour-washed old houses.

30. Enchanting Lavenham

One of the finest surviving examples of a small medieval town, this lovely little place has delightfully rickety-looking 14th- and 15th-c timbered buildings wherever you look; many now house tearooms or antiques shops. The old wool hall has been incorporated into the ancient timbered Swan Hotel, well worth a look despite its prices. Self-guided audio tours of the town are available from the pharmacy, 98 High St; (01787) 247284; £3. The A1141 through Monks Eleigh and then the B1115 to Hitcham, through Chelsworth (where the prettily set Peacock has enjoyable food), is an attractive drive.

   Guildhall (Market Pl) Picturesque 16th-c timbered building, at various stages in its life a town hall, prison, workhouse and wool store; its beamed interior has interesting local history displays. Disabled access to tearoom (cl Mon) and shop; cl Dec–Feb, plus Mon and Tues Mar–May and Oct–Nov; (01787) 247646; £3; NT. The Angel opposite is very good for lunch.

Little Hall (Market Pl) Delightful 14th-c house, attractively presented, showcasing the Gayer-Anderson collection of books, pictures and antiques, with a pleasant enclosed garden. Open pm Weds, Thurs, wknds and bank hols Easter–Oct; (01787) 247179; £1.50. There's a good wildlife art gallery nearby.

31. Long Melford – completing this trio of exceptional villages

A very nice old place to stroll around: the fine green and exceptionally long main Hall St are lined with buildings from various eras, many with lovely timbering. Lots are now antiques shops (not cheap, but interesting). The **church** of Holy Trinity is glorious, with ornate carvings and dozens of spectacular windows; very attractive when floodlit at night. The Bull Hotel, one of the finer old buildings here, does good light lunches; the Crown, Cock & Bell and George & Dragon are also useful for food.

Kentwell Hall Beautiful Tudor mansion with genuinely friendly lived-in feel, best during their enthusiastic re-creations of Elizabethan and 1940s life (several wknds Apr–Sept), when everything is done as closely as possible to the way it would have been done then – even the speech. It's surrounded by a broad carp-filled moat, and there's a rare breeds farm in the grounds. Meals, snacks and picnic area, shop, disabled access; house cl am, plus late Sept–mid-July (exc Sun Apr–Oct and Easter week); (01787) 310207; most re-creations cost around £9, though the Great Annual one is £12. On non-event days entry is £6.50, or £4.50 garden and farm only.

Melford Hall Turreted Tudor house mostly unchanged externally since Elizabeth I with hundreds of servants and courtiers stayed here in 1578; it also still has the original panelled banqueting hall. Fine collection of Chinese porcelain and Beatrix Potter memorabilia; the gardens have a Tudor banqueting house. Some disabled access; cl am, also Mon and Tues exc bank hols, wkdys Mar and Oct, and all Nov–Feb; (01787) 880286; £4.50; NT.

32. Remarkable and lively collection of historic buildings

Museum of East Anglian Life (Stowmarket; Iliffe Way, opposite Asda) Excellent 70-acre open-air museum. Children look at the reconstructed buildings with a genuine sense of astonishment, and even the 1950s domestic room settings seem prehistoric to fresher eyes. Most of the buildings have been removed from their original settings and rebuilt here; the oldest is a splendid 13th-c timber barn, now housing a collection of horse-drawn vehicles. Among the rest are an old schoolroom, a smithy, chapel, windpump, and a very pretty watermill. They're quite spread out, so a fair bit of walking is involved. Also wandering around are various traditional farm animals, and on some Suns they often have demonstrations of local crafts and skills like wood-turning and basket-making; their occasional event days with extra children's activities are usually around the spring and summer bank hols. There's a decent rustic-style adventure play area, and it's great for a picnic; dogs are welcome on a lead. They have a big fireworks display near Guy Fawkes night (1 Nov this year). Snacks, shop, disabled access; cl end Oct–Mar; (01449) 612229; £5.

33. England in the Dark Ages

Sutton Hoo is one of the most famous archaeological sites in the country. The 1939 discovery here of an Anglo-Saxon ship burial and burial ground of an early 7th-c ruler made historians completely reinterpret the Dark Ages. £5 million has recently been spent on improving access to the site and new visitor facilities. A modern-looking reinterpretation of an Anglo-Saxon Hall houses a permanent exhibition on the site's history, inc a full-size reconstruction of part of the ship, complete with replica treasures. Another houses changing exhibitions (which should run from Mar–Oct), with finds from the site on loan from the British Museum; also new restaurant, visitor centre and shop. Guided tours at wknds for an extra charge (they advise you to book). Excellent disabled access; facilities cl Nov–21 Mar exc wknds, also cl wkdys Mar–May and Oct exc half terms; (01394) 389700; *£4. The site is open every day throughout the year; £2.50 car parking when facilities are closed. A turn off the B1083 S takes you to the Ramsholt Arms at Ramsholt for lunch among waterside pinewoods, with quiet walks along the Deben estuary.

34. Renewable energy, 18th-c style

Tide Mill (Woodbridge) Restored 18th-c mill on busy quayside, its wheel usually working when tides allow. Schemes to use tidal power for sustainable energy make headlines as new thinking these days, but this mill was using the rise and fall of the tides as its source of power hundreds of years ago. Shop, disabled access to ground floor only; cl Oct–Apr exc wknds Oct and Apr; £1.50. The Wilford Bridge Hotel nearby at Melton is a good lunch stop – and well placed for river walks.

35. Bet you didn't know how fascinating gunpowder could be . . .

Royal Gunpowder Mills (Waltham Abbey; Beaulieu Drive, off A121) Though a visit to these former gunpowder works can be absorbing enough at any time (with plenty for anyone not particularly interested in military history), it's the excellent programme of weekend events that really makes it a good choice for families. And what's particularly impressive is that none of the ones we've seen have involved an extra charge. One weekend a month they have costumed re-enactments, with demonstrations of weapons, manoeuvres and skirmishes from periods as diverse as the reign of Charles II, World War II and the American Civil War. The following weekend they have what they call Igniting Ideas, a series of workshops where children aged 7–14 can make models of radios, telephones and the like to find out how they work. The next week is a bit more specialist, with slideshows and a lecture on a particular theme, then the next weekend they have family activities aimed at children between 4 and 12: trails, games and some sort of art or craft. In the summer holidays they generally have extra activities one day every week – in 2002 that was Wednesday, when children were admitted free, and could take part in free activities such as quizzes, mask-making and nature trails; they may do this on more days next year. Their website, www.royalgunpowdermills.com, has full details of the schedule. The works were established in the 17th c and acquired by the Crown in 1787; they had an international reputation because of their superior production methods, and in World War I 5,000 people were employed here. Many of the restored old buildings around the site are open, and there are good displays on the evolution of explosives and development of the mills, with a film, and a nice mix of traditional and hands-on exhibits, with costumes to try on, and cogs and wheels to turn. Changing displays (not all of which are open every day) might look at fireworks, or small arms. It's a massive site, and even on a non-event day you'll need two or three hours to make the most of the 175 acres of surrounding parkland. Part of this is now a nature reserve, well laid out with boardwalks, bridges and footpaths, and now home to the area's largest colony of herons, as well as muntjac deer and otters. For £1 extra, they usually have guided tractor trailer rides throughout the day. If you're planning to explore properly, comfortable walking shoes are a must. A tower on the edge of the woodland offers good views of the area, with a mural showing the sort of animals you might be able to see. No dogs (except guide dogs). Meals, snacks, shop, disabled access; open late Mar–Oct, plus special events round Christmas; (01992) 707370; £5.90 adults, £3.25 children 5–16. The family ticket, for two adults and up to three children, is good value at £17. The Lee Valley Park attractions can make this a fuller day out.

36. Colchester, capital of Roman Britain

Britain's oldest recorded town, Roman Britain's administrative centre. You can trace the Roman wall (the Hole in the Wall, Balkerne Gdns, is a decent pub built into the one surviving fragmentary gatehouse). The High St has handsome buildings, some extravagantly timbered, and plenty more historical buildings inc **St Botolph's**, the oldest Augustinian priory in the country. The good **Minories Art Gallery** at no 74, (01206) 577067, has recently been awarded a lottery grant; they plan to create a contemporary art space in the town, and work should start on the project this year. Town tours leave the Tourist Information Centre (Queen St) at 11am (Jun–Sept; £2.50), and they also do themed tours (6pm Sat; £3.50), with costumed guides. The Tudor Rose & Crown (East St) is good for lunch.

   Colchester Castle Museum (Castle Park, off High St) Great for families: they let you try on Roman togas and helmets, or touch 2,000-year-old pottery excavated nearby; also splendid collection of Roman relics from jewellery to military tombstones. The castle itself has the biggest Norman keep in Europe, and stands on the site of a colossal Roman temple (you can still see the vaults). They go to some lengths to bring grisly moments in its history to life: you can hear a dramatisation of one of the forced confessions of the suspect witches incarcerated here. For £1.20 extra a guided castle tour takes you up on the roof as well as to the vaults and chapel. Snacks, good shop, mostly disabled access (to castle museum but not to vaults or castle roof); cl 25–26 Dec and 1 Jan; (01206) 282939; £4.

37. The prettiest village in Essex

Finchingfield has an interesting variety of charming houses spread generously around a sloping green that dips to a stream and pond; just off stands a pristine-looking small windmill. The Tudor Red Lion, opposite the churchyard and 15th-c guildhall, has sensibly priced food. There's a pleasant easily followed path along the Finchingfield Brook to nearby Great Bardfield.

38. The dark side of very recent history

Secret Nuclear Bunker (Kelvedon Hatch, off A128) Who'd have thought that a three-storey Cold War underground complex lay beneath this innocuous 1950s bungalow? Knowledgeable tours take you through all parts of this clinically self-sufficient little world, and are done with real relish, so you can't help feeling relieved when you're back in the surrounding woodland. Audio tour, film shows (one showing what you needed to do in case of a nuclear bomb alert), wknd meals, snacks, shop; cl Mon–Weds Nov–Feb and 25 Dec, best to check; (01277) 364883; £5. The Black Horse in Pilgrims Hatch is a good handy dining pub.

39. An enjoyable look at Norman life

Mountfitchet Castle & 1066 Village (Stansted) Intriguing, an authentically reconstructed Norman castle and village, complete with thatched houses, and deer, sheep, goats and chickens wandering around between them. The castle includes a small chunk of the original, and dummies display gruesome tortures and punishments. Cheerful and enthusiastic rather than particularly sophisticated, it's a good introduction to life a thousand years ago, though you will need to visit on a dry day. Snacks (and space for picnics), shop, some disabled access; cl mid-Nov to mid-Mar; (01279) 813237; £5. A good **toy museum** under the same management is five mins' walk up the hill.

   Stansted Mountfitchet Windmill The nearby well preserved 18th-c windmill still has much of its original equipment (though isn't working). Shop; open pm first Sun of month Apr–Oct, and pm bank hol Sun and Mon; 50p.

40. Splendid Knebworth House, a family favourite

(Old Knebworth) With its turrets, domes and gargoyles, the house is magnificent; it was originally a straightforward Tudor mansion, but was spectacularly embellished by Victorian author Edward Bulwer-Lytton (best known today for coining the phrase 'the pen is mightier than the sword'), who wanted it to be a castle fit for the romantic characters in his novels. The same family have lived here for 500 years, so the guided tours take in rooms and exhibits from a variety of periods; highlights include the marvellous Jacobean great hall, an exhibition on the glory days of the Raj, and mementoes of former guests like Dickens and Churchill. A huge draw in themselves, the well restored gardens were designed by Lutyens, and include a herb garden laid out to plans by Gertrude

Jekyll, and a delightful rose garden. An intriguing pet cemetery has memorials dating back to the mid-19th c. Lots of special events such as craft fairs and even jousting. The 250-acre park also has lovely woodland walks, and a church with a nave and chancel dating back to the 12th c. This is one of very few historic estates that appeals to children just as much as it does to adults, thanks to its great adventure playground, big enough to keep most active boys and girls busy for quite some time. In addition to the usual wooden climbing equipment and so forth, there are quite a few exciting slides, including the fantastic monorail suspension slide (where you hang on to a rope and slide back down to the ground), and the twisting corkscrew. Younger children get their own enclosure, Fort Knebworth (you can just see it as you go past on the motorway). Best of all, as there's no extra charge for this area, you can keep coming back during your visit; you may find a vintage London bus runs you between the house and the playground. All the play equipment is outdoors, so it's not ideal in wet weather, when they may close some of the features. Children also enjoy the miniature railway (which has a nice little steam train on bank hols and event Sundays), and the Victorian maze, and with lots of space in the park for a picnic, to run around or kick a ball about, there's enough here to occupy families for a good lump of the day. Dogs allowed in the park on a lead. Meals, snacks, limited disabled access; open wknds Easter–Sept, and daily in July, Aug, and spring and summer school hols – house open only in the afternoons; (01438) 812661; an all-in ticket is £7 for adults (£6.50 children), with a family ticket (two adults, two children) not bad value at £23.50. A grounds-only ticket (which includes the play areas and gardens) is £5.50, or £19 for families.

41. Jacobean grandeur, and a model army

Hatfield House (Hatfield) A great Jacobean house built in 1611 on the site of a childhood home of Elizabeth I; the splendid State Rooms include portraits of that Queen, and even her gloves. Also the National Collection of Model Soldiers, with over 3,000 exhibits. The scented garden and knot garden contain plants that were typical in the 15th and 16th c. Alongside is an extensive park. Meals, snacks, shop, disabled access; open Easter Sat–Sept, house cl am, and sometimes during special events. Guided tours wkdys only; (01707) 287010; £7, £2 park only. The nearby church has a window by Burne-Jones, and the attractive village of Old Hatfield has a handsome old pub (the Eight Bells). Beyond is the extensive modern built-up area that has now taken the Hatfield name.

42. Lots to discover in St Albans

Though modern shops dominate your first impressions, corners of real antiquity are tucked away between and behind them. This was one of the most important Roman towns in northern Europe, and has some fine well excavated remains in peaceful surroundings. A stroll in search of other notable buildings (the Tourist Information Office in the Town Hall, Market Pl, has helpful guide maps) is rewarded by the surprisingly large number of decent pubs here. Down between the abbey gate and park, the Fighting Cocks is based on an ancient building which had some connection with the abbey, and its interesting layout includes the clearly discernible shape of a cockpit. In the quietly attractive largely Georgian St Michael's St, the Rose & Crown is very civilised, and the Six Bells is on the site of a Roman bath house, though not visibly so. The Cock (Hatfield Rd) is worth looking out for because of its bizarre history; its floors rest on thick foundations of human bones, probably dating from the second Battle of St Albans, in 1461.

Roman Theatre of Verulamium Most impressive; not large by the standards of some others in England (room for over 2,000), but taking into account its good state of preservation it's unique. Shop, limited disabled access; cl 25–26 Dec, 1 Jan; (01727) 835035; £1.50.

St Albans Cathedral Up on a mound above the Roman city, this has good views; its 11th-c reddish exterior uses bricks recycled from the Roman remains. Once the country's premier abbey, it suffered a little after the Reformation, and its fortunes didn't revive until Victorian times. It was touched up a lot then, but the majestic building does have many earlier features, inc 13th- and 14th-c wall paintings in the long nave, the Norman central tower, and some Saxon transept pillars. Meals, snacks, shop, disabled access; cl pm 25 Dec, and during services Sun am; cathedral free, around £1.50 for audio-visual show. The great 14th-c abbey gatehouse beyond leads down to a neat park, its lake and willow-edged stream packed with ducks.

Verulamium This was the name of the Roman city; its remains are down in the SW corner of town, past the cathedral and attractive park (coming from outside, most easily reached by the A4147 off the Hemel Hempstead exit from M1 junction 7). The place to start is the excellent Verulamium Museum (St Michael's) with its lively interpretation of everyday Roman life, as well as jewellery, wall paintings and domestic items found nearby. Shop, disabled access; cl am Sun, 24–26 Dec; (01727) 751810; £3.30. Unfortunately the best site outside is closed (we hope temporarily) because of vandals, but signs take you to a well preserved section of the Roman town wall.

43. A 200-year-old garden fantasy, and vintage flying machines

Old Warden is an attractive village, built deliberately quaintly in the 19th c. The village church has a number of European wood carvings, inc some from the private chapel of Henry VIII's wife, Anne of Cleves. The Hare & Hounds has imaginative food, and a play area in its nice garden.

Swiss Garden (Old Warden Park) Early 19th-c romantic wilderness garden, a nice place for a wander, with pretty vistas and colourful trees and shrubs. Meals, snacks, shop, disabled access; open Sun and bank hols Jan, Feb and Oct, plus pm Mar–Sept; (01767) 627666; £3.

Shuttleworth Collection (in the grounds of Shuttleworth Mansion) Nearly 40 working historic aeroplanes covering the early history of aviation, from 1909 Bleriot to 1942 Spitfire in purpose-built hangars on a classic grass aerodrome. Several exhibits are the only surviving examples of their type, and it's worth trying to go on one on the days when some of them are flown (usually the first Sun of the month and Sat evenings, May–Oct; best to phone). Meals, snacks, shop, disabled access; cl Christmas wk; (01767) 627288; £6. A triple ticket (not on special event days) includes with the Garden and the Collection an impressive lakeside birds of prey centre, with flying displays. There are pleasant picnic areas in the grounds.

44. Eye-catching grandeur in a magnificent stately home

Woburn Abbey is one of England's grandest stately homes – everything from the lovely English and French 18th-c furniture to the splendid range of silver seems to have the edge over most assemblages elsewhere, and the art collection, taking in sumptuous paintings by Rembrandt, Van Dyck and Gainsborough, is outstanding (where else can you see 21 Canalettos in just one room?). The 3,000 acres of surrounding parkland were landscaped by Humphrey Repton, and today are home to several varieties of deer. Swans, ducks and other waterfowl on the lake; pottery and huge antiques centre, as well as Woburn Safari Park. Meals, snacks, shop, disabled access (stairs to gold and silver vaults); open wknds Jan–Mar and Oct, daily Apr–Sept; (01525) 290666; £8.00. Readers recommend the attractive drive into the park through Froxfield, which has masses of rhododendrons in June.

45. A refuge for endangered historic buildings

Chiltern Open-Air Museum (Newland Park, Gorelands Lane, Chalfont St Giles) This collection of re-assembled historic buildings makes a relaxed, quietly instructive family trip out, free from queues, crowds, and overflowing car parks. The 30 or so buildings dotted around have been painstakingly dismantled and rebuilt here piece by piece to avoid demolition. That may not sound too exciting for children, but in fact a lot of effort is put into bringing the buildings and their heritage to life; you might come across historic cooking on an open hearth, or be able to join in brick- or candle-making (ring in advance for what's on when). During school holidays they have a whole range of hands-on activities and demonstrations designed with children in mind; it's especially lively then. And at any time the 45 acres of woods and parkland are a delight to explore; they happily encourage children to run around, and there's a decent children's playground. You can pick up themed guidesheets to the sculpture trail, environmental trail, and pretty woodland walk at the ticket office. The buildings themselves are fascinating: structures as diverse as an Iron Age house (its design based on excavations in the area), Victorian farmyard complete with animals, intriguing oddities like the 18th-c well head and Edwardian public convenience, and a 1940s prefab, with useful displays on their original use. You can explore the site in a couple of hours, but even when there's nothing special going on it's easy to spend a fair bit longer; the site is ideal for a picnic. One 19th-c barn is a centre of the Hawk and Owl Trust, and though they don't keep any captive birds, they run regular demonstrations and after-schools clubs, when you may be lucky enough to see some of the wild birds of prey that live in the grounds. As you'll spend most of your time outdoors, the museum isn't really a place to come in wet weather. Dogs are welcome on a lead. Snacks, picnic area, mostly disabled access; open Apr–Oct (and usually for events around Christmas); (01494) 87117; £5.50 adults, £3 children 5–16. A family ticket for two adults and two children is £15.

Milton's Cottage (Deanway, in the village) The writer brought his family to this timber-framed 16th-c cottage to escape the Plague in 1665, and while here completed *Paradise Lost* and began *Paradise Regained*. Displays of first editions, other rare books and memorabilia, and a charming cottage garden full of plants and flowers mentioned by Milton in his poetry. Shop, disabled access to ground floor; cl 1–2pm, all day Mon (exc bank hols), and Nov–Feb; (01494) 872313; £2.50. The nearby White Hart (Three Households) has decent food.

46. Where the Nazi codes were cracked

Bletchley Park (Bletchley; turn off B4034 at Eight Bells pub, then right into Wilton Ave) Victorian mansion featured in the Robert Harris novel *Enigma*, where 12,000 men and women worked cracking German codes during World War II. It now has a series of genuine and untouristy wartime exhibitions and displays. Some of the code-breaking bits are a little technical, but there's plenty more to see, inc a toy collection, landscaped grounds, wartime fire engines and military vehicles. Meals, snacks, shop, disabled access; usually open wknds and bank hols (plus wkdys for the guided tour at 2pm) Feb–Nov; (01908) 640404; £6. The Crooked Billet (Westbrook End, Newton Longville) has good food and wines.

47. Benjamin Disraeli and Rupert Brooke

Hughenden Manor (Hughenden) The home of Benjamin Disraeli until his death in 1881, this imposing house still has many of the ex-Prime Minister's books and other possessions, as well as related memorabilia, portraits of friends, and formal gardens; he's buried in the grounds. Meals, snacks, shop, some disabled access; open pm Weds–Sun and bank hols Apr–Oct, wknds only in March; surrounding woodlands open all year; special events and performances throughout the summer (01494) 755565; £4.50, £1.60 garden only, NT. The Red Lion at Great Kingshill does good fish lunches.

   Lacey Green Smockmill (Lacey Green, a few miles NW, off A4010) The oldest surviving smock mill in the country, and indeed the third-oldest windmill of any type, built around 1650. It's been well restored. Open pm Sun and bank hols May–Sept; (01844) 343560; *£1.00. The Pink & Lily nearby does good food – and has kept its little tap room much as Rupert Brooke enjoyed it. One poem he wrote here, about himself and a hiking friend, suggests quite a deal of liquid inspiration:

Never there came to the Pink
Two such men as we think
Never there came to the Lily
Two men quite so richly silly.

48. Vanity Fair

Claydon House (Middle Claydon) The wonderfully over-the-top rococo décor is the prime attraction of this mainly 18th-c house (featured in BBC's *Vanity Fair*) – quite a surprise given the classical simplicity of the exterior). Highlights are the carvings by Luke Lightfoot and the fantastic walls, ceilings and overmantels, though there are also portraits by Lely and Van Dyck, and mementoes of Florence Nightingale, a frequent guest. The original owner's tastes were considerably richer than his pockets, and his ambitious plans for the house eventually bankrupted him, though his family still live here. Meals, snacks, secondhand bookshop, disabled access to ground floor; open pm Sat–Weds Apr–Oct; (01296) 730349; £4.40; NT. The Old Thatched Inn over at Adstock has enjoyable food.

49. One of Britain's grandest landscape gardens

Stowe Landscape Gardens (Stowe) Stunning gardens stretching over 350 acres, first laid out between 1713 and 1725. Capability Brown was head gardener for ten years, and the monuments and temples that adorn the grounds are by the likes of James Gibb, Sir John Vanbrugh and William Kent. There's a continuing programme of restoration, and in recent years they've replanted thousands of new trees and shrubs. Several suitably grand events throughout the year, but at any time this is a spectacular place to visit, the scale of its artistry quite staggering. Meals, snacks, shop, disabled access (inc electric-powered cars at no extra charge); open Weds–Sun Mar–Dec; (01280) 822850; £4.80; NT. The house itself (a public school since 1923) is open pm daily (exc some wknds) during the Easter and summer hols (phone to check extra opening times (01280) 818000). You may feel it's outclassed by its surroundings, though it is very elegant from the outside; £3. The Wheatsheaf at Maids Moreton does good lunches, and the Queens Head at Chackmore is even handier.

50. Dark deeds in an interesting National Trust village

The whole village of **West Wycombe** was bought by the NT in 1929 when it was threatened with road-widening. It's still beleaguered by traffic, and you risk getting run over as you step back to admire the architecture along the village street – all the sites we mention are just off street. The busy and ancient George & Dragon is popular for lunch. A visit to the caves and village here can be easily combined with a walk into the beechwoods just N; the pretty village of Bradenham makes a good objective for longer circular walks.

West Wycombe Park 300 acres of beautifully laid-out parkland surround this splendid Palladian home of naughty 18th-c local squire Sir Francis Dashwood, parts of which are currently being restored. The magnificent rooms have a good collection of tapestries, furniture and paintings, and the Italianate painted ceilings are particularly notable. Disabled access to ground floor only, Braille guide; house and grounds open pm Sun–Thurs Jun–Aug, grounds also open pm Sun–Thurs Apr–May; (01494) 513569; £5, £2.60 grounds only; NT.

Hell Fire Caves Great fun, these spooky old caves were extended in the 1750s by Sir Francis to provide work for the unemployed. Legend has it that the Hell Fire Club he founded met in the tunnels for their drinking, whoring and sorcery. Once through the atmospheric Gothic entrance, the tunnels extend for about a third of a mile underground, and are filled with colourful models and tableaux. Underground café, shop; cl wkdys Nov–Feb; (01494) 533739; £3.75.

St Lawrence church On the site of an Iron Age fort, adapted by Sir Francis, and crowned with a golden ball so big (it can seat six people) that it too served as a meeting-place for the Hell Fire Club. The view from the top of the tower is impressive.

51. Blenheim Palace, a magnificently rewarding visit

Blenheim Palace (A44, Woodstock) Few stately homes can rival this extraordinary estate for its range of things to see, splendidly opulent grandeur, or just its sheer scale: the house itself covers 14 acres, and the grounds stretch for well over 2,000 (that's nearly four square miles). As well as being one of Britain's most impressive historic houses, it's also one of the best organised for visitors, which is just as well: thousands flock through the gates in summer, and most people stay all day. The land was given to the Duke of Marlborough by Queen Anne as a reward for his victory over the forces of Louis XIV; the Queen promised to pay for the house's construction, but, thanks to the politics of the court, the Duke eventually stumped up most of the cash himself. It's quite astonishingly grand: highlights include the sumptuous State Rooms, 56-metre (183-ft) Long Library, and elaborate ceiling in the Great Hall, along with plenty of luxurious furnishings and sculpture. You can walk around on your own, or half-hour guided tours leave every 5-10 minutes. The very extensive parkland, landscaped by Capability Brown, is no less majestic, though not stuffily so: you can picnic just about anywhere, saving you venturing into the slightly expensive restaurants. Various monuments and statues are dotted around the grounds, and the formal gardens are magnificent, particularly the water terraces and Italian garden. Included in the price are a miniature railway, and butterfly house with free-flying butterflies and other insects, but there's a small extra charge to cover the rest of the family activities: the Maze (a good big one, its design inspired by some of Grinling Gibbons's carvings in the palace), a model village based on Woodstock and its surroundings, and play areas with swings, ropes and slides. There's enough space to absorb the crowds (Sunday is busiest, while Wednesday is popular with overseas students), but you'll find the house usually gets quieter after about 3pm. And you can avoid queuing for tickets by arriving early: though most parts are closed till 10.30am, the gates and ticket office open at 9. Churchill was born here in 1874, and there's a straightforward exhibition on his life. You can hire rowing boats or, with notice, arrange coarse fishing on the lake. Dogs on a lead are welcome in the park, which is just as pleasant out of season, though the house is closed then, and there isn't so much for families. Meals and snacks (three different restaurants), several shops and plant centre, some disabled access; house and most attractions open mid-Mar to Oct, park open all year; (01993) 811325; a full ticket is £10 adults (£5 children 5–15), with an extra £1.50 (£1 children) for the maze, play areas and model village. Entry to just the park is £6.50 a carload – or £2 (£1 children) for pedestrians. For a brief taste of the estate, a public right of way runs through it, with pleasant walks (for example from the attractive village of Combe).

Woodstock outside the gates is a civilised and prosperous small town, with good antiques shops and fine stone buildings. The Black Prince (riverside garden), Star (food all day) and grander Feathers Hotel are all good. The graveyard of nearby Bladon church, where Churchill is buried, has views over Blenheim Park.

52. From 18th-c taste to William Morris

Buscot Park (A417, Buscot) What makes this 18th-c house really special is the amazing collection of art and furnishings amassed by its owners; paintings by Reynolds, Gainsborough, Rembrandt,

Murillo and several of the Pre-Raphaelites (inc a splendid series by Burne-Jones), with some more recent pictures too. The attractive grounds have formal water gardens and a walled kitchen garden, and perhaps pick-your-own in summer. Teas (when house is open); open pm Weds–Fri and bank hols (plus pm Mon and Tues garden only) and pms every 2nd and 4th wknd in the month Apr–Sept (plus 3rd wknd in Apr, and 1st wknd in May and Jul), best to check; (01367) 240786; £5, £4 grounds only; NT. The Thames-side Trout (A417 towards Lechlade) is popular for lunch.

Kelmscott Manor (along the Thames at Kelmscott) The summer home of William Morris until his death in 1896, now with one of the best assemblages of Morris memorabilia, standing out all the more for its domestic setting. Works by other Pre-Raphaelite artists include splendid paintings by Rossetti, who initially shared the lease. Meals, snacks, shop, disabled access; open Weds (exc 1–2 pm), and pm third Sat of month Apr–Sept, plus pm first and third Sat July–Aug; (01367) 252486; £7. There's a nice Thames-side walk of 1½m E to the Swan at Radcot Bridge.

53. Elizabethan beauty by the Thames

Mapledurham House (Mapledurham) Impressive Elizabethan mansion in pretty Thames-side parkland, with paintings and family portraits, great oak staircases, and moulded Elizabethan ceilings. In the grounds is the last **watermill** on the Thames to use wooden machinery; dating from 1423, it still produces flour, bran and semolina. Also riverside walks and island with picnic area. Teas, shop, disabled access to ground floor only; open pm wknds and bank hols Easter–Sept; (0118) 972 3350; £6 house and watermill, £4 house only, £3 watermill only. You can stay in one of the lovely cottages on the estate (some thatched).

54. The best of historic Oxford

On first impression Oxford can seem quite a frenetic city: the ancient university buildings with their medieval lanes and scholarly corners are surrounded by a bustling largely industrialised town, with a formidable amount of traffic. Some of the major city centre thoroughfares have been pedestrianised in a bid to relieve the nightmarish congestion problems (you can't drive your car through the centre btween 7am and 6.30pm). If you don't come by train or coach, it's certainly a good idea to leave your car at one of the Park and Rides around the ring road; £1 parking, and £1.60 return on the buses. Guided walks around the city (£6.50) usually leave from the Tourist Information Centre (Old School pub, Gloucester Green) at 11 and 2 daily (more often in the summer), exc 25–26 Dec. For first-time visitors, hop-on-and-off **tour buses** take in all the best sites and last about an hour (£8.50). Many of the city's oldest or most interesting buildings are grouped around the Bodleian Library, the Sheldonian Theatre and the splendid domed Radcliffe Camera (also a library). This partly cobbled central university area is most attractive, but does sometimes overfill with visitors. In the streets and lanes leading off, the honey-coloured stone makes for a harmony that unites different styles and different centuries. There are a few good shops dotted about; Blackwells is the main bookseller, with several branches around the Broad St area, and the Tourist Information Centre on Broad St has a leaflet on the best antiquarian book shops here.

Most **colleges** allow visitors into at least some of their quads, and do have a wonderful timeless appeal. One of the few they failed to impress was William Cobbett, who wrote in his *Rural Rides* that he 'could not help reflecting on the drones that they contain, and the wasps they send forth'. Newcomers are often surprised to discover that the colleges are all separate bodies with little in common, each firmly maintaining its own dons, rules and traditions; the university itself is little more than an administrative umbrella. Several now charge admission, notably Christ Church, New, Magdalen, Trinity and Brasenose. Access may be more limited in term-time. A few may let you in only with a guide; ideally though, it's worth trying to explore at your own pace away from the crowds – afternoons are best, with more colleges open then. Besides colleges we pick out individually, more are tucked down some of the town's prettiest streets, such as charming Exeter, Jesus and Lincoln down Turl St, and Corpus Christi and Oriel around Merton Lane and Oriel Sq. This last college has a very attractive and unusual entrance to its dining hall. Trinity on Broad St though not large is very grand. Around Radcliffe Sq Brasenose is quaint (and has good views of the surrounding skyline from its quads), and Hertford has its Bridge of Sighs over New College St, in itself worth exploring for some more unusual and less busy views and a good look at the gargoyles on the backs of some of the buildings. Worcester has particularly nice gardens, and many of the other colleges' private Fellows' gardens not usually open to visitors can be seen under the National Gardens Scheme.

Christ Church (St Aldates) The best-known college, a magnificently stately place begun by Cardinal Wolsey in the 16th c, but soon taken over by Henry VIII. The main entrance is through Tom Tower, designed by Christopher Wren and named after its famous bell that rings out 101 times at nine o'clock every night – in less liberal times the hour when students were due back in their rooms. The hall is worth a look, with its remarkable hammerbeam roof, paintings of alumni and benefactors by all the most expensive portrait-painters of the period, and the long tables laid out with silver for meals. The elaborate little cathedral is England's smallest, and doubles as the college chapel. It has some excellent stained glass by Burne-Jones, fantastic pendent vaulting in the choir, and some of the original Norman priory work. Entry into the college may be limited on Sun. A hidden treasure unnoticed by most visitors is the college's Picture Gallery (Canterbury Quad), with an important collection of Old Master paintings and drawings, and various temporary exhibitions. Shop; cl 1–2pm, am Sun, and end Mar; guided tours by arrangement; (01865) 276172; £2 (free on Mons).

Keble College (Parks Rd) Brightly Victorian and very red-brick, with perhaps the most famous Pre-Raphaelite painting of all, Holman Hunt's *Light of the World*, in its chapel.

Magdalen College (High St) The most beautiful college, its tower a dramatic sight for visitors entering the city from the S. The quads and cloisters are very pleasant to stroll through, but the chief attraction is the deer park, an unexpected haven in the heart of the bustling city. There's a circular path around this meadow (you can't go in) called Addison's Walk; in spring it's a mass of snowdrops and daffodils, then has hundreds of thousands of fritillaries in later spring, and after that the deer. Over a small bridge is the Fellows' Garden with a small ornamental lake – a very peaceful, sheltered spot.

Bodleian Library (Broad St) One of the oldest in Europe, its splendidly grand quad dominated by the Tower of the Five Orders. Most of it is closed to the public, but guided tours take in the beautifully vaulted 15th-c Divinity School, which shows some of the library's treasures inc the Chancellor's Court, Convocation House and Duke Humfrey's Library, the oldest reading room. (Tours usually leave at 10.30, 11.30, 2 and 3 mid-Mar–Oct; 2 and 3 only wkdys in winter); (01865) 277224; no under-14s; excellent shop, limited disabled access (with notice); cl Sat pm and all Sun; £3.50. Altogether the library houses over 6,500,000 books, going down six storeys under the centre of the city.

Sheldonian Theatre (Broad St) A grand classical building, with a lovely painted ceiling. In its time it's been used for parliaments, and nowadays university ceremonies are held here; you may see gowned students heading for these on some wknds, though the theatre is closed to the public then. Nearby, the Kings Arms is a famous university haunt.

St Michael at the North Gate (Cornmarket St) Oxford's oldest building, this Saxon church has displays of silver, clocks and bells; great views from the tower. Shop, disabled access to church; cl Sun am, 25 Dec and Good Fri; £1.50.

55. Classic 18th-c gardens around a delightful house

Rousham House (Rousham) Nicely unspoilt 17th-c house embellished by court artists and architects, and remodelled in the 18th c by William Kent to give the external appearance of a Gothic Tudor mansion. It still has Civil War shooting holes in the door. Excellent 18th-c classically landscaped garden with buildings, cascades, statues and vistas in 30 acres of hanging woods above the River Cherwell, and walled flower and vegetable gardens. No children under 15. Some disabled access to grounds; house open pm Weds, Sun and bank hols Apr–Sept, gardens open daily all year; (01869) 347110; £3 house, £3 garden. There's a 12th-c church, and the Bell in a pretty square of thatched cottages at Lower Heyford has enjoyable food, and canal walks nearby.

56. Iron Age traditions on the edge of the Downs

Uffington Castle (Uffington) High above the village, this Iron Age fort covered eight acres but had only one gateway; great views over the vale below. On the hillside a 115-metre (375-ft) **white horse** carved into the chalk is now thought to be around 3,000 years old; it's a striking design, very Celtic (local hunt supporters who in 2002 added a huntsman and hounds used biodegradable colours which have quickly faded). If you stand in the centre of the eye and turn around three times with your eyes closed, any reasonable wish will be granted. This is one good setting-off point for the Ridgeway. The flat-topped little hill below is said to be where George killed the dragon. A bit over a mile E, off the B4507, the turning off up towards the downs opposite the Kingston Lisle road almost immediately passes a cottage on the left which has outside a huge pitted flint rock, locally known as the blowing stone: if you blow in the right hole and in the right way you can produce a splendid deep blast of sound. A popular nearby pub/restaurant is named after it.

Wayland's Smithy Midway along the Ridgeway between the Uffington White Horse and the B4000 above pretty thatched Ashbury (where the Rose & Crown is ideally placed for walkers), this was even in Saxon times reputed to be the forge of a magic blacksmith, who would invisibly shoe your horse overnight if you left it there with a silver coin – and exact horrid penalties if you tried to slip by without paying. It's an impressive place, alone on the downs, an excavated neolithic burial chamber rather over 5,000 years old, made with massive sarsen stones each weighing several tons; free.

57. Royal Windsor

Well worth an expedition (though a tremendous magnet for visitors), **Windsor** is dominated by its famous castle, the largest inhabited one in the world. The little streets to the S have many pretty timber-framed or Georgian-fronted houses and shops. The High St, by contrast, is wide and busy. You can walk by the Thames (for example, from Home Park, beyond the station); or across to Eton. The good evening racecourse is best approached by boat –

shuttle services run from Barry Avenue Promenade; (01753) 865234 for race dates. The Two Brewers in pretty Park St is a good food pub, and in the quieter nearby Thames-side village of Old Windsor the Union has good bar food.

Windsor Castle A mass of towers, ramparts and pinnacles, this awesome palace is the official residence of the monarch, though it's changed considerably since William the Conqueror built his original wooden fort here. Henry II constructed the first stone buildings, inc the familiar Round Tower, but for many the highlight is the magnificent **St George's Chapel**, a splendid example of Perpendicular architecture, with intricate carvings on the choir stalls, fine ironwork, an amazing fan-vaulted ceiling, and the arms and pennants of every knight entered into the Order of the Knights of the Garter. This is closed Sun and occasional other dates, often at short notice – best to check on the number below. The **State Apartments**, used for ceremonial and official occasions, are decorated with carvings by Grinling Gibbons and ceilings by Verrio, and full of superb paintings from the Royal collection (inc notable Rembrandts and Van Dycks), porcelain, armour, and exceptionally fine furniture. This part may be closed when the Queen is in residence. Although everything is well signed, readers recommend buying a guidebook, and if you visit in one of their quieter periods the helpful staff take time to point out details you might not notice. Entrance to **Queen Mary's Doll's House**, an exquisite creation by Edwin Lutyens, built for Queen Mary in the 1920s, with perfectly scaled furniture and decoration, is also included in the general admission price. The approach to the castle has recently been enhanced by the creation of a new Royal garden to celebrate the Golden Jubilee. It's designed to complement the castle rather than be an attraction in its own right, and when there are enough people they take groups round – ask at reception when you arrive. Shop, (a new farm shop too), disabled access (exc Doll's House); occasionally closed for official events, so best to phone (020) 7321 2233; £11.50. The guards generally change daily Mon–Sat (alternate days only in winter), at 11 o'clock – again, phone for exact dates.

Eton, so close to Windsor it's pretty much part of it, has a restrained and decorous High St with a mix of interesting old shops and houses. Its glory is **Eton College**, the famous public school, whose stately Tudor and later buildings in graceful precincts are marvellously calm during the school's holidays. The Chapel is an outstanding late Gothic building in the Perpendicular style, and a museum tells the story of the school from its foundation in 1440 up to the present, with fascinating videos on life for pupils here today (inc Prince Harry). Bizarre information is turned up by the various historical documents – in the 17th c, for example, smoking was compulsory for all scholars as a protection against bubonic plague. The Brewhouse Gallery has some good changing exhibitions, and next door there's a collection of Egyptian antiquities. Shop, some disabled access; cl am in term-time, and Oct–Mar; (01753) 671177; from £3.50 (guided tours from £4.50). The college runs residential courses in summer on a wide range of topics. Gilbeys (High St) does good imaginative light meals.

58. A classical mansion and wild flower meadow

Basildon Park (Lower Basildon, off A329 NW of Pangbourne) Elegant Bath stone Palladian mansion, with delicate plasterwork on the ceilings and walls, unusual Octagon room, and intriguing collection of rare sea shells in the Shell Room. Outside are old-fashioned roses, a pretty terrace, and pleasant grounds beyond. The classical frontage is particularly impressive. Summer teas, light lunches, shop, disabled access to garden and grounds only; open pm Weds–Sun and bank hols, Apr–Oct; (0118) 984 3040; £4.40,

£2 grounds only; NT.

   Pangbourne Meadow (Pangbourne) Traditional meadow by the Thames, scythed after flowering and seeding to preserve its wide range of wild flowers. The attractive riverside Swan has food all day, and the village has some decent shops; it was the home of Kenneth Grahame, who perhaps found inspiration around here for *The Wind in the Willows*.

59. When steam was king

Steam (Kemble Drive, Swindon, next to the well signed Great Western Designer Outlet Centre) In the former works of the Great Western Railway, this brings to life the sights and sounds of the railway age, when 12,000 people used to work here to produce everything needed to keep it running. It has good reconstructions and up-to-date display techniques to get you really involved – as well, of course, as several of the locomotives built here. Particularly good fun is a simulator that re-creates the experience of riding on a steam train footplate, even down to the hisses, whistles, jolts and swaying as the countryside rushes by. There's as much emphasis on the people who worked and travelled on the railways as there is on the trains, and there may be lively talks by people who used to work here. Children have plenty to keep them amused, from the various touch-screen games and hands-on activities to a track layout where younger visitors have fun shunting the trucks. Other displays focus on Isambard Kingdom Brunel and the GWR's days as the 'holiday line', and you can watch restoration work on old engines and carriages. This has much wider appeal than many steam-themed collections, and all ages seem to get something out of it. There's a good programme of special events, particularly in the summer holidays, when actors re-create anything from real-life railway dramas to Victorian music-hall. Meals, snacks, shop, disabled access; cl 25–26 Dec, 1 Jan; (01793) 466646; £5.95 (£3.80 children). A family ticket, for two adults and two children, is £14.70. There are lots of bargains at the outlet shopping centre next door, and decent food in the Old Pattern Shop.

60. Stonehenge

(off A344) One of the most famous prehistoric monuments in the world; everyone knows what it looks like, and how they got the stones here has been pretty much sorted out (the larger ones local, the smaller ones all the way from South Wales), but nobody's really sure exactly what Stonehenge (with its careful astronomical alignments) was for. In the interests of conservation, you can't normally go right up to the stones (see below), but you can get pretty close, and the fact that people are kept back means that your photos won't be cluttered by the crowds. The best views are very early in the morning from the track from Larkhill, on the other side of the A344, or on a cold clear winter evening looking W past the monument towards the sunset; the ancient stones look very impressive silhouetted against the sky. Even in the crowded light of day the place never quite loses its power to inspire awe. The car park area and busy main roads nearby detract a little, but great improvements here and to the visitor centre are in the pipeline, and may be completed by 2006. Snacks, shop, disabled access (and a Braille guide); (01980) 624715 – but beware, it's a very long-winded answering machine; cl 24–26 Dec, 1 Jan; £4.40 (inc very good audio tour); EH. Private access outside normal hours (not Oct–Nov) can be booked in advance, phone (01980) 626267 (£10 for an hour visit); or Astral Travels (0870) 902 0908 organise day trips from London (£52). Good walks from here around associated ancient monuments (leaflet available in the car park). There's good pick-your-own fruit late Jun–late July at Rolleston Manor Farm on the B3086 NW.

Woodhenge The scant traces of another prehistoric monument further E which consisted of six rings of timber posts in a ditch; the positions are now marked by concrete posts, and a cairn marks the central spot where the tomb of a little girl ceremoniously axed to death was found.

61. Even more striking than Stonehenge?

Avebury Stone Circle (Avebury) This spectacular 4,500-year-old henge monument encompasses the pretty village – where Stones does good vegetarian food. It's the largest stone circle in Europe, the 200 surviving stones enclosed in a massive earthen rampart nearly a mile in circumference. Originally, there were two smaller internal stone circles, too. The site was excavated in the 1920s and 1930s, in the most unusual way. A marmalade magnate bought the entire village, and had the stones re-erected – many had become buried or dilapidated. The **Alexander Keiller Museum** named after him gives a succinct introduction to the archaeological wonders of the area, inc a new interactive barn gallery exhibition. Meals, snacks, shop, disabled access; cl 24–26 Dec; (01672) 539250; *£4; NT.

West Kennett Avenue Leading away from the circle is this 1½-mile avenue of stones, virtually destroyed by ploughing and mostly replaced by modern concrete posts. It leads to the site of the Sanctuary, a stone circle (on the site of an earlier wooden temple) that was similarly razed, then marked out with posts in modern times.

Silbury Hill This towering prehistoric mound, purpose unknown, is the largest man-made mound in Europe – it would have taken a thousand men about ten years to build. There's a parking and viewing area, or you can walk the short distance from Avebury car park; there's no access to the top of the hill (where a huge shaft, perhaps a relic of 1776 treasure-hunters, has suddenly opened up, threatening further collapses).

West Kennett Long Barrow The prehistoric remains of a 5,000-year-old chambered tomb and barrow (one of the largest in the country), where several dozen people were buried. Take a torch if you want to venture in behind the massive entrance stone: the chamber with two side chapels runs some 9 metres (30 ft) or more into the barrow. You have to park in either the car park next to Silbury Hill or the layby at the bottom of the field next to the A4, and then walk about half a mile up the track. The Waggon & Horses at Beckhampton (of *Pickwick Papers* fame) is quite handy.

Windmill Hill Reached by footpath NW, this, the earliest monument in the area, is a neolithic enclosure dating back some 5,000 years. There's not a great deal to see apart from mild lumps, but the site is quite evocative.

62. A golden stone wool town

Bradford-on-Avon is an attractive hillside town given a distinguished air by the same sort of golden stone as was used in Bath; it's very steep, and has some handsome buildings reflecting its past wealth as a wool town – and quite a few serious antiques shops. Nr the Norman parish church is a tall narrow late **Saxon church**, unusual for having virtually no later additions. The Dandy Lion (Market St) is good for lunch. From here you can cycle around 11m E to Devizes or 10m W to Bath along the towpath of the Kennet & Avon Canal. Cycle hire from TF Cycles, at the Lock Inn (Frome Rd); £5 for 1st hour, then £1.10 an hour after that; canoe (£10 for 2 hours) and boat hire too; (01225) 867187.

Westwood Manor (above Avoncliff, just SW) Fully furnished

15th-c stone manor house with its original Gothic and Jacobean windows, fine 17th-c plasterwork, and modern topiary garden. No facilities, cl am, and Mon, Thurs–Sat and Oct–Mar; (01225) 863374; £4.20; NT. The church in Westwood village has some interesting late medieval stained glass.

63. Glorious parkland around the mansion where oxygen was discovered

Bowood (Calne, off A4) The extensive Capability Brown parkland and colourful pleasure gardens are the glory of Bowood, with their temples, cascades and hermit's cave shielded from the outside world by further miles of partly wooded grounds; in May a woodland garden is open for rhododendron walks. Much of the main building was demolished in 1955, but there's plenty left, inc the impressive library designed by Robert Adam. Joseph Priestley discovered oxygen here in 1772 and it's home to an excellent collection of watercolours. There's an outstanding adventure playground and new soft play area. Meals, snacks, shop, limited disabled access; cl Nov–Mar; (01249) 812102; £6.05. The Lansdowne Arms at Derry Hill, nr the house, is nice for lunch, and Calne also has a **motor museum**.

64. Perhaps Britain's prettiest village

Castle Combe is for many people the prettiest village in Britain. It has a classic group of stone-tiled Cotswoldy cottages by the turreted church, at the bottom of a tree-clad hill running down to a trout stream and its ancient stone bridge. Preservation of the village is taken so seriously that you won't even see television aerials on the houses; several villagers occasionally open their beautifully kept gardens for charity. Best of all during the week out of season; at other times it does get a great many visitors, even though the car park is some way up the hill. The charming old Castle Inn has good food. The village has surroundings that are equally appealing, and attractive paths along deep peaceful valleys.

65. Another contender for prettiest village title

Lacock is a favourite of both visitors and film-makers (see for instance the first Harry Potter film). Its grid of quiet and narrow streets is a delightful harmony of mellow brickwork, lichened stone and timber-and-plaster. The church is 15th c, and nothing in the village looks more recent than 18th c. It's remained so remarkably unspoilt because most of its buildings were owned for centuries by the Talbot family, until they left them to the NT in 1944. It gets very busy in summer, but the Trust has preserved it against a surfeit of antiques shops (you'll find all you want in the nearby old market town of Melksham). The village does on the other hand have a splendid collection of pubs – the George is the best.

Lacock Abbey Tranquil spread of mellow stone buildings around a central timber-gabled courtyard, based on the little-altered 13th-c abbey. Tudor additions include a romantic octagonal tower, and there was a successful 18th-c Gothicisation. Surrounded by quiet meadows and trees, this was the setting for Fox Talbot's experiments which in 1835 led to the creation of the world's first photographic negative – a picture of part of the abbey itself. There's an interesting museum devoted to this in a 16th-c barn at the gates, and the gardens are evidence of Fox Talbot's skills in other fields. Limited disabled access; cl Good Fri, Tues and Nov–Mar, Abbey also cl ams; (01249) 730227; £6.20, £4; museum, grounds and cloisters only NT. The photography museum is also open winter wknds (exc Christmas–New Year).

66. The all-singing all-dancing stately home

Longleat (off A362 4m W of Warminster) Few places can boast such a range of activities for families, and the Passport Ticket allows you to spread the attractions over more than one visit. Children will probably get most excited about the safari park, which as well as the famous lions has rhinos, camels, elephants and a rare white tiger. Unusually, you can walk through some parts, and if you haven't got a car you can go by bus (it gets booked up very quickly, so go early in the day). A boat trip leads to Gorilla Island, where two gorillas live in a miniature stately home. Also displays of parrots and butterflies, a narrow-gauge railway, simulator ride, pets corner, and an elaborate play area in a full-size mock castle. Older visitors may prefer the collection of doll's houses or the peaceful formal gardens laid out by Capability Brown, and of course there's the handsome 16th-c house itself, much restored inside, but with impressively grand formal rooms, and the individual murals of the colourful current Marquis of Bath. He has had several mazes and labyrinths built around the grounds: the yew hedge maze is the world's longest, and one new maze is the prize design of a 12-year-old *Blue Peter* winner. Changing exhibitions, lots of extra events, and you can get coarse fishing permits. Meals, snacks, shop, disabled access; largely cl Nov–early Apr, phone to check; (01985) 844400. You can get individual tickets for the attractions, but it works out much cheaper to buy the all-in Passport Ticket, £15 adults, £11 children.

67. A perfect cathedral close

Salisbury is a beautiful and gently relaxed city, with a good many fine old buildings, particularly around the lovely cathedral close. The most extensive close in the country, it's always been a distinct area of town, and the gates to it are still locked each night. The buildings cover a variety of architectural styles from the 13th c to the present, and while of course its great glory is the elegant cathedral itself, you can't help being struck by how impeccably mown the lawns are. Outside the close, there are some interesting antiques and other little independent shops, and the broad Market Sq still has a traditional market each Tues and Sat; parking in town can be tricky then, so it's a good idea to take advantage of the Park and Ride system (parking at Old Sarum to the N on the A345). The Haunch of Venison (Minster St) is an interesting old town tavern.

Salisbury Cathedral Begun in 1220 and completed in only 38 years – giving a rare uniformity of style. The magnificent spire (added in 1315 along with the tower) is at 123 metres (404 ft) the tallest in the country, and many would say the finest in the world. 332 winding spiral steps take you to the top of the tower, giving spectacular views of the city and surrounding countryside – and you can peer up into the spire, with its internal medieval scaffolding. Also notable are a fascinating floor-mounted 14th-c clock (the oldest working mechanical clock in the world), and the tomb of the first Earl of Salisbury, who gave the church one of only four surviving editions of the Magna Carta; it's still on show in the Chapter House, alongside remarkable early silver. The cloisters stand out too. Meals and snacks (with good views of the spire), shop, disabled access; (01722) 555120; £3.50 suggested donation, tower tour £3. The guides are entertaining and knowledgeable. There's a classic view of the cathedral from across the water meadows, where the Old Mill has decent food.

Mompesson House (The Close) Exquisite Queen Anne building, probably the most interesting in the close, with period furnishings, china and paintings, remarkable collection of 18th-c drinking glasses, and interestingly carved oak staircase. Tearoom with nice home-made cakes, disabled access to ground floor; cl

Thurs–Fri and Oct–Mar; (01722) 335659; £3.90, 80p gardens only; NT. The NT shop is a couple of minutes' walk away on the High St. The close also includes striking St Anne's Gate, a regimental museum (cl Mon Feb–Mar and Nov and Dec–Jan; (01722) 414536; *£2.75).

68. A must-see stately home

Wilton House (Wilton, just W of Salisbury) Particularly satisfying to visit, well organised and friendly, and usually free from too many crowds. The original house was damaged by a fire in 1647, and superbly redesigned by John Webb and Inigo Jones, the latter responsible for the magnificent Double Cube room, considered by many to be one of the country's finest surviving rooms from this period; it's full of splendid works by Van Dyck. The Tudor kitchen and Victorian laundry have both been well restored to give a good impression of their original use. The furnishings and art are exquisite, and a lovely doll's house re-creates some parts of the house in miniature. For children the highlight of the 21-acre grounds is the bigger-than-average adventure playground; there's also plenty of space for picnics, as well as water and rose gardens, a restful cloister garden, a striking Palladian bridge, and woodland walks. Meals, snacks, shop, disabled access; cl Nov–Mar; (01722) 746720; £9.25. The ornately Italianate 19th-c **church** incorporates all sorts of treasures, esp its magnificent medieval continental stained glass and 2,000-year-old marble pillars. Wiltons (Market Pl) is good for lunch, and the charming Victoria & Albert in nearby Netherhampton is nicely off the tourist track, with a pleasant riverside walk into Salisbury.

69. Wiltshire's only working windmill

Wilton windmill (off A338 E of Burbage) Built in 1821 after the construction of the Kennet & Avon Canal had diverted the water previously used to power mills. Now restored, it's beautifully floodlit most evenings. Shop (sells flour milled on site); open pm Sun and bank hols Easter–Sept; (01672) 870266; £2. This little village of Wilton (not to be confused with the larger town nr Salisbury) is attractive; the Swan has good if not cheap food.

70. The Isle of Wight's medieval castle

Carisbrooke Castle (Carisbrooke) Ruins of the only medieval castle on the island, between 1647 and 1648 home to the imprisoned Charles I (his daughter died here in 1650). Some later buildings behind the imposing gatehouse and walls, and entertaining demonstrations of how donkeys drew water from one of the medieval wells. Shop, summer café, disabled access to ground floor; cl 24–26 Dec, 1 Jan; (01983) 522107; £4.50; EH. The Eight Bells above the waterfowl lake has decent food and good Solent views.

71. Queen Victoria's favourite residence

Osborne House (1m SE of East Cowes) Where Queen Victoria died in 1901; the state and private apartments haven't changed much since. Designed to resemble an Italian villa, by her consort Prince Albert with professional help from Thomas Cubitt, it's a striking place. Albert and his wife were also responsible for the original layout of the fine formal gardens, which seem filled with every conceivable English tree, masses of roses and clematis. The refurbished Durbar Wing is filled with opulent gifts to Victoria from the people of India. Swiss Cottage is where the Royal children learnt cooking and gardening. The house featured in the film *Mrs Brown*. Snacks, shop, some disabled access; cl 25–26 Dec, Jan 1; (01983) 200022; *£7.50; EH. Down on the River Medina, the beautifully placed Folly Inn has an appropriately nautical atmosphere.

72. Lakeside stately home and national motor museum

Beaulieu Abbey (Beaulieu) Palace House is a fine old mansion based around the gatehouse of the huge Cistercian Abbey that stood here until the Reformation (still with what are thought to be the original monastic fan-vaulted ceilings). The surrounding lakeside parkland and gardens are rewarding to explore, with ruins of other abbey buildings, and an exhibition on the monks who lived here. What helps to make this a great day out for families is its centrepiece National Motor Museum, a collection that from humble beginnings has become one of the most comprehensive in the world; they've recently opened a new motorsport gallery. Other features have a motoring theme too: a hands-on gallery explains how cars work, and Wheels is probably the highlight for children – you sit in a pod-like vehicle and trundle through 100 years of motoring. For an extra charge a simulator ride gives you a more robust driving experience. A monorail whizzes round the grounds, and in summer you can ride on a replica 1912 London bus. Also go-kart style mini-bikes, and radio-controlled cars. Meals, snacks, shops, disabled access; cl 25 Dec; (01590) 612345; £11.95. In the village facing the Palace House gates, Montys is popular for lunch, and a pleasant marked trail leads from here down the waterside to Bucklers Hard, run by the same people.

73. Gilbert White and Jane Austen

Gilbert White's House (The Wakes, Selborne) Impressive 18th-c home of naturalist Gilbert White, furnished in period style. The restoration of the extensive gardens to their original form is almost complete, and separate galleries commemorate the explorers Captain Oates and Frank Oates. Impressive teas and 18th-c-style snacks, good shop, plant sales, disabled access to ground floor and garden; cl 25–31 Dec; (01420) 511275; *£4.50. The Queens Hotel is handy for lunch. There are good pockets of scenery nearby – the countryside White recorded in such detail. The zigzag path he created with his brother in 1753 still climbs Selborne Hanger (the hangers hereabouts are beechwoods which cling to the abrupt escarpments). Noar Hill close by has been designated a nature reserve for its chalkland flora, and from Selborne churchyard, a path leads into the Lythe, a wooded hillside that was another favourite haunt of White's.

Jane Austen's House (Chawton) Enjoyable unpretentious 17th-c house where the author lived and worked 1809–17, still with some of her letters and possessions. Rooms are furnished in period style, and the pleasant garden is good for picnics. Good bookshop, disabled access to ground floor and garden; cl wkdys Dec–Feb, 25–26 Dec; (01420) 83262; *£4. The Greyfriar opposite has reasonably priced food, and there are good walks here. Just up the road, Chawton House, the former home of Jane Austen's brother Edward, is now the Centre for the Study of Early English Women's Writing.

74. An isolated Tudor castle by the sea

Hurst Castle One of the most sophisticated fortresses when built by Henry VIII, on a long spit commanding the Solent, and best reached by summer ferry from Keyhaven, or perhaps on foot (there's a pleasant walk from the 17th-c Gun pub – good value food). Fortified again in the 19th c, it still has two huge 38-ton guns. Summer snacks, shop, disabled access to ground floor; cl wkdys Nov–Mar, 25–26 Dec; (01590) 642344; £2.80.

75. When Britain ruled the waves

Portsmouth Historic Dockyard The main stop for most visitors to Portsmouth, with lots to see. It's home to **HMS Victory**, the **Mary Rose**, **HMS Warrior**, and the **Royal Naval Museum**. The flagship is HMS Victory, which is still in commission; guided tours (not in school holidays) bring those Trafalgar days very close, and include the spot where Nelson died. The raising of the Mary Rose from the Solent silt where she had sat for 437 years provided a wealth of material and information about the Tudor period. The discoveries are well shown in the Mary Rose Museum, while the great oak hull itself is in a separate hall, sprayed constantly to prevent the timbers from drying out (there are plans to build a new ship hall as part of the harbour redevelopment). HMS Warrior, when launched 140 years ago, was the most fearsome battleship in the world; she's been immaculately restored. A bit like a games arcade, **Action Stations** gives a new look at the modern Navy through a large format film and interactive displays; a big hit with children, there can be lengthy queues in the holidays. Housed in handsome 18th-c dockside buildings, the **Royal Naval Museum** has lively displays on the development and history of the Navy up to and beyond the Falklands War (or as it's called here the South Atlantic Campaign), with interactive galleries looking at Nelson, the sailing Navy, and HMS Victory (and its role in the Battle of Trafalgar). An inclusive ticket lumping in all the attractions costs £13.75 (you don't have to see them all in one day); a family ticket (2 adults and up to 3 children) is £44. The site – which itself costs nothing to enter, after a security check – has a restaurant, cafés and shops, and there's limited disabled access to all the ships; cl 25 Dec; (023) 9272 7562.

Southsea Castle The fortifications in defence of Portsmouth Harbour, here, around Gosport, and up on Portsdown, give a remarkably complete picture of the development of defensive strategy from Tudor times to the fears of French invasion in the 1860s, though they have more appeal to people interested in warfare than to those who like the romantic idea of a regular 'castle'. Southsea Castle and Museum is the best place to start, built in 1545 as part of Henry VIII's coastal defences. Good displays on Portsmouth's military history, and a time-tunnel experience of the history of the castle; special events (esp summer). Shop; cl Nov–Mar; (023) 9282 7261; £2.50. On the seaward side of Southsea are sturdy Tudor and later towers, bastions and batteries, alongside the resort's gardens and entertainments, giving interesting sea views. Good guided walks around the Tudor fortifications and the best parts of the Old Town leave the Square Tower at 2pm on Sun (mid-Apr to late Sept); (023) 9282 6722; £1.

Spitbank Fort Wind up an exploration of Portsmouth's naval past with the boat trip from the Naval Base to this granite, iron and brick fortress a mile out to sea. Its two floors are linked by a maze of passages, and there's a 130-metre (420-ft) deep well which still draws fresh water. The inner courtyard is now a sheltered terrace for summer refreshments from the café and bar. Open Sun in summer for day visits which include the boat trip (£6.95, ferries leave from the Historic Dockyard and Gunwharf Quay in Portsmouth). They also do popular pub nights with – of course – a spit-roast (£15, ferries leave from Gosport ferry terminal and the Hard in Portsmouth); phone for more information; (023) 9250 4207.

76. Roman city with a 1½ mile city wall

Calleva (Silchester) The site of Roman town Calleva Atrebatum has been excavated; 1½ miles of city wall to walk along (tricky in places), as well as a 9,000-seat amphitheatre, 12th-c church on the site of the Roman temples, and a small **museum** giving a pictorial account of the site; some disabled access; cl 25 Dec; free. The Calleva Arms (with a family dining conservatory) does cheap lunches, and sells a guide to the site. Over at Little London the Plough (good snack lunches) is handy for Pamber Forest walks.

77. England's Saxon capital

Winchester has a compact and fascinating medieval centre, still with two city gates intact; it was England's capital in Saxon times. The most attractive part is the glorious and peaceful cathedral close, surrounded by a very harmonious and distinguished collection of buildings; the handsome old Eclipse Inn nr the NE edge is a useful refreshment break. The Brooks Shopping Centre has a few jolly dioramas and displays on the city's history (free), with the chance for children to make their own Roman mosaic. Guided walks around the sights from the Tourist Information Centre at 11am Mon–Sat (plus 2.30pm Sat in Apr, 2.30pm Sat and Sun May–Jun, and 2.30pm Mon–Sun Jul–Oct, exc Sun in Oct), Sat only Nov–Mar; £3. There's a multi-storey car park at the top of the High St, or a Park & Ride nr the junction with the M3. There are pleasant walks up rounded St Catherine's Hill, which has a small medieval turf maze and traces of a hill fort.

Winchester Cathedral Awesome and full of interest – one of Europe's finest, with the longest of all Gothic naves, and quite a mixture of architectural styles. Among many rare books and manuscripts in its library is a wonderful 12th-c illuminated Bible, while the sculpture gallery contains some outstanding late Gothic work. William of Wykeham paid for much of the rebuilding, so his tomb is appropriately the finest; also memorials and monuments to Jane Austen, King Canute and St Swithun. The cathedral hosts changing exhibitions of modern art through the summer, and a sculpture by Antony 'Angel of the North' Gormley beautifully exploits reflections in the winter flood waters of the crypt. Good guided tours, and first-rate visitor centre in 16th-c coach house, with very good meals and snacks (not cheap) and distinguished shop, disabled access; £3.50 suggested donation. The recently created Dean Garnier Garden between the deanery and the cathedral reflects the cathedral's architecture; open all day; free; for more info ring Sally Curtis (01962) 732246 or the cathedral office (01962) 857202. Close by are the appreciable remains of Wolvesey Castle, the original Bishop's Palace begun in the 12th c, and beside it (not open, but a handsome sight), the present Bishop's Palace of 1684. The best way out of the Close is through the medieval King's Gate, which includes the upper-floor church of St Swithun. This takes you into Kingsgate St, calm and old-fashioned, with an excellent dining pub, the Wykeham Arms. Down on the left a lovely riverside path takes you along to the City Mill and a mighty statue of King Alfred.

City Mill (Bridge St) Restored and working 18th-c watermill, with timbered and raftered ceilings and a pretty little island garden. They are planning milling displays for this year (and to sell the flour they mill), but as we went to press they were unsure of times, so best phone to check. Shop, disabled access; open wknds in Mar, Weds–Sun Apr–Jun and Sept–Oct, daily Jul–Aug; (01962) 870057; £2; NT.

Great Hall of Winchester Castle All that now remains is its huge 13th-c great hall, where Raleigh was tried and condemned to death; hanging on one wall is a round table they call King Arthur's (actually much the same date as the castle, and painted with its Arthurian scenes later). Restored roof, stone parapets and stained glass, and there's a small but interesting re-created medieval garden S of the hall. Shop, disabled access; cl 25–26 Dec; (01962) 846476; free.

Hospital of St Cross Very attractively set around two quadrangles, the quaint 15th-c almshouses still provide bread and ale to travellers who ask at the massive gate (you have to ask for 'wayfarer's dole'). 19th-c scandals here inspired Trollope's *The Warden*. Summer snacks, shop, disabled access; cl Sun, Good Fri and 25 Dec; (01962) 851375; £2. The Bell here is useful for lunch, and the stroll out from the city centre, along the ancient water meadows by the River Itchen, is one of the nicest short walks in southern Britain.

78. High society a century ago

Polesden Lacey (off A246 S of Great Bookham) Attractive Regency house once at the centre of Edwardian high society, now with photographs of some of the notable guests, as well as splendid tapestries, porcelain, Old Masters and other art. The spacious grounds have a walled rose garden and open-air theatre. Meals, snacks, shop, disabled access; house cl Mon and Tues exc bank hols, and all Nov–Mar, grounds open all year; (01372) 458203; £3 house only, £4 grounds only; NT. On the other side of the extended commuter village, the Bookham Commons, with a mixture of thorny scrub (full of birds), small lakes, marshy bits and oak woods, are well wooded and attractive. In Effingham nearby, the Plough has honest home cooking.

79. Guildford — more historic than you might guess

The biggest town (despite having a cathedral – it's not a city) in the area, Guildford is older than you might at first think; although many of the buildings are Georgian-fronted, what's behind often dates back much further. The sloping High St has attractive parts as well as its briskly modern shops, with interesting buildings inc the **Abbots Hospital** and the **Grammar School**. Tunsgate Arch is the start for free guided walks of the city – 2.30pm every Sun, Mon and Weds May–Sept, also 7.30 Thurs till end Aug.

Guildhall (High St) Mainly Tudor, with one of the few surviving sets of Elizabethan standard measures. Disabled access to ground floor only; usually open only for guided tours at 2, 3 and 4pm Tues and Thurs; (01483) 444035; free.

Loseley Park (off B3000, 3 miles SW) Most people are familiar with the name from the yoghurts and ice-cream produced here (try the white chocolate and butterscotch). The stately Elizabethan stately home was built in 1562, and has fine panelling, paintings and tapestries. The walled gardens include an amazing rose garden with over 1,000 bushes, and a fountain garden. Meals, snacks, shop and plant sales, limited disabled access; cl Mon exc bank hols, Tues, house open pm Jun–Aug, gardens open May–Sept; (01483) 304440; £6 house and gardens, £3 gardens only.

River Wey & Godalming Navigation This 17th-c canal, passing through some fine scenery, by 1763 linked Godalming (where the wharf has some handsome Georgian buildings) with the Thames. A visitor centre at **Dapdune Wharf** here has interactive exhibitions on the waterway and the people who lived and worked on it, housed in a restored Wey barge. There's a new hands-on activity area in an old gunpowder store; they also have children's trails, guided nature walks and various special events, and you can take a 40-min boat trip from here (£2, best to phone for dates).

Snacks and picnic areas, shop, disabled access; cl Tues, Weds and Nov–21 Mar; (01483) 561389; *£3. The locks and towpath have been restored by the NT, and you can walk all the way from Godalming to Weybridge, some 20 miles, or hire boats from Farncombe Boat House; Mar–Nov; (01483) 421306.

80. Reigate's underground surprise

Barons Cave Below the peaceful castle grounds is a network of old tunnels, prime among them this splendid cavernous passageway with all sorts of myths and stories attached. Enthusiastic and entertaining tours are available; for an appointment ring the Wealden Cave and Mine Society (Malcolm Tadd) on (01737) 823456, for full details and dates; around £1.50. Among the few surviving original buildings in this mainly modern town are one or two timber-framed houses around the High St, where the beamed Red Cross has decent food.

81. Where it all went down in 1066

Battle takes its name from certainly the most celebrated and perhaps the most disorganised skirmish in English history, thrashed out here in 1066 and giving the Norman invaders from France control of England. The main street (carrying a fair bit of traffic, so not exactly peaceful) has a lot of attractive old buildings, several housing antiques shops and cafés; beyond them the town extends into spreading new estates. The **church** of St Mary has some 13th-c wall paintings, and the Squirrel (A269) has generous cheap home cooking and a big family garden.

The **battlefield** has a mile-long walk around it with a good audio tour explaining what happened. Four years after the bloodshed William built an abbey on the site as penance, the altar reputedly on the very spot where Harold fell. Not much is left of the original **Battle Abbey**, but later remains include the monks' dormitory and common room, and the great 14th-c gatehouse which looms over the small market square. Snacks, shop, mostly disabled access; cl 24–26 Dec, 1 Jan; (01424) 773792; £4.50; EH.

82. A vast Roman palace

Roman Palace (Salthill Rd, Fishbourne) This magnificent villa with its 100 or so rooms was occupied from the 1st to the 3rd c, and is the largest known residence from the period in Britain. Some archaeologists now think the Romans first landed here (and not in Kent as was originally supposed), to reinstate the recently evicted king. They probably built his successor this place. You can see 25 mosaic floors (some are quite remarkable, and it's a bigger collection than anywhere else in Britain), and a garden has been laid out according to its 1st-c plan. Much of the palace is buried beneath nearby housing. Snacks, shop, disabled access; cl wkdys mid-Dec to Jan; (01243) 785859; £4.70. The Bulls Head has good food.

83. . . . and a peaceful Roman villa

Roman Villa & Museum (Bignor) One of the largest villas discovered so far, with marvellous mosaics housed in quaint thatched buildings erected by the farmer on whose land the site was found in 1811. One mosaic, 25 metres (82 ft) long and still in its original position, is the longest in Britain. Snacks, shop, some disabled access, and largely under cover; cl Mon (exc bank hols and May–Sept), and all Nov–Feb; (01798) 869259; £3.65. The White Horse at nearby Sutton has good food (and good value bedrooms), and the top of Bignor Hill (just S of the Villa; not signed) is excellent for picnics and views. Here you can follow Stane St, a highly evocative Roman road (now a path with some of the original ditch and surface in evidence), taking a strikingly straight course SW towards Chichester through attractive landscapes.

84. Kipling Country

The single main street of the ridge village of **Burwash** has many attractively restored tile-hung cottages, inc an antiques centre with a teashop, with lime trees along its brick pavement. The graveyard of the Norman-towered church gives fine views over the Dudwell Valley, and the flower-decked Bell is useful for lunch. Around here the intricate landscapes of the Sussex Weald show steep slopes and valleys, ancient woods and hedgerows punctuated by great oaks, pretty villages, tile-hung or weatherboarded oast houses and wood-and-tile barns with their long cats'-slide roofs.

Batemans (off A265) Handsome early 17th-c stone-built ironmaster's house, home to Rudyard Kipling 1902–1936. His study is kept much as it was then, as is the hefty pipework he installed for a pioneer hydro-electric lighting plant. The attractive gardens have a quaint operating watermill, grinding flour every Sat at 2pm (though as we went to press it and the millpond were awaiting overhaul, so phone to check it's open). Dog crèche, snacks, shop, disabled access to ground floor only; cl Thurs, Fri (exc Good Fri), and Oct–Feb; (01435) 882302; *£5.20 (*£2.60 1–23 Mar as only Wild Garden open then); NT. Good little-used walks up the wholly unspoilt valley from here, where you can look for Kipling landmarks such as Pook's Hill and Willingford Bridge (aka Weland's Ford). The valley, now so peaceful, was a busy centre of the iron and glass industries from Roman times onwards.

85. Two Iron Age downland landmarks

Cissbury Ring A huge ramparted Iron Age hill peppered with much earlier flint mines, and good views over to the Isle of Wight (looking surprisingly near). It's quite close to Findon, where the Gun is good for lunch. There's a pleasant walk from here to Chanctonbury Ring.

Chanctonbury Ring Another of the great South Downs landmarks, a Romano-British temple site within an Iron Age earthwork, now a prominent hilltop clump of trees: a bracing walk, best reached from Steyning (the Tudor Chequer has generous food) or Washington – or from Cissbury Ring.

86. A Georgian city with much older landmarks

Chichester is partly pedestrianised and easy to get around. This handsome former Roman city is one of the country's finest examples of Georgian town planning and architecture. Useful central pubs for food are the Fountain (Southgate), Nags (St Pancras), Dolphin & Anchor (West St), and lively Toad (redundant church, West St).

Chichester Cathedral Mostly Norman, and unusual for rising straight out of the town's streets rather than a secluded close. The spire collapsed in 1861 (the latest in a long line of structural problems), and was rebuilt, but even now the scaffolding always seems to be up as restoration work continues. Highlights include the 14th-c choir stalls, John Piper's Aubusson tapestry, and the window by Chagall. Guided tours (not Sun) at 11.15am and 2.30pm Easter–end Oct. Meals, snacks, shop in the medieval bell tower, disabled access; cl only for special services and events; (01243) 782595; £2 suggested donation. The Bishop's Palace gardens are very pleasant.

87. An ancient fishing town

The seaside core of **Hastings** (though surrounded by sprawling deprived areas) has a really dramatic setting in the cliffs, unique in the south-east, with the aptly named Old Town huddled below the ruins of the castle. The labyrinth of alleys and stepped paths threading through its former fishermen's quarter make for highly enjoyable wandering, and it's refreshingly not over-tidy. Down below, the fishermen still haul their boats up on to the beach and sell excellent fresh fish by the unusual tall black wooden net huts. At each end of the cliffs is a steep funicular railway down to sea level (90p). The First In Last Out in the Old Town has interesting food and brews its own beer. The rest of the town is a busy shopping town, rather run-down in parts, with 19th-c resort buildings nearer the seafront, seaside hotels and B&Bs, a good prom (with miles of cycle path), and shingle beach.

Fishermen's Museum (Rock-a-Nore Rd) Interestingly housed in a former fishermen's church, and crammed full of stuff; the centrepiece is a 29-ft sailing lugger; there's a new audio-visual presentation, and a huge stuffed albatross; shop, disabled access, cl 25 Dec; (01424) 461446; donations.

Hastings Castle Bracingly set above crumbling cliffs and the tracked lift, the evocative Norman ruins (which encompass, unusually, a collegiate church) are close to the site of William the Conqueror's first English motte and bailey castle. There's a lively audio-visual exhibition on the Battle of Hastings. Shop, some disabled access; cl 24–26 Dec; (01424) 781112; £3.20.

88. Great art in a splendid mansion

Petworth House The magnificent rooms are filled with one of the most impressive art collections in the country, inc Dutch Old

Masters and 20 pictures by Turner, a frequent visitor. Other highlights include the 13th-c chapel, grand staircase with frescoes, and the carved room, elegantly decorated by Grinling Gibbons. You can see extra rooms Mon–Weds. Meals, snacks, shop, disabled access; cl Thurs, Fri and Nov–Mar; (01798) 342207; £7; NT. The deer park, with stately trees and prospects still recognisable as those glorified by Turner, is open all year; free. The town (cruelly carved up by busy traffic) is now an antiques honey-pot, with dozens of antiques shops in its narrow streets of attractive old houses. The Angel Hotel fits in well, and has a good wknd carvery; the Well Diggers (A283 E – almost a museum of the rural 1920s) and stylish Badgers (A285 S) have good food too.

89. A classic steam railway

Bluebell Line (Sheffield Park Station, A275) Earliest preserved standard gauge steam railway in Britain, and one of the best; 9-mile trips from Sheffield Park via Horsted Keynes to Kingscote (where there are wknd bus connections to East Grinstead), with splendid stations decked out with period advertisements and wonderful genuine period carriages. The journey passes woodlands that are a mass of bluebells in late spring, usually at their best in mid-May – hence the name of the line. Part of the station houses the region's largest railway collection, inc some 30 locomotives. The Revd W Awdry based his Fat Controller on the man who organised the railway's restoration in the late 1950s. Pullman dining specials, Santa specials, shop, café, disabled access (with notice); trains wknds all yr, daily May–Sept and school hols – (01825) 720800 for timetable; £8. Depending on which direction you're coming from, the Griffin at Fletching and Sloop at Scaynes Hill are good for lunch.

90. Nostalgic remnants of a medieval port

Winchelsea is a rare example of a planned medieval town (now decidedly village-like in character), ranged around a grid of peaceful streets, and an interesting contrast in style to nearby Rye. Storms, French raids and the Black Death put paid to Winchelsea's commercial importance. Most of the buildings are post-medieval: there are fine 17th-c and 18th-c houses with much older vaulted cellars in their basements, while the tranquil church of St Thomas is elaborately decorated, with some fine old stained glass and medieval tombs. There are three town gates: one of them, the New Gate, is in a field some way S, and in view from the well waymarked 1066 Country Walk, which gives some wide views over Romney Marsh and the sea; it's worth taking this path to the Queens Head at Icklesham, which has good food. The Royal Military Canal, from here to Hythe in Kent, was a never-used Napoleonic defence meant as a sort of glorified coastal moat – now a peaceful spot for coarse fishing. The New Inn is popular for lunch.

91. The best of Canterbury

Canterbury is at its most atmospheric out of season, as its compact and easily walked historic centre does get almost unpleasantly packed in summer. The most rewarding area is in the cathedral precincts, and the admission charge brings a measure of peace to one of Britain's greatest religious sites; the choicest parts elsewhere need a bit of seeking out. Good guided walks leave from the helpful Visitor Information Centre, 12 Sun St (2pm Apr–Oct, plus 11.30 July–Aug; (01227) 459779; £3.75), and every Fri and Sat at 8pm there are Ghost Tours (meet opposite Alberrys Wine Bar, Margaret St; (01843) 299460; £5). Summer boat trips leave daily from Kings Bridge; (07790) 534744; £5. If you're making your own way, don't miss Palace St, Burgate with the Buttermarket Sq, and St Peter's St, all of which have fine buildings, and you can follow quite a lot of the ancient city wall on a walk passing the remains of the Norman castle (some info panels, usually open). The city's Roman and ecclesiastical heritage is well known, but there are other remains here too, notably a prehistoric tumulus in Dane John Garden. The `Whitefriars area of town is currently being redeveloped to include a new shopping centre and library, and they hope to open up archaeological excavations of the site to the public by spring 2003. There are good car parks on the fringes of the old centre. Canterbury Tales (just off St Peter's St) is a useful central pub for lunch.

Canterbury Cathedral Dramatically floodlit at night, this spectacularly lives up to expectations. The earliest parts are Norman, with much added in the 12th and 15th c. Rewarding features are everywhere – an airily impressive nave, fascinating stained glass, the Bell Harry Tower, lovely cloisters, and the shrine of Thomas à Becket, murdered here in the 12th c. In the crypt are some wonderfully grotesque carvings, full of strange animals are fantastic fighting monsters. The precincts are particularly rewarding, containing buildings connected to the cathedral, inc the ruins of the former monastery in Green Court, the impressive Norman Staircase and the medieval Kings School. Summer snacks, shop, disabled access; may be closed for services at certain times, limited opening Sun; (01227) 762862; £3.50 – note this isn't a donation, you'll be charged this just to enter the precincts. There are additional charges for guided tours, audio tours, audio-visuals, and photo permits. Entry to the services is free, and the choir's singing is then a bonus.

Roman Museum (Longmarket) Splendid underground museum, incorporating the remains of a Roman town house; lively reconstructions of a market and kitchen, as well as lots of hands-on and hi-tech displays. The mosaic floor is very well displayed. Shop, disabled access; cl Sun (exc Jun–Oct), Good Fri and Christmas wk; (01227) 785575; £2.60.

St Augustine's Abbey (Longport) Founded at the end of the 6th c, but most of the remaining ruins date from the Benedictine rebuilding in the 11th c. A free audio tour takes you around the ruins and adjacent museum. Snacks, shop, disabled access; cl 24–26 Dec, 1 Jan; (01227) 767345; £3; EH.

St Martin's church (North Holmes Rd) The country's oldest church in continual use; the Venerable Bede says it was built by the Romans, and there are certainly Roman bricks in the walls.

West Gate Towers (where St Peter's St meets St Dunstan's St) The city's last remaining fortified gatehouse, built in the late 14th c, with interesting cells, and excellent views from the battlements. Children can do brass rubbing or try on replica armour. Shop; cl 12.30–1.30, all day Sun, Good Fri, Christmas wk; (01227) 452747; £1.

92. 18th-c showpiece of naval power

Historic Dockyard (Chatham) Excellent 80-acre working museum in the most complete Georgian dockyard in the world – a visit here can easily fill most of the day. Lots to see and do: the Wooden Walls exhibition uses sights, sounds and smells to show how 18th-c warships such as HMS *Victory* were built here. Guided tours of the restored 1944 destroyer HMS *Cavalier*. You can also look around the Cold War submarine *Ocelot*, and watch the restoration of the Victorian sloop *Gannet*, which should be completed sometime in 2003. An exhibition on the RNLI has 16 lifeboats. An exhibition centre in the Flagship Brewery even explores the role of beer in the Navy (disabled access; open most wkdys, with new naval theme pub nearby in Harbourmaster's House; free), and a gallery charts Chatham's historic relationship with the Navy. Also restorations, rope-making demonstrations, craft workshops, interactive exhibitions, and lively events. Meals, snacks, shop, disabled access; open daily Apr–Oct, plus wknds and Weds in Nov, Feb and Mar; (01634) 823807; £9.50. You can get a ticket that includes **boat trips** on the paddle steamer *Kingswear Castle*. There's a new visitor centre, and you can now travel between attractions on heritage buses (it's a big place), that are similar to those that would have taken workers to and from the dockyard in the 1960s.

Fort Amherst (Dock Rd) Perhaps the finest surviving 18th-c fort in the country, with massive ditches, gun emplacements, a warren of tunnels and a firing gun battery. 18 acres of parkland, and occasional live re-enactments on Sun. Meals, snacks, shop; cl wkdys Nov–Easter, 25–26 Dec, and 1 Jan; (01634) 847747; £4.50. The Command House just below by the water does limited but decent food.

93. An unspoilt Tudor village

Chiddingstone, a favourite village in lovely Kentish countryside, is an unspoilt cluster of Tudor houses and buildings owned by the NT. The church and the mysterious stone which one story claims gives the village its name are worth a look. The Castle Inn has decent food all day.

Chiddingstone Castle 17th-c house rebuilt in castle style at the start of the 19th-c; renowned paintings and antiquities from England, Egypt and the Orient, inc fine collections of japanese swords and Buddhist art. Attractively restored landscaped grounds, and you can fish in the lake (£8 a day for two rods). Tearoom, shop, disabled access to ground floor only; open pm

Weds–Fri and Sun Easter–Sept, Sun and public hols only at Easter and in spring; (01892) 870347; £4.

94. Two of Henry VIII's mighty coastal fortresses

Deal Castle (Deal) The biggest in Henry VIII's chain of coastal defences, uniquely shaped like a Tudor rose with every wall rounded to deflect shot. Snacks, good audio tour, shop, disabled access to ground floor only; cl Mon and Tues Sept–Mar, and 24 Dec–1 Jan; (01304) 372762; £3.20; EH.

   Walmer Castle (just S) Another of Henry VIII's coastal defence fortresses, later the official residence of the Lord Warden of the Cinque Ports (one was the Duke of Wellington, who left behind his famous boot). It became more stately home than fortress, with rooms furnished in 18th-c style, and pretty gardens laid out mainly by a niece of William Pitt (one designed by Penelope Hobhouse is dedicated to the late Queen Mother). Snacks, shop, some disabled access; cl Mon and Tues Nov–Dec and Mar, wkdys Jan and Feb, 24–26 Dec, 1 Jan and whenever Lord Warden is in residence; (01304) 364288; £5; EH.

95. Time-hop through three civilisations

The village of **Eynsford** neatly takes you from Roman and the earliest Christian days through Norman times to the Middle Ages and the first Tudors. The Malt Shovel (Station Rd) has good seafood.

   Eynsford Castle Norman fortress with impressive 9-metre (30-ft) walls, and remains of the hall and ditch; cl 24–26 Dec, and 1 Jan; (01322) 863467; free. There are organised trails from the nearby countryside centre at Lullingstone Park, with various special events such as nature rambles, and bat evenings; phone to book; (01322) 865995; from £2.

Lullingstone Castle Historic family mansion with fine state rooms, great hall, staircase and library, and beautiful grounds. The 15th-c gate tower was one of the first buildings to be made entirely of brick. Shop, disabled access; open pm wknds and bank hols May–Aug; (01322) 862114; £5.

Lullingstone Roman Villa (just SE off A225) Remains of 1st- and 2nd-c family's villa, with exceptionally well preserved floor mosaics and an extensive bath complex. Also an early Christian chapel – the only one so far found in a private house. Snacks, shop, limited disabled access; cl 24–26 Dec, and 1 Jan; (01322) 863467; £2.80.

96. Showpiece lakeside castle

Leeds Castle (Leeds) Long renowned as one of the loveliest castles in the country, perfectly placed on two little islands in the middle of a lake in 500 acres of landscaped parkland. It dates from the 9th c, and was converted into a Royal residence by Henry VIII. Lots of paintings, furniture and tapestries, and a unique dog-collar museum in the gatehouse. The enormous grounds have gardens (inc a Mediterranean one), a maze and grotto, duck enclosure and aviary (well liked by readers), and a golf course; as this suggests, it's a busy place, not quite as idyllic as it appears from a distance, but very satisfying for a day out. Special events from food and wine festivals to open-air concerts. Meals, snacks, shop, good disabled access; cl 28 Jun, 5 Jul, and 25 Dec; (01622) 765400; £11 Mar–Oct, otherwise £9.50. The Windmill at Eyhorne St is good value for lunch.

97. Where to find Britain's oldest door – and much more

The busy town of **Rochester** is well worth walking round, with several attractive buildings besides those we mention; one of the quaintest is Kent's oldest pub, the Coopers Arms (St Margaret's St; cheap lunches), and many of those on the High St feature in Dickens's novels. Casa-Lina (High St) has nice Italian family cooking.

Rochester Castle One of the best examples of 12th-c military architecture – dramatic too; the great square keep is one of the tallest in England. Shop; cl a few days over Christmas; (01634) 402276; £3.90, audio tour 50p; EH.

Rochester Cathedral Spectacularly Norman, with original richly carved door, vaulted crypt, St Gundulf's tower, tombs and effigies, and huge 15th-c window. A new fresco to be finished by Easter 2003 is the first to be painted in an English cathedral for 800 years; by contrast the Gundulf Door now turns out to be England's oldest, with wood dating from 822. The choir sings Evensong at 5.30 wkdys, 3.15 wknds. Snacks, shop, good disabled access; (01634) 401301; £3 suggested donation.

Restoration House (Crow Lane) From Tudor beginnings to recent conservation work, you can trace the development of this city mansion where Charles II stayed and Dickens reputedly found inspiration for the home of Miss Haversham in *Great Expectations*; fine furniture and pictures inc works by Kneller, Reynolds and Gainsborough. Pepys kissed a shopkeeper's wife in the very English interlinked walled gardens. Open Thurs and Fri Jun–Sept, phone to check; (01634) 848520; £5 (inc a guidebook), £2 gardens only.

Charles Dickens Centre (High St) Late Tudor house used in both *Pickwick Papers* and *Edwin Drood*, with scenes and characters from the author's books brought vividly to life using impressive hi-tech effects. Shop; cl 24–26 Dec, and 1 Jan; (01634) 844176; £3.90.

98. Churchill's home, and a nearby charmer

Chartwell (off B2026 S of Westerham) The home of Winston Churchill until his death. Still much as he left them, the rooms are full of his possessions and reminders of his career, and the gardens are attractive, with the famous black swans on the lakes. Though this is one of the NT's most popular houses, and even more so after the screening of the BBC's Churchill film *The Gathering Storm* which was largely set here, you need at least a passing interest in the statesman really to enjoy it. Entry is by timed ticket. Meals, snacks, shop, disabled access; house and garden cl Mon and Tues (exc bank hols), and Nov–Mar; (01732) 866368; £5.80 house and garden, £2.90 gardens and studio only; NT. This is good walking country.

Squerryes Court Overshadowed by its more famous neighbour Chartwell but for some people more satisfying, this fine 17th-c manor house overlooks attractive grounds and has excellent collections of paintings, china and furniture. The formal garden, first recorded in 1686, has being painstakingly restored to the design laid out in 1709. Teas, shop, limited disabled access; open pm Weds, wknds and bank hols Apr–Sept; (01959) 562345; £4.60, £3 grounds only.

99. Buckingham Palace

In a marvellous position almost surrounded by Royal Parks, this looks commandingly along the stately Mall towards Admiralty Arch. At the grand front palace gates the guards still keep their unflinchingly solemn positions: you can watch the **changing of the guard** every day Apr–Jul (every other day in winter) at 11.30am; the ceremony may be late or even cancelled in exceptionally wet weather.

Buckingham Palace tour Now firmly established as one of London's most visited attractions, usually drawing around 400,000 visitors in the eight weeks it's open. The main appeal is that this is where the Queen actually lives – her official London residence, and where she meets other Heads of State; the Royal Standard flies above it when she's home. But beyond that, while perhaps not the most satisfying of the Royal palaces, it does pile a magnificent series of opulent sights into your walk through the state rooms. Highlights include the beautiful Picture Gallery, 46 metres (150 ft) long and filled with paintings from the Royal Collection, the spectacular Grand Staircase, and the throne room with its predominant impression of gold, red and splendour. Tours are unguided, and there aren't many clues to help you, so it's definitely worth buying the guide book. Theoretically you see everything at your own pace, but in practice you're likely to be carried along in the stream of other people, and you won't get much of a chance to linger. You leave the palace with a short walk through a section of the 42-acre gardens, with a good view of the Garden Front of the Palace and the 19th-c lake. Tickets are sold from an office opposite the palace by the entrance to Green Park, though it's advisable to book a day or two in advance, on (020) 7321 2233. Shop, disabled access (with notice); open early Aug–Sept; £11.50.

100. The Houses of Parliament

Across the road from St Margaret's church, these buildings are now, of course, the main seat of British government, but until Henry VIII moved to Whitehall Palace in 1529, the site was the main residence of the monarch – when they answer the phone today they still call it the Palace of Westminster. The present 19th-c building was designed by Charles Barry, though the 'gothick' detail which has given so much life to what would otherwise be rather a tiresomely deadpan classical façade is by Pugin. One end of the extraordinary 286-metre (940-ft) structure finishes in a lofty Victorian tower (which flies the Union Jack when Parliament is in session), and the other in the clock tower which contains **Big Ben**, the 3½-ton bell whose sonorous hourly rings are one of the best-known sounds in the world. Inside, over two miles of passages link the central hall and two chambers – the Houses of Lords and Commons to the N and S of the building respectively. The Commons sits from 2.30pm Mon–Weds, all day from 11.30am to 7.30pm Thurs, and 9.30am to 2pm some Fri; to watch the antics from the Strangers' Galleries, you'll need to queue by St Stephen's Gate (on the left for the Commons, right for the Lords – rather appropriate in a way) – or arrange it first with your MP. A letter from your MP can also give access to what's called the Line of Route, going through both Houses and the Members' Lobby and Divisions Lobby, to Westminster Hall, from 1224 to 1882 the chief law court of the country. It witnessed such trials as those of Sir Thomas More and Charles I, and organising admission is worth the trouble even just to admire the magnificent hammerbeam roof, the earliest surviving example of its kind; alternatively you can book yourself in for a good (if rather hurried) guided tour during the summer recess, early Aug to late Sept. There are proposals to change the sitting hours radically, so check before you visit; (0870) 906 3773; £7.50. The Westminster Arms in Storeys Gate across the square is a good pub, and you're likely to see politicians in the imposing Albert up Victoria St.

Mounting the Guard (Whitehall) A survival of the kind of Royal pageantry which once filled this area can be seen in this daily ceremony at Horse Guards Parade, 11am Mon–Sat and 10am Sun.

101. Westminster Abbey

Surely one of the most impressive pieces of architecture to survive from the Middle Ages: Edward the Confessor transformed it into the crowning place of English kings, and his body now lies in the great shrine of the present building, erected in the 13th c on the site of his original. Pretty much every king and queen up to George II is buried here; Henry VII's chapel is particularly impressive, and there are splendid tombs erected by James I for his mother Mary, Queen of Scots, and his predecessor Elizabeth I, under whose orders Mary had been executed. Perhaps it's in revenge for this that Elizabeth was lumped in with her sister Mary I, with whom she never got on. The loosely named Poets' Corner takes in a wide range of cultural figures. There's a small medieval garden in the charming tranquil cloisters. Snacks, shop, disabled access, cl 25 Dec and Good Fri, and Sun (exc for services); £6; £2 audio tour. If you like history the **museum** in the Norman undercroft shouldn't be missed – it has effigies of many ancestors of the Royal Family made from their death masks, and often wearing their own clothes; (020) 7654 4889; £2.50 (which also includes entry to the Chapter House and Pyx Chamber).

102. Where World War II was won

Cabinet War Rooms (King Charles St, just off Whitehall) An intriguing series of 21 rooms built to provide Sir Winston Churchill, the War Cabinet and his Chiefs of Staff with a safe place from which to plan their strategies during World War II. The Cabinet Room, Map Room and Prime Minister's Room were preserved intact from the end of the war, and the other rooms have been authentically restored since. Quite basic, they're very evocative, with sound-effects adding to the atmosphere. A museum dedicated to Churchill's life will open here in 2005. Shop, disabled access; cl 24–26 Dec; (020) 7930 6961; *£5.80, children free.

103. One of London's hidden highlights

Sir John Soane's Museum (13 Lincoln's Inn Fields, WC2) One of London's hidden highlights, built by the architect for his splendid collection of pictures, books and antiquities. It's most eccentric, full of architectural tricks and mirrors, which form a complex natural-lighting system for the antiquities covering most of the walls. There's a lovely picture by Turner and an Egyptian sarcophagus, but the highlights are Hogarth's acid series on *The Rake's Progress* and *The Election*. When you've seen them the guide swings open the hinged 'walls' and further treasures emerge inc choice Piranesi drawings and a scale model of the Bank of England. At the back of the Picture Room is a monument to his dog ('Alas, poor Fanny!'); you ring the bell to get in, and sign a visitors' book. The guides are very friendly and helpful, and the guidebook worthwhile. Shop, phone for disabled access; cl Sun, Mon, bank hols and 24–26 Dec; open first Tues evening of every month; (020) 7405 2107; free (donations welcome). The breakfast room of Soane's first house, no 12 next door, can also be visited.

104. Home of a great 18th-c wordsmith

Dr Johnson's House (17 Gough Sq, EC4) A perfect example of early 18th-c architecture, just as Dr Johnson himself was a perfect example of 18th-c barbed slightly flawed gentility. Between 1749 and 1755, toiling as he said 'at the lower employments of life', he wrote his great *Dictionary of the English Language* here, and there are various memorabilia from his learned life on show. Shop; cl Sun and bank hols; (020) 7353 3745; £4. The passages and walkways around here are a good reminder of how London's streets used to be laid out. The 17th-c Olde Cheshire Cheese nearby is a splendid old tavern; over the years Congreve, Pope, Voltaire, Thackeray, Dickens, Conan Doyle, Yeats and perhaps even Dr Johnson himself have called in.

105. A Tudor enclave

Middle Temple Hall (The Temple, EC4) Of all the Inns of Court, this is perhaps the most impressive, and it boasts many famous literary figures among its former members. Most of the buildings date from after the reign of Elizabeth I or the Great Fire, but the name points to an older history: the land was owned by the Knights Templar from about 1160. The hall is a fine example of Tudor architecture, with a double hammerbeam roof and beautiful stained glass. There is a table made from timber from Sir Francis Drake's Golden Hind – he was a member of the Middle Temple – while a single oak tree from Windsor Forest supplied the wood for the 9-metre (29-ft) long High Table. Open 10–11.30am and 3–4pm wkdys (exc bank hols, Easter wk, Whitsun wk, Aug and 2 wks at Christmas); (020) 7427 4800; free. The Temple has an unusual round church. Up on Fleet St the Old Bank of England is a spectacular pub conversion.

106. St Paul's Cathedral

Despite the attempts of brasher, taller modern buildings to take over, and now the completion of the controversial Paternoster Square development just NE, this masterpiece still asserts itself proudly as the area's real landmark, its unmistakable shape repeatedly looming out above the streets. Its huge dome is a pleasing shape after the stolid self-satisfaction of the Victorian and Edwardian masonry which dominates this area. Originally the cathedral was Gothic in style, with a towering 150-metre (500-ft) spire. It fell into disrepair and Wren was assigned to work on its renovation. He didn't relish the job, and no doubt was delighted when the Great Fire of London swept the old church away, allowing him to construct something entirely new. His mainly classical design is unlike any other cathedral in Britain, and took just 35 years to build. The setting for various State occasions, it's full of interesting monuments – the one to John Donne was the only complete figure to be salvaged from the Great Fire. Look out for the wonderful carving on the exterior – some of which is by Grinling Gibbons, who also did the choir stalls. Other highlights include the dizzying Whispering Gallery, the panoramic views from the top, and the crypt, full of tombs and memorials to notable figures from British history. Snacks, shop, disabled access; cl Sun, Good Fri, 25 Dec and for occasional services; (020) 7236 4128; £6. The City Pipe by the tube station is an enjoyable wkdy wine bar, and the heavy-beamed Olde Watling (Watling St) was knocked up by Wren as a commissariat for his site workers.

107. The Tower of London

(Tower Hill, EC3) Picturesque classic castle, the most notable building to survive the Great Fire of London. A lot of fun to look at even superficially, it dates back to the late 11th c, though the site had been used as a defensive position by the Romans much earlier. It's witnessed all sorts of gruesome goings-on, with not even the highest or mightiest safe from imprisonment or even execution: Walter Raleigh, Lady Jane Grey and two of Henry VIII's wives spent their last days in the Tower. There's a mass of things to see, inc enough medieval weaponry and armour to glut the appetite of even the most bloodthirsty, and not forgetting the Beefeaters and the ravens – you need a fair bit of time to see everything properly. The Jewel House shows off the Crown Jewels to dazzling effect; on the busiest days those tempted to linger are gently drawn along by moving floorways. Two towers that were part of Edward I's medieval palace are furnished in period style, and peopled with appropriately costumed helpful guides; one room in this part has been left untouched to show what a difficult job the restoration was. A reorganisation of the oldest part, the White Tower, has revealed that the inside of the fortress when built was much less imposing than was suggested by the formidable exterior – they were clearly just trying to intimidate the locals. You can also walk along the elevated battlements. Meals, snacks, shop, some disabled access; cl 24–26 Dec, 1 Jan; (020) 7709 0765; £11.50.

108. 18th-c London life

Dennis Severs House (18 Folgate St, E1) Guided tours of a quite remarkable house now named after the man who made it such fun to visit – but be warned, this is no ordinary guided tour, and one far more suited to adults than children. It doesn't do the place justice to say that it's been furnished and decorated in period style – to all intents and purposes you are back in the 18th c, with candles and firelight flickering away, food and drink laid out on the table, even urine in the chamber-pots. Open 2–5pm first and third Sun of month (£8) and 12noon–2pm on the Mon following the first and third Sun (£5); (020) 7247 4013. Elaborate candlelit tours Mon evening (booking required); £12. Dirty Dicks (Bishopsgate) re-creates a traditional City cellar tavern, also fun for visitors.

109. A little-known museum in 18th-c almshouses

Geffrye Museum (Kingsland Rd, E2) One of London's most friendly and interesting museums, yet least-known; 18th-c almshouses converted to show the changing style of the English domestic interior. Displays go from lovely 17th-c oak panelling and furniture through elegant Georgian reconstructions and Victorian parlours to the latest in interior design inc a contemporary loft-style dwelling, though not all is as it seems – out of sight inside the shell of a vintage radio, for example, there's actually a distinctly modern CD player. They've given the gardens similar treatment, showing trends in domestic horticulture through the ages, inc a notable herb garden. Excellent programme of exhibitions, special events, talks and activities. Well worth tracking down. Meals, snacks, shop, disabled access; cl Sun am, all day Mon (exc pm bank hols), 24–26 Dec, 1 Jan, Good Fri; (020) 7739 9893; free.

110. Shakespeare's theatre reconstructed

Globe Theatre (Park St, SE1) The most famous of Southwark's 1600s theatres, Shakespeare's Globe has been reconstructed on its original site, where it was open from 1599 to 1642 (when the Puritans closed it down). It couldn't be more different from the West End: shaped like an O, the three-tiered open-topped theatre is 30 metres (100 ft) in diameter, seating audiences of 1,500 with a further 500 promenaders. Shakespeare's works are performed almost the way they were in the early 1600s – no spotlights, canned music or elaborate sets. Anyone who tells you the seats are uncomfortable has rather missed the point (and you can hire cushions). There are entertaining tours during the day, and displays on the Globes old and new – a good substitute if you can't make a performance. An exhibition under the building looks at the life and works of Shakespeare. Very good café and restaurant with river views, shop, disabled access; tours daily, although there are no tours summer pms; (020) 7902 1500; £8. The 17th-c galleried George in Borough High St, back past London Bridge station, gives another idea of how the area's buildings used to look back then; NT.

111. Southwark Cathedral

(Montague Cl, SE1) Off the busy main road and quite a contrast to the buildings cluttered all around it, this is well worth a look, with parts over 600 years older than the present late 19th-c nave. There are interesting memorials to William Shakespeare (whose brother is buried here) and the poet John Gower, and a chapel is dedicated to John Harvard, founder of the American university named for him, who was baptised here in 1607. An exhibition in the visitor centre uses touch-screen computers to show finds from recent excavations at the cathedral, while interactive tower-top cameras give views of London (you can contrast these with various views recorded from the 16th c onwards from the same viewpoint), and a mini-theatre has a film on the cathedral's history. Meals, snacks, shop, disabled access; cl 25 Dec, Easter Sun and Good Fri and occasionally during services; (020) 7367 6700; £2.50 suggested donation, £2.50 for audio guide, £3 exhibition (discount voucher valid for this).

A short walk from here is the **George** (off 77 Borough High St); unique in central London as a 17th-c galleried coaching inn – originally much larger, but the substantial and substantially unspoiled remains give an excellent impression of what Southwark's inns were like, in the days when this was London's entertainment centre.

112. Kensington Palace

State Apartments (Kensington Gardens, W8) Once-humble town house remodelled by Sir Christopher Wren and then enlarged by William Kent, the birthplace of Queen Victoria, and principal private Royal residence until the death of George II. Princess Margaret and Princess Diana lived here, and it's still the home of Prince and Princess Michael of Kent. The state rooms are quite magnificent, with elaborate furnishings and décor, while other rooms are interesting for their comparatively restrained understatement and personal history. Make sure you look up at the ceilings: some are exquisitely painted, inc an effective trompe-l'oeil dome (a couple of the patterns transfer very nicely to stationery in the gift shop). There are pictures and furniture from the Royal collection, and this is home to the Royal Ceremonial Dress Collection, with items of Royal, ceremonial and court dress dating from the 18th c to today, inc a display of the Queen's dresses and Diana's evening gowns. There's a small formal sunken garden. Café in imposing Orangery, shop, disabled access to the dress collection only; cl 24–26 Dec; (020) 7937 9561; £10.

113. A stately home in West London

Syon Park (London Rd, Brentford) The London home of the Duke of Northumberland, this was built on the site of a medieval abbey and remodelled from its Tudor original by Robert Adam – it's widely considered to be one of his finest works. The ceiling by Cipriani and the magnificent Scagliola floor are particular highlights, but a visit here can keep the whole family entertained, with 40 acres of grounds to stroll around (landscaped by Capability Brown), Thames-side water meadows, and a giant indoor adventure playground. Snacks, shop, disabled access to café and gardens only; house open Weds, Thurs, Sun and bank hol Mon (and all Easter wknd) mid-Mar to Oct, gardens open daily exc 25–26 Dec; (020) 8560 0882; £6.95 house and gardens, £3.50 gardens only. Also in the grounds is the London Butterfly House (shop, disabled access; cl 25–26 Dec; (020) 8560 0378; £4.95) and, with a range of endangered species, the **Aquatic Experience** (shop, disabled access; cl 24–26 Dec, 1 Jan; (0208) 8474730; £4).

114. The perfect Royal Palace

Hampton Court Palace (Hampton Court) An amazing place, just as a Royal palace should be. Begun by Cardinal Wolsey in the early 16th c, the house's splendour soon so pricked Henry VIII's jealousy that Wolsey felt compelled to present it to his king in an attempt to appease him. Successive monarchs have left their architectural marks: the hammerbeamed hall and kitchens were Henry's addition, the Fountain Court was designed by Wren for William and Mary, and much comes from the work of the Victorians (the chimneys mostly date from then). The rooms have managed to keep their distinctive styles, from the starkly imposing Tudor kitchens (themselves taking up 50 rooms) to the elaborate grandeur of the Georgian chambers. The King's Staircase is wonderfully over the top, and the Picture Gallery has the finest Renaissance works from the Royal collection, inc Pieter Bruegel the Elder's fascinating *Massacre of the Innocents*. Look out too for the carvings by Grinling Gibbons and the cartoons by Mantegna in the Lower Orangery. There are several excellent audio guides you can pick up and listen to as you go along, at no extra charge. Meals, snacks, shops, disabled access; cl 24–26 Dec; (0870) 752 7777; £11 inc entry to Privy Garden and maze.

Elaborately landscaped, the Palace Gardens are a fine mix of formal and informal (esp the Wilderness, full of spring flowers), bounded by a deer park with golf course. William III's quiet Privy Garden has been restored to its intricate 1702 design, with fountains, stonework, topiary and elaborate sand patterns cut into lawn. The famous maze swallows up 300,000 people a year, and the annual flower show here is one of the world's biggest. Open as palace; Privy Garden and maze £3 each (unless you are also visiting the palace, see above), gardens free. The Kings Arms (Lion Gate) is a decent food stop.

HISTORIC PLACES TO STAY

Berkshire

TAPLOW Cliveden *Taplow, Maidenhead, Berkshire SL6 0JF (01628) 668561* **£250** (plus £7 each paid to National Trust), plus special breaks; 39 luxurious, individual rms with maid unpacking service and a butler's tray. Superb Grade I listed stately home with gracious, comfortable public rooms, fine paintings, tapestries and armour, and a surprisingly unstuffy atmosphere; lovely views over the magnificent NT Thames-side parkland and formal gardens (open to the public); imaginative food in the two no smoking restaurants with lighter meals in the conservatory, friendly breakfasts around a huge table, and impeccable staff; pavilion with swimming pool, gym etc.; tennis, squash, croquet, riding, coarse fishing, a new golf course 5 minutes away reached by chauffeur-driven car, and boats for river trips; they are kind to children; good disabled access; dogs welcome away from eating areas

WINDSOR Oakley Court *Windsor Rd, Water Oakley, Windsor, Berkshire SL4 5UR (01753) 609988* **£165***w, plus special breaks; 118 spacious, individually furnished rms. Splendid Victorian country-house hotel in 35 acres of grounds by the Thames with 9-hole golf course, croquet lawn, tennis, fishing, boating, and health club; log fires in the elegant lounges, a panelled library, and particularly good food in smart restaurant; used in 200 films, notably the 'St Trinians' series and Hammer 'Dracula' films; disabled access

Buckinghamshire

AYLESBURY Hartwell House *Oxford Rd, Aylesbury, Buckinghamshire HP17 8NL (01296) 747444* **£235**, plus special breaks; 46 rms, some huge and well equipped, others with four-posters and fine panelling, inc ten secluded suites in restored 18th-c stables with private garden and statues. Elegant Grade I listed building with Jacobean and Georgian façades, wonderful decorative plasterwork and panelling, fine paintings and antiques, a marvellous Gothic central staircase, splendid morning room, and library, exceptional service, pricey wines, and excellent food; 90 acres of parkland with ruined church, lake and statues, and spa with indoor swimming pool, saunas, gym and beauty rooms, and informal restaurant; croquet, fishing; children over 8; good disabled access; dogs in Hartwell Court

Cambridgeshire

STILTON Bell *7 High St, Stilton, Peterborough, Cambridgeshire PE7 3RA (01733) 241066* **£89.50***; 19 rms. Elegant, carefully restored coaching inn with attractive rambling bars, big log fire, generous helpings of good food using the famous cheese (which was first sold from here), and seats in the sheltered cobbled and flagstoned courtyard; cl 25 Dec

Essex

BROXTED Whitehall *Church End, Broxted, Dunmow, Essex CM6 2BZ (01279) 850603* **£125**, plus special breaks; 26 pretty rms. Fine Elizabethan manor house in lovely walled gardens, with restful spacious lounge, a smaller cosier one with log fire, pleasant bar, good food in big, heavily timbered restaurant, and friendly service; cl 26–31 Dec

Kent

CANTERBURY Cathedral Gate *36 Burgate, Canterbury, Kent CT1 2HA (01227) 464381* **£88**, plus special breaks; 27 rms, 12 with own bthrm and some overlooking cathedral. 15th-c hotel that predates the adjoining sculpted cathedral gateway; bow windows, massive oak beams, sloping floors, antiques and fresh flowers, continental breakfast in little dining room or your own room, and a restful atmosphere; municipal car parks a few minutes away; dogs welcome but bring own bedding

CHIDDINGSTONE HOATH Hoath House *Penshurst Rd, Chiddingstone Hoath, Edenbridge, Kent TN8 7DB (01342) 850362* **£55**; 4 rms, 1 with own bthrm. Wonderful medieval house – added to over the years – with huge beams and plastered walls in the sitting room, family portraits, open fire in the library, heaps of interest and atmosphere, homely suppers, welcoming owners, and a big garden with fine views; they are kind to children; cl Christmas

FRITTENDEN Maplehurst Mill *Mill Lane, Frittenden, Cranbrook, Kent TN17 2DT (01580) 852203* **£90**; 3 rms with views over the water and surrounding countryside. Carefully restored 18th-c watermill attached to 15th-c mill house with original machinery, millstones and waterwheel; big comfortable drawing room, delicious imaginative food using home-grown organic produce in candlelit beamed dining room, and 11 acres of gardens and grounds with heated outdoor swimming pool; no smoking; cl Christmas and New Year; children over 12; disabled access

Leicestershire and Rutland

ROTHLEY Rothley Court *Westfield Lane, Rothley, Leicester LE7 7LG (0116) 237 4141* **£105**; 32 rms (the ones in the main house have more character). Mentioned in the Domesday Book, this carefully run manor house with its beautifully preserved 13th-c chapel has some fine oak panelling, open fires, a comfortable bar, conservatory, and courteous staff; seats out on the terrace and in the garden; disabled access; dogs welcome in bedrooms

Norfolk

MORSTON Morston Hall *The Street, Morston, Holt, Norfolk NR25 7AA (01263) 741041* **£190** inc dinner, plus special breaks; 6 comfortable rms with country views. Attractive 17th-c flint-walled house in tidal village, with lovely quiet gardens, two small lounges, one with an antique fireplace, a conservatory, and hard-working friendly young owners; particularly fine modern English cooking (they also run cookery demonstrations and hold wine and food events), a thoughtful small wine list, and super breakfasts; croquet; cl Jan; they are kind to families; partial disabled access; dogs welcome in bedrooms

Oxfordshire

BURFORD Lamb *Sheep St, Burford, Oxfordshire OX18 4LR (01993) 823155* **£120**, plus special breaks; 15 rms. Very attractive 500-year-old Cotswold inn with lovely restful atmosphere, spacious beamed, flagstoned and elegantly furnished lounge, classic civilised public bar, bunches of flowers on good oak and elm tables, three winter log fires, antiques, imaginative food in airy restaurant, and pretty little walled garden; cl 25–26 Dec; dogs welcome away from dining room

HORTON-CUM-STUDLEY Studley Priory *Horton-cum-Studley, Oxford OX33 1AZ (01865) 351203* **£165**, plus special breaks; 18 rather luxurious rms. Once a Benedictine nunnery, this lovely Elizabethan manor stands in 13 wooded acres; fine panelling, 16th- and 17th-c stained-glass windows, antiques, big log fires, and good sofas and armchairs in the elegant drawing room and cosy bar, smartly uniformed friendly service, and seasonally changing menus in attractive high-beamed restaurant, hung with lots of landscape prints; grass tennis court and croquet; dogs welcome in bedrooms

SHIPTON-UNDER-WYCHWOOD Shaven Crown *High St, Shipton-under-Wychwood, Chipping Norton, Oxfordshire OX7 6BA* (01993) 830330 **£95**, plus special breaks; 8 comfortable rms. Densely beamed, ancient stone hospice built around striking medieval courtyard with old-fashioned seats on cobbles, lily pool and roses; impressive medieval hall with a magnificent lofty ceiling, sweeping stairway and old stone walls, log fire in comfortable bar, intimate candlelit restaurant, well chosen wine list, good friendly service, warm relaxed atmosphere, and bowling green; children over 5 in evening dining room; disabled access; dogs welcome away from restaurant

Suffolk

BURSTALL Mulberry Hall *Burstall, Ipswich, Suffolk IP8 3DP* (01473) 652348 **£50***; 2 comfortable rms. Once owned by Cardinal Wolsey, this lovely old farmhouse has a fine garden, an inglenook fireplace in the big beamed sitting room, excellent food (ordered in advance) in pretty dining room, very good breakfasts with home-baked bread and preserves, and helpful friendly owners; tennis and croquet; cl Christmas week

LAVENHAM Lavenham Priory *Water St, Lavenham, Sudbury, Suffolk CO10 9RW* **£78**; 6 big rms with sloping beamed ceilings, antiques, fresh flowers, and pretty bthrms. Dating back to the 13th c, this is a lovely Grade I listed house once owned by Benedictine monks: Elizabethan wall paintings, beams and oak floors, a huge flagstoned Great Hall, inglenook fireplaces, and all lavishly restored; lovely civilised breakfasts, evening meals by arrangement, and helpful, friendly owners; a charming garden with herb beds, kitchen garden and some fine trees; cl 25 Dec–1 Jan; children over 10

NEEDHAM MARKET Pipps Ford *Norwich Rd, Needham Market, Ipswich, Suffolk IP6 8LJ (01449) 760208* **£77**, plus winter breaks; 8 pretty rms with antiques and fine old beds, 4 in converted Stables Cottage. Lovely 16th-c farmhouse in quiet garden surrounded by farmland alongside attractive river; log fires in big inglenook fireplaces, good imaginative food using home-baked bread, locally produced meats, honey, eggs, and preserves, and organic local veg and herbs, and conservatory with subtropical plants (some meals can be communal); cl 2 wks over Christmas; children over 5; disabled access

Sussex

AMBERLEY Amberley Castle *Church St, Amberley, Arundel, West Sussex BN18 9ND (01798) 831992* **£155**; 19 very well equipped charming rms. Magnificent 900-year-old castle with suits of armour and weapons in the day rooms – as well as antiques, roaring fires and panelling; friendly service, imaginative food in no smoking 13th-c dining room, and exceptionally pretty gardens; children over 12

CLIMPING Bailiffscourt *Climping St, Climping, Littlehampton, East Sussex BN17 5RW (01903) 723511* **£160**, plus special breaks; 32 rms, many with four-poster beds and winter log fires, and with super views. Mock 13th-c manor built only 60 years ago but with tremendous character – fine old iron-studded doors, huge fireplaces, heavy beams and so forth – in 30 acres of coastal pastures and walled gardens: elegant furnishings, enjoyable modern English and French food, fine wines, a relaxed atmosphere, and outdoor swimming pool, tennis and croquet; children over 7 in restaurant; disabled access; dogs welcome away from restaurant

HARTFIELD Bolebroke Mill *Perry Hill, Edenbridge Rd, Hartfield, East Sussex TN7 4JP (01892) 770425* **£66**, plus special breaks; 5 rms, some in the mill and some in adjoining Elizabethan miller's barn. A working mill until 1948, this ancient place was mentioned in Domesday Book, and is surrounded by mill streams and woodland; the internal machinery has been kept intact and steep narrow stairs lead to bedrooms that were once big corn bins; both this and the barn have their own sitting room, breakfasts are marvellous (good nearby pubs and restaurants for other meals), and the owners very friendly; no smoking; cl 20 Dec–12 Feb; children over 8

RYE Jeakes House *Mermaid St, Rye, East Sussex TN31 7ET (01797) 222828* **£84**; 12 rms overlooking the rooftops of this medieval town or across the marsh to the sea, 10 with own bthrm. Fine 16th-c building, well run and friendly, with good breakfasts, lots of well worn books, comfortable furnishings, linen and lace, a warm fire, and lovely peaceful atmosphere; children over 11; dogs welcome in bedrooms

Warwickshire

LOXLEY Loxley Farm *Stratford Rd, Loxley, Warwick, Warwickshire CV35 9JN (01789) 840265* **£64***; 2 suites with their own sitting rooms in attractive barn conversion. Not far from Stratford, this tucked-away, thatched and half-timbered partly 14th-c house has low beams, wonky walls and floors, antiques and dried flowers, open fire, helpful friendly owners, and good Aga-cooked breakfasts; peaceful garden, and fine old village church; cl Christmas and New Year; dogs welcome in bedrooms

SUTTON COLDFIELD New Hall *New Hall Drive, Sutton Coldfield, West Midlands B76 1QX (0121) 378 2442* **£153**w, plus special breaks; 60 lovely rms (the ones in the manor house are the best). England's oldest moated manor house, in 26 beautiful acres, with luxurious day rooms, a graceful panelled restaurant with carefully cooked imaginative food using the freshest (often home-grown) produce, and excellent service; they can hold wedding ceremonies, and have a leisure club; children over 8; disabled access; dogs welcome in bedrooms

Wiltshire

MALMESBURY Old Bell *Abbey Row, Malmesbury, Wiltshire SN16 0BW (01666) 822344* **£130***, plus special breaks; 31 rms. With some claim to being one of England's oldest hotels and standing in the shadow of the Norman abbey, this fine wisteria-clad building has traditionally furnished rooms with Edwardian pictures, an early 13th-c hooded stone fireplace, two good fires and plenty of comfortable sofas, magazines and newspapers; cheerful helpful service, very good food, and attractively old-fashioned garden; particularly well organised for families; disabled access to ground floor bedroom; dogs welcome in bedrooms

South-West England & Southern Wales

Including Southern Wales, Herefordshire, Worcestershire, Gloucestershire, Somerset, Dorset, Devon and Cornwall.

◆ ◆ ◆

115. Caverns where Iron Age people lived

National Showcave Centre for Wales (A4067 just N of Craig-y-Nos) Fascinating series of caves, well lit to emphasise the extraordinary rock formations. The Cathedral Cave is the largest single chamber open to the public in any British showcave, while 3,000 years ago Bone Cave was lived in by humans. There's also a dinosaur park, Iron Age farm, shire horse centre, and artificial ski-slope, so lots to see. Meals, snacks, shops; cl Nov–Apr (open Feb half-term); (01639) 730284; £8. The Tafarn y Garreg just N does decent food.

116. Mine gold where the Romans did

Dolaucothi Gold Mines (Pumsaint, off A482) 2,000 years of gold-mining are the focus of this unusual mine, in use since Roman times; tours of both the Roman adits, Victorian, and 1930s workings, complete with miners' lamps and helmets. Visitor centre, woodland walks, and the chance to have a go at panning for gold. Stout footwear recommended. Meals, snacks, shop; site open

Apr–mid Sept. *£2.80; NT. Underground tours; (01558) 650177. Estate events – monthly walks and talks Apr–Sept; Roman and archaeology activity days for families, fishing, self-catering, B&B and cycle hire on the estate; (01558) 650707. The nearby Brunant Arms in fine scenery at Caio has good value food (inc prime Welsh black steak), and opposite the pub is a Roman fort and red kite information centre.

117. Britain's oldest cathedral community

St David's has had a community in residence around its cathedral for longer than any other in Britain, but thanks to the relative isolation of the place it's stayed undeveloped, so that St David's today is little more than a village – with lots of colourful flowers in spring. It's a good area for coastal walks, perhaps to ancient sites such as the neolithic burial chambers up by St David's Head to the S or over towards Solva, to St Non's Chapel, or W to St Justinian (another chapel here, looking over Ramsey Island). The cheerful Farmers Arms by the cathedral gate has good value food. The beach at Whitesands Bay is good. In summer there are boat trips from the lifeboat station around or to rocky Ramsey Island, where seabirds nest in great numbers.

St David's Cathedral The Norman church had largely collapsed by the 15th c, and elaborate repairs had to be made; the resulting roof is an impressive lace-like oak affair, and oak features in most of the rest of the church too. There's a fine collection of Celtic sculptured crosses. Shop, disabled access; cl Sun am; free, though donation welcome.

Bishop's Palace Impressive ruins, clearly once very grand: plenty of quadrangles, stairways and splendid arcaded walls, with all sorts of intricate and often entertaining details (like the carvings below the arcaded parapets). Atmospheric and tranquil, particularly out of season when you may have it largely to yourself. Shop, limited disabled access; cl winter Suns am, 24–26 Dec, 1 Jan; (01437) 720517; £2.50; Cadw.

118. Medieval walled town and Ice Age cave

Tenby is a pleasantly restrained family seaside resort, with nice sheltered beaches and rock coves. It's a walled town, the splendidly preserved 13th-c wall still with many of its towers left, as well as a magnificent 14th-c arched barbican gateway; a moat used to run the whole length of what is now a tree-lined street. The medieval Plantagenet House has good interesting food.

Hoyle's Mouth Cave (off A4139 just SW, Trefloyne Lane towards St Florence; short path through wood on left after 500 yds) Running more than 30 metres (100 ft) back into the hillside, this spooky place has yielded Ice Age mammoth bones, as well as human tools dating back over 10,000 years. Take a torch, but don't go in winter – you'd disturb the hibernating bats.

119. When coal powered Welsh life

Rhondda Heritage Park (Trehafod, off A470) Based around the last colliery buildings in the area, this well organised centre uses lively multi-media exhibitions to re-create the golden days of the coal-mining industry, evoking sights, sounds and smells from the life and work of the miners. The excellent underground tour showing what it was like to work a shift is uncannily realistic, and the twisting simulated trip back to the surface is a definite highlight. Other displays look at the wider social heritage of the valley, with art by locals, a re-created village street, and (Easter–Sept) an excellent themed adventure play area for children. A good excursion whatever the weather. Meals, snacks, shop, good disabled access (even underground); cl Mon Oct–Easter, and 25–26 Dec; (01443) 682036; £5.60.

120. Go down to the coal face in this World Heritage Site

The industrial village of **Blaenavon** was until 20 years ago the centre for mining and ironwork in the Gwent valleys.

Big Pit Mining Museum (B4248) This was a working pit for 200 years, until 1980, and the tour guides are all former miners; their anecdotes and expertise, and the underground atmosphere, make a visit here quite special. There are plenty of colliery workings to explore on the surface, but it's the hour-long pit tours that stand out; armed with a hard hat and lamp, you get into the pit cage and descend 90 metres (300 ft) into the inky blackness that was daily life for generations of local men. Wrap up warmly (even in summer) and wear sensible footwear. They don't allow under-5s, or anyone under a metre tall. Back on the surface there's a reconstructed miner's cottage, and an exhibition in the old pithead baths. The whole site takes around 2½ hrs to see properly. Meals, snacks, shop, disabled access (even underground, though you must book); usually cl Dec–mid-Feb; (01495) 790311; free.

Blaenavon Ironworks (North St) Appreciable ruins of five 1788–89 steam-powered blast furnaces, driven out of business by the advent of steel in the following century. A water-balance tower (which provided power to move materials around the site) and workers' cottages also survive. Site exhibition; open Apr–Oct; (01495) 792615; £2; Cadw. Tours through the Pontfaen Museum, Pontypool.

121. A mighty moated medieval fortress

Caerphilly Castle (Caerphilly) One of the largest medieval fortresses in Britain, begun in 1268, with extensive land and water defences. Rising sheer from its broad outer moat, it's a proper picture-book castle, pleasing for this reason to the most casual visitor. It also enthrals serious students of castle architecture with its remarkably complex design of concentric defences. Look out for the incredible leaning tower, which appears ready to topple any second; audio-visual display and replica medieval siege engines; new visitors centre. Shop, disabled access to ground floor; cl 24–26 Dec, 1 Jan; (029) 2088 3143; £2.50; Cadw. In the oddly strung-out small town, the ancient Courthouse overlooking the castle has reasonably priced food.

122. A fairytale castle in Cardiff itself

Cardiff Castle (Castle St) Despite their fairytale medieval appearance, the main buildings are largely 19th-c, when the Marquess of Bute employed William Burges to rebuild and restore the place, adding richly romantic wall paintings, stained glass and carvings. Some parts are much older, and in the grounds there's even a piece of a Roman wall 3 metres (10 ft) thick. The Norman keep survives, as does a 13th-c tower – these two look like proper castle architecture, perched on a little mound. Also two military museums. Snacks, shop; usually cl 25–26 Dec, 1 Jan only, though major development over the next five years may affect opening times – best to phone; (029) 2087 8100; *£5.50 for full guided tour, *£2.75 grounds only.

123. A vibrant show of Welsh life through the ages

Museum of Welsh Life (St Fagans, A4232 4m W of Cardiff) Excellent 100-acre open-air museum, with a variety of recon-structed buildings illustrating styles and living conditions through-out the ages. Buildings have come from all over Wales, and there are some remarkable exhibits, inc a homely gas-lit Edwardian farmhouse and a Celtic village. You can buy things from a period grocery store, ride on horse and cart or have a go at making your own pot. Also crafts, regular demonstrations and lots of seasonal events – there's plenty to fascinate here, and the grounds are pretty too. Meals and snacks (in 1920s tearoom), shops, limited disabled access; cl 24–25 Dec; (029) 2057 3500; free. The Plymouth Arms is very handy for good value food.

124. Was this Roman garrison the court of King Arthur?

Roman Fortress Baths, Amphitheatre & Barracks (Caerleon) The site of the 50-acre Roman fortress of Isca, established in AD 75 as the permanent base of the 5,500-strong Second Augustan Legion. One of the best examples of an amphitheatre in the country, alongside impressive remains of the fortress baths, barrack blocks (the only examples currently visible in all Europe), and fortress wall. Shop, disabled access; cl 24–26 Dec, 1 Jan; (01554) 890104; £2; Cadw. Caerleon is reckoned in these parts to have been the site of the court of King Arthur. Near the Tourist Information Centre on the High St is a little art gallery, with various craft workshops in an 18th-c walled garden; the Hanbury Arms has generous food.

125. A classic romantic ruin by the River Wye

Tintern Abbey (Tintern, off A466) Remarkably well preserved, these 14th-c ruins were considered an essential spot for 18th-c artists and poets to visit, lying as they do in a lovely part of the steeply wooded Wye Valley. Wordsworth was just one of many to find inspiration here. Shop, disabled access; cl 24–26 Dec, 1 Jan; (01291) 689251; £2.50; Cadw. The Moon & Sixpence overlooking it and the river has good value food, and the ancient tucked-away Cherry Tree (signed off the main road) does bargain lunches. The Abbey Mill has been converted into a craft and visitor centre. Demonstrations, restaurant and coffee shop; cl 25–26 Dec; free. A visitor centre at Tintern Old Station can help you make the most of the surrounding hills and woodland; open Apr–Oct; free.

126. Norman castle remains, great for exploring

Goodrich Castle (Goodrich) This proper-looking 12th-c castle (built using the same red sandstone rock it stands on so that it seems almost to grow out of the ground) appeals a lot to readers. Still plenty to see, with towers, passageways, dungeon and marvellous views of the surrounding countryside. Snacks (summer only), shop; cl 1–2pm, Mon–Tues in Nov–Mar, 24–26 Dec, 1 Jan; (01600) 890538; £3.60. These formidable ruins are a feasible objective for stout-hearted walkers from Symonds Yat, or could be a starting point for Wye Valley gorge walks. The partly Norman Mill Race at Walford has good value food.

127. Hereford, a classic market town of yesteryear

Hereford grew as a regional market centre, and still has its livestock and general market every Weds. For the rest of the week it feels very quiet-paced and old-fashioned, its streets, some pedestrianised, lined with handsome Georgian and other buildings; Church St is almost wholly medieval. The local council, unhappy with the city's rather too peaceful reputation, want to rebrand Hereford 'City of Living Crafts': Church St and Capuchin Yard will be developed as a crafts quarter, and they'll be adding tree sculptures too. Guided walks leave the Tourist Information Centre every day mid-May to mid-Sept at 11am (2.30pm Sun); they also do a ghost walk (7.15pm Weds Jun–Sept; £2). Wye-side walks give a pleasing view of the city, its spires and towers. The Bay Horse (Kings Acre Rd), Gilbies (St Peters Cl), Green Dragon Hotel (Broad St) and Stagecoach (West St) are all useful for lunch.

Hereford Cathedral This largely Norman building has a lovely 13th- and 15th-c chapel, as well as the country's biggest chained library (the second biggest is at All Saints church, at the opposite end of the main street), and the famous Mappa Mundi, the largest surviving 13th-c world map. There's a splendid interpretative exhibition, with some computer displays; the map itself is shown in a specially dimmed room to preserve it. Meals, snacks, shop, disabled access; cl winter Suns, most of Jan, Good Fri, 25 Dec (tower only open July–Aug); (01432) 374200; Mappa Mundi exhibition and chained library £4, suggested donation for cathedral £2. Guided tours at 11am and 2pm Mon–Sat Easter to end Sept (£2.50).

St John Medieval Museum and Coningsby Hospital (Widemarsh St) Little museum and chapel dating back to 13th c, with armour and relics relating to the Order of St John and the Crusades, and a display on the pensioners who lived at the hospital in the 17th c; in the rose garden you can see the ruins of Black Friars Monastery, and a rare preaching cross. They usually do guided tours, ask the friendly staff; disabled access; cl am, Mon, Fri and Sun, Oct–Easter; (01432) 267821; £2.

128. Seven centuries of Worcestershire buildings

Avoncroft Museum of Historic Buildings (Stoke Prior, 2m S of Bromsgrove, by A38 bypass and B4091) An enjoyable place to spend a relaxing afternoon. Around 25 buildings from the last seven centuries have been saved from demolition and rebuilt here: there's a timber-framed merchant's house, a Victorian church and gaol, even a 1946 prefab. A lovely working windmill is particularly popular with children and, more incongruously, there's a unique collection of telephone kiosks, from Tardis-style police boxes to unlovely modern hutches, with everything in between. Also a play area, and donkeys and chickens wander about. Several of the buildings are furnished inside, but it's very much a place to visit on a dry day, when children can make the most of the open space the museum stands on. Meals, snacks, picnic area, shop, disabled access; cl Dec–Mar, Mon Mar–Jun and Sept–Nov, also Fri Mar and Nov; (01527) 831363; £5.20. The nearby Country Girl has enjoyable food, and is handy for walks on Dodderhill Common.

129. Historic Evesham

The pedestrianised market square has some fine buildings around it, inc a 12th-c abbey gateway; the church's striking 16th-c bell tower is well preserved, and some altogether more ruined remnants in the town park beyond lead to riverside meadows. The Tourist Information Centre is in another attractive abbey building, the Almonry, a Tudor timbered house with a museum and nice gardens (cl Christmas–New Year and Sun pm Nov–Jan; £2). The Green Dragon (Oat St), visibly brewing its own ales, has inexpensive food. In Apr or early May the orchard drive through Harvington, the Lenches, Badgers Hill, Fladbury Cross, Wood Norton and Chadbury is pretty.

130. A warren of secret hidey-holes in a moated manor

Harvington Hall (Harvington) Moated Elizabethan manor house with secret chapels, the largest number of priest hides in England, and original wall paintings. Also herb garden and picnic area; restaurant, shop, ground floor disabled access; cl Mon, Tues, wkdys Mar and Oct, and Nov–Feb; (01562) 777846; *£4.20. The village is one of the area's oldest, brilliantly black and white. The Golden Cross has nice food.

131. Where England's most English composer was born

Elgar Birthplace Museum (Crown East Lane, Lower Broadheath) Modest cottage where the composer was born in 1857; now, as he wanted, a museum of his life and work, with displays of photographs and letters, and the desk where he did his writing. A visitor centre concentrates on his music and inspirations, with audio and visual displays, manuscripts, musical scores, concert programmes and other memorabilia. Shop (with CDs), disabled access to centre, gardens, and ground floor of cottage; cl 23 Dec–end Jan; (01905) 333224; £3.75 (audio tour £1). You can pick up routes and information here about the Elgar Trail around the area. The Bear & Ragged Staff over at Bransford is a good dining pub.

132. Worcester's treasures

Though it's a busy commercial centre, Worcester has some splendid medieval buildings dotted about, with lots of half-timbered houses, particularly around Friar St, where the Lemon Tree has good food, and New St (the King Charles here is a good restaurant). Plenty of shops, inc some nice specialist ones and cafés in Hopmarket Yard, a former coaching inn. You can visit handsome

Georgian Guildhall (usually cl Sun); free.

Worcester Cathedral Founded on the site of a Saxon monastery, in a calm and peaceful setting overlooking the river. It took from 1084 to 1375 to build, and has an attractive 14th-c tower, Norman crypt, and the tombs of Prince Arthur and King John, the latter topped by the oldest Royal effigy in the country. Lots of Victorian stained glass, and some monastic buildings. Guided tours, (book on (01905) 28854), snacks, shop, some disabled access; £3 suggested donation.

Greyfriars (Friar St) Beautiful and carefully restored medieval timber-framed town house (still lived in), with delightful walled garden. Cl am, Fri–Tues and Nov–Mar; (01905) 23571; £3; NT.

Museum of Worcester Porcelain (Severn St) Home of Royal Worcester, the country's oldest continuous producer of porcelain, with wkdy factory tours (no under-11s), period room settings, and displays of porcelain dating back to the 18th c. Meals, snacks, shop, disabled access to museum only; cl 25–26 Dec and Easter Sun; (01905) 746000; factory tour £5, tour of the museum and visitor centre £4.50, museum £3. The Potters Wheel opposite has decent food.

133. Perhaps Britain's oldest mining caverns

Clearwell Caves (Clearwell, off B4228) A good way to spend an hour or so rather than a whole day, these caverns are great for children who like to be spooked and don't mind going underground. It's quite low-key, and not overly developed, so if you're after great facilities and dramatic effects it's not for you, but if you haven't toured many caves before and want to discover a bit about Britain's mining history, you should find it enthralling. You find your own way around nine caverns, reckoned to be some of the oldest underground workings in Britain. Generations of miners

– many of them (like the owners) freeminers, with an ancient birthright allowing them to dig for minerals here – worked the site for iron ore, but today the very small-scale mining produces pigments used in allergy-free paints. In places, artificial pools make it seem as if you're in a natural cave, and the years of work down here have resulted in some unique shapes and colourful patterns. It's quite a labyrinth, so stout shoes are recommended and, like most caves, it can feel dark and damp at times (you are 30 metres – 100 ft – below ground, after all), so wrap up well. If you can get a group together, very good guided tours take you down a little deeper. In the run-up to Christmas, young children will get more out of the caves than geologists, as they're transformed into a festive walk-through grotto. Other events might include subterranean Shakespeare performances. There are also displays of mining equipment and engines. Meals, snacks, shop; usually open Mar–Oct, plus the run-up to Christmas and wknds Jan–Feb; (01594) 832535; £3.80 adults, £2.40 children 5–16. A family ticket (two adults, two children) is £11 (discount voucher not valid for bank hols and end of Nov–Dec).

134. Tombs from 4,000 years ago

There's a pleasant walk up to **Belas Knap**, a massive 4,000-year-old barrow – one of England's best-preserved prehistoric burial sites, complete with original dry-stone walling enclosing four internal chambers. Great views from the Craven Arms in Brockhampton (a good pub, with a nice garden in a lovely setting); this could be tied in with a walk past some very surprising ruins of a Roman villa tucked away in the woods.

135. Regency elegance

Cheltenham is a beautiful spa town, useful for exploring the Cotswolds, shopping, or admiring the elegant Regency architecture of its tree-lined avenues. These days Cheltenham is best known for its races, and the racecourse at Prestbury Park (N on A435) has an exhibition on Gold Cup winners; (01242) 513014; cl wknds; free. Lots of antiques shops, esp around the Montpellier area. Tailors (Cambray Pl), the Montpellier Wine Bar (Montpellier St), Mitres (Sandford St) and Belgian Monk (Clarence St) have decent food, and the well run café in the beautiful Imperial Gardens is good for families.

   Pittville Pump Room (Pittville Park) A short walk from the centre, this is the town's finest building, a 19th-c Greek Revival with a colonnaded façade and balconied hall. It's easy to imagine the place's Regency heyday, especially strolling around the super park and gardens, or during concerts in the July music festival. On some summer Suns they may have teas accompanied by live music, also occasional art and craft exhibitions. You can still sample the spa water – rather salty. Meals, snacks, shop, disabled access to ground floor only; cl Tues; (01242) 523852; free.

136. The Cotswolds' most charming town

Chipping Campden is extremely attractive, with interesting old buildings inc an ancient covered open-sided market hall, a grand Perpendicular church typical of the area's rich 'wool churches', enjoyable shops, and fine old inns. Many of our contributors would put it among the country's most delightful small towns, though until they get the cars out of the centre not all would agree. The Eight Bells, Volunteer, Kings Arms, Noel Arms and Lygon Arms are all good for lunch. The **Cotswold Way**, a 100-mile path from here all the way to Bath, carefully picks out some of the choicest Cotswold scenery – a worthwhile aid for those planning a shorter stroll.

137. Gloucester's glory – and where Harry Potter went to school

Gloucester Cathedral Towering majestically over the city's more recent buildings, this has lovely fan-vaulted cloisters, the second-largest medieval stained-glass window in the country, and a fine collection of church plate in the Treasury. In 1330 the Abbot astutely purchased the remains of murdered Edward II, and the resulting stream of pilgrims paid for elaborate rebuilding, an early example of Perpendicular style. The cloisters' temporary transformation into parts of Harry Potter's Hogwarts school for wizards may persuade normally philistine younger visitors to spend some time here; sadly in the news more recently when mindless vandals smashed up some of the stained glass. Meals, snacks, shop, some disabled access; (01452) 508210; £2.50 recommended donation.

138. Fascinating tours of an unfinished mansion

Woodchester Mansion (Nympsfield, B4066) Construction of this splendid unfinished Gothic mansion was inexplicably abandoned virtually overnight in 1870. It's being repaired but not finished, and you can usually see traditional building techniques such as stonemasonry. Readers have high praise for the guided tours. Five species of bat have made this their home, and infra-red CCTV in their colonies (the only such installation in Britain) lets you watch them. Snacks, shop, disabled access to ground floor only; open first wknd of month Easter–Oct, plus bank hol wknds, Sun July–Sept, plus Sat July–Aug, though best to check; (01453) 750455; £4. The NT-owned 500-acre park is open all year (a herd of pigs, introduced to eat up brambles and nettles, made the news when they unearthed archaeological remains here). The walk up Coaley Peak gives tremendous views over the Severn Valley. In the village the Rose & Crown is a good value dining pub.

139. Hidden in the woods, a lovely Roman villa

Chedworth Roman Villa (Yanworth) The best example of a 2nd-c Roman house in Britain, excavated in 1864 and nicely set in secluded woodland. Well preserved rooms, bath houses, 4th-c mosaics, and a water shrine, with smaller remains in the deliberately Victorian-feeling museum. Snacks, shop, some disabled access; cl Mon (exc bank hols), and mid Nov–Feb; (01242) 890256; £3.80; NT. The riverside Mill at Withington and Seven Tuns in pretty Upper Chedworth are quite handy for lunch, and the walk from each is very picturesque and unspoilt, with Chedworth Woods providing further scope for short walks.

140. Beautiful Bath

For many Bath is England's most rewarding old town, though its throngs of summer visitors tend to mask its charms a bit then. Many places enjoyably recall the days of Beau Nash and the building of Bath as a fashionable resort; other draws go back to the Roman Baths, and come right up to date with the city's interesting and unusual shops. The new Bath Spa complex, opening in February, will bring taking the spa waters into the 21st century. In the meantime our favourite places to visit are the Roman Baths, Museum of Costume at the Assembly Rooms (these attractions offer a good value joint ticket), Pump Room, Building of Bath Museum, Industrial Heritage Centre, No 1 Royal Crescent, and Bath Abbey. The American Museum on the edge of the city at

Claverton is very special. Parts not to be missed include the great showpieces of 18th-c town planning, Queen Sq, the Circus and the Royal Crescent; the quieter Abbey Green and cobbled Abbey St and Queen St; and the great Pulteney Bridge (there's a fine view of it from the bridge at the end of North Parade, or the riverside Parade Gardens, where brass bands play in summer). The narrow little lanes between the main streets can be fascinating. The Old Green Tree (Green St) is a good pub with decent food. Walcot St has a good flea market (Sat am), and every Sat a farmers' market by Green Park Station has lots of fresh fruit and vegetables. The beautifully restored historic **Theatre Royal** presents more pre-West End productions than anywhere else in the country. Don't try to drive around the city: Bath's streets were laid out for travel by sedan chair, not car, and a tortuous one-way system seems designed to deter drivers rather than to make traffic flow more easily. It's better to leave your car at one of the city's four park-and-ride sites and take the shuttle bus in. Walking around Bath is a delight; there are flat parts, though to make the most of it you have to be prepared to slog up some of the steeper streets. Readers particularly enjoy the somewhat irreverent **Bizarre Bath** walking tours that leave the Huntsman Inn on North Parade Passage at 8pm daily, Apr–Sept (£5) – more street theatre than a typical tour; or you can go on one of the free daily walking tours which leave from outside the Roman Baths at 10.30am and 2pm (10.30 only on Sats). The rush of a day trip doesn't do justice to the host of things worth seeing; it is best to stay, preferably out of season. On summer days crowds of trippers and school parties tend to spoil the best-known parts, and if you want to visit during Bath's early summer Music Festival, book accommodation well ahead. The Bath Pass, giving entry to several places here, plus bike hire and canoeing, for £19 (£29 for a 2-day pass), is worth considering if you want to pack lots into a visit; details from Tourist Information Centre, (01225) 477101.

Roman Baths Founded by AD 75, and undoubtedly one of Britain's most remarkable Roman sites. They were built to service pilgrims visiting a temple to Sulis Minerva, which had been constructed around a sacred hot spring. After this the spring played a dual role – as both a focus for worship, and a reservoir supplying the baths with spa water. The temple and baths were all but forgotten until the 18th c, when workmen chanced upon a bust of Minerva, and it was not until 1878 that most of what you see today was uncovered. The main baths are pretty much intact, though the columns are 19th-c reconstructions. In July and Aug they're open at night and quite beautifully floodlit. A **museum** shows finds made during excavations, inc the bust of Minerva, a remarkable Gorgon's Head pediment, and lead tablets inscribed with messages and thrown into the spring by pilgrims; also models and an audio guide. Meals, snacks, shop, some disabled access (though not to baths themselves); cl 25–26 Dec; (01225) 477785; £8, inc an audio guide.

Bath Abbey & Abbey Heritage Vaults Particularly renowned for its fan vaulting, the current building is the third great church to be built on this site, begun in 1499. The Elizabethans called it the Lantern of the West because of its profusion of stained glass. Most impressive is the great E window, depicting 56 scenes from the life of Christ. On one side of this is a finely carved memorial to Bartholomew Barnes (1608), and on the other the beautiful medieval carving of the Prior Birde chantry. Restoration has returned the interior's gradually blackened Bath stone to its more appealing honey colour. Bookshop, disabled access; cl Good Fri, 24–26 Dec, 1 Jan, and during private services (usually Sun); £2 suggested donation. The carefully restored 18th-c vaults have a very good exhibition on the abbey's history. Disabled access; cl Sun; (01225) 422462; £2.

No 1 Royal Crescent The most splendid example of the

architecture that sprang up in the town's Georgian heyday. In 1768 it was the first house built in Bath's most regal terrace, and now has two floors restored and beautifully furnished in the style of that time. Shop; cl Mon (exc bank hols), and end Nov to mid-Feb; (01225) 428126; £4. The Crescent is closed to traffic at one end, with the hope of reducing damage inflicted by tour buses.

Jane Austen Centre (Gay St) Jane Austen lived in this street 1801–6, and this enjoyable centre takes a comprehensive look at the novelist's life, as well as the ways in which the city influenced her writing. Displays include re-creations of a Georgian shop-front and town garden, exhibitions on places mentioned in her novels, and elegant costumes; also news on Austen-related events and walking tours (£3.50 extra). Shop (selling every Austen-related book in print), disabled access; cl 24–26 Dec; (01225) 443000; £3.95.

Prior Park Landscape Garden (Ralph Allen Drive, off A3062 S) In a sweeping valley, this striking 18th-c landscaped garden is being comprehensively restored by the National Trust. Capability Brown and Alexander Pope originally helped with the design, and there are plenty of unique ornamental features (inc 18th-c graffiti on the Palladian bridge). Woodland walks offer unusual views over Bath (ring for details of events). Note you can't drive all the way here: there's no car parking on site or nearby (though there are some spaces for disabled visitors; phone to book). You can walk from town, but the hill is very steep, so best to take the number 2 or 4 bus. Cl Tues Feb–Nov, Mon–Thurs Dec–Jan, 25–26 Dec, 1 Jan; (01225) 833422; £4 (£1 off if show bus or train ticket or cycle); NT. There's decent food at the Cross Keys on Midford Rd.

141. Snapshots of Bristol's distinguished past

This busy city has parts with handsome buildings, great waterfront panoramas, hilly parts with interesting alleys and sudden leafy quarters, and plenty of cafés, pubs and bars. The city's prosperity still stems from its port, though aerospace now predominates among many other manufacturing interests. There are some striking buildings around the centre, notably the Corn Exchange and the Old Council House on Corn St, and on Broad St the Grand Hotel (1869), the Guildhall (1843) and the art nouveau façade of the former Edward Everard printing house. The Theatre Royal, opened in 1766, is one of the oldest working theatres in the country. A good part for leisurely strolls is the elegant suburb of Clifton, with handsome Georgian terraces (it's got more Georgian buildings than Bath) and its famous suspension bridge. Useful central places for a cheapish lunchtime bite are the Commercial Rooms (Corn St), Cottage (Cumberland Rd), Llandoger Trow (King St), Old Fish Market (Broad St) and Horts City Tavern (Broad St).

Bristol Cathedral This was originally an Augustinian monastery, founded on what's supposedly the spot where St Augustine met the Celtic Christians in the early 7th c. It's a real mix of architectural styles, and perhaps the country's most splendid example of a hall church, where the nave, choir and aisles are all the same height. Highlights include the Chapter House (one of the finest Norman rooms in Britain), and the candlesticks given in thanks by the privateers who rescued Alexander Selkirk (whose adventures inspired Daniel Defoe to write *Robinson Crusoe*). Snacks, shop; (0117) 926 4879; free (donations welcomed).

New Room – John Wesley's Chapel (Horsefair) Incongruously set in a shopping centre, but much as it was when Wesley preached here (from his famous double-decked pulpit, as well as a less-known predecessor, returned here from Anglesey in 1999); the oldest Methodist chapel in the world, built in 1739 and rebuilt in 1748. Guided tours by arrangement. Shop, disabled access to ground floor only; cl Sun, Good Fri, and 25–26 Dec;

(0117) 926 4740; free (£2.80 tour).

Red Lodge (Park St) The house was altered in the 18th c, but on its first floor still has the last surviving suite of 16th-c rooms in Bristol, as well as a wonderful carved stone chimney-piece, plasterwork ceilings and fine oak panelling. They occasionally open the reconstructed Tudor-style garden. Open Sat–Weds and most bank hols Jun–Oct; (0117) 921 1360; free. There are several elegant Georgian streets round here, notably Great George St, where the **Georgian House**, built in 1790 for a wealthy sugar merchant, is a fine illustration of a typical town house of the day. Three floors are decorated in period style, inc the below-stairs area with kitchen, laundry and housekeeper's room. Times as for Red Lodge; (0117) 921 1362; free.

Historic Boat Trips (from Princes Wharf) The 1860s steam-tug *Mayflower*, the 1930s fireboat *Pyronaut* and the tug *John King* give interesting trips round the dock in the summer – best to check times with the Industrial Museum; (0117) 925 1470; £3. From Apr to Oct the **pleasure steamers** *Waverley* and *Balmoral* run fairly frequent day cruises from here, along the Avon and Severn or to Devon, Wales or Lundy; (0141) 221 8152 for timetable.

142. Legends galore here

Tales of King Arthur can be found all over the country, but are especially prominent in **Glastonbury**; they like to say that bones reinterred in the abbey in 1191 were those of Arthur and Guinevere. The best approach is by the B3151, showing the town below the famous Tor. The NT has begun work on improving access to the Tor; you can walk there (it takes about 25 mins) or catch a park-and-ride bus from the Abbey car park (Magdalene St, Easter–Sept; £1), as there is no parking at the Tor. Glastonbury has quite a New Age feel, probably due to all the legends and the famous annual rock festival. The brasserie of the Hawthorns Hotel (Northload St) is good for lunch, and the medieval carved façade of the George & Pilgrims is one of the sights of the town, which the bypass has made much more pleasurable.

Glastonbury Abbey These noble ruins are said to mark the location of the birth of Christianity in this country. The story goes that Joseph of Arimathaea struck his staff into Wearyall Hill, where it took root. Offshoots of the tree, the famous Glastonbury Thorn, have flourished to this day, with a fine specimen here. The remains of the church date mainly from 1539, though the Lady Chapel is much older. An interpretation area has a good range of stories connected with the site, and in the summer, a monk actor will tell you more about how the monks used to live. Snacks July–Aug, shop, disabled access; cl 25 Dec; (01458) 832267; *£3.50.

Glastonbury Tribunal (High St) Glastonbury was formerly an island rising from a vast inland lake, and you can almost see this from the top of the Tor, the highest point of the hills and ridges among which the little town nestles, with fantastic views. Excavations here have revealed a prehistoric **lake village** covering three or four acres below it, consisting of nearly a hundred mounds surrounded by a wooden palisade. Lots of items and timbers from the village have been unusually well preserved, thanks to the waterlogged state of the site, and some of the finds, giving a fascinating insight into the life of the settlement, are shown in this fine 15th-c merchant's house. The Tourist Information Centre is here too, and there's some notable plasterwork in the lower back room. Shop, cl 25–26 Dec; (01458) 832954; £2; EH.

143. England's smallest city

With a population of only 9,500, **Wells** wouldn't normally even qualify as a big town, but in fact this delightful place is England's smallest city. The **Vicars Close** is said to be one of the oldest complete medieval streets in Europe; the cathedral's Vicars Choral still live here, passing the 15th-c Chain Gate to the cathedral itself. The Fountain, a good nearby dining pub, is popular with the choir – you may even be served by a Vicar Choral. There are a good few other attractive old buildings, many now used as offices and shops (inc several antiques shops), and several grouped around the Market Pl; the City Arms is a pleasant place for lunch. The High St and Saddler St have recently been made more pedestrian friendly. The B3139 through Wedmore and side roads off it give a good feel of the dead flatness of the Somerset Levels.

Wells Cathedral Stunning structure right in the centre, its three towers stretching up against the Mendip foothills. The spectacular W front is reckoned by many to be the finest cathedral façade in the country; dating from the 13th c, it carries 293 pieces of medieval sculpture. Unmissable oddities inside include the wonderful scissors-shaped inverted arches, the north transept's 14th-c clock where horsemen still joust every ½ hour, and the fine carvings in the south transept, inc various victims of toothache and four graphic scenes of an old man stealing fruit and getting what for. The embroidered stallbacks in the choir (1937–1948) are a riot of colour, and the library, with documents dating back to the 10th c, is at 51 metres (168 ft) the longest medieval library building in England. Evensong is at 5.15 wkdys (not Weds), 3pm Sun. Meals, snacks, shop, disabled access; £4.50 suggested donation.

Bishop's Palace Moated and fortified, approached through a 14th-c gatehouse; it's quite dramatic going across the drawbridge. The beautiful series of buildings still has some original 13th-c parts, notably the banqueting hall and undercroft, as well as several state rooms and a long gallery hung with portraits of former bishops. The grounds are the site of the wells that give the city its name, producing on average 150 litres (40 gallons) of water a second. Also lovely gardens, decent arboretum, and a pair of swans trained to ring a little bell under the gatehouse window when they're hungry (so many people feed them in summer that this isn't terribly often). Meals (May–Sept), snacks, shop, disabled access to ground floor; open Tues–Fri plus bank hols and pm Sun Apr–Oct, most days in Aug; (01749) 678691; £3.50, perhaps more for special exhibitions.

144. A lovely village below a naughty giant

Cerne Abbas is famed above all for its prehistoric giant cut into the chalk above, giving no doubts as to his virility; best seen from the signed layby on the A352 N. The village itself is most attractive in its own right: a fine church, fragments of the old abbey, good pubs such as the picturesque Royal Oak, some 500 years old. There's a working **pottery** (cl Mons, phone Nov–Easter; (01300) 341865) on the way up to the giant; above it, the old Dorchester–Middlemarsh ridge road has some bracing views.

145. Britain's longest parish church

Christchurch Priory Magnificent medieval monastic church, at well over 90 metres (300 ft) the longest parish church in the country; very striking inside, with remarkable carving. The 'Miraculous Beam' apparently fitted in the roof only with divine assistance, so prompting the renaming of the borough to Christchurch (it used to be called Twynham). Shop, mostly disabled access; cl 25 Dec and Sun during services; (01202) 485804;

donations. The church has a small museum open in the summer, and good views from the tower (£1, only when a member of staff is available) – though with 176 spiral steps you have to earn them.

146. A spectacular ruined castle

Corfe Castle One of the most memorable ruins in England, the spiky remains of the castle rise on a hill in a breach in the Purbeck ridge, above the village of the same name; superb views from its dramatic hilltop position. Until it was seized in the Civil War and blown up, it was a veritable skyscraper; its demolition has left the masonry leaning at unlikely-looking angles, and there are remnants of portcullises and menacing murder holes. Much of the stone was re-used in buildings in the village. Meals, snacks, shop; cl 25–26 Dec; (01929) 481294; £4.40; NT.

147. A mighty pre-Roman fortress in Thomas Hardy country

Maiden Castle (off A354 S of Dorchester; no access from bypass) Europe's most famous Iron Age fort, a series of massive grassy ramparts covering 47 acres, and once home to some 200 families; the Romans captured it after a particularly bloody battle. It's so vast that the tour of its grassy ramparts almost qualifies as a fully fledged walk; free.

Nearby **Dorchester** is the thriving though rather traffic-ridden county town which features as Casterbridge in Hardy's novels; busy shopping streets, Weds market, and several worthwhile antiques and print shops. Though most of the more attractive Georgian buildings are just out of the bustle, there are a few distinguished buildings on the main streets, inc the timbered building of **Judge Jeffreys' Lodgings** in High West St; he stayed here during his notorious Bloody Assizes (the Oak Room in Antelope Passage, with good teas and cakes, is the courtroom where the Monmouth rebels were tried). The trial of the Tolpuddle Martyrs also took place on High West St, in the **Old Crown Court**, preserved as a memorial; for an extra £1.50 you can look round some of the cells (open wkdy pms in summer). There are one or two traces of the Romans' occupation, inc the fragmentary remains of a town house behind the County Hall (which has a booklet on its history), and of an amphitheatre (Maumbury Rings), rather tucked away on Weymouth Ave. The Napper's Mite restaurant (South St), a former almshouse, is good value, and the Blue Raddle (Church St) is popular for pub lunches.

Hardy's Cottage (Higher Bockhampton, just off A35 3m E) All alone by a sandy track inside the edge of a forest, the thatched cottage where Thomas Hardy was born in 1840 hasn't changed much since. Shop, disabled access to ground floor only; cl Fri and Sat and Nov–Mar; (01305) 262366; *£2.80; NT. The forest was heath in Hardy's day, but you can walk through the plantations SE of the cottage to find open heathland much as he knew it on Black Heath and Duddle Heath, parts of the 'untamed and untameable' Egdon Heath of his novels. From the Hardy's Cottage car park, it's a shortish walk to the cottage; a nature trail takes a slightly longer but prettier route via Thorncombe Wood. The 16th-c thatched Wise Man at West Stafford has good value food. See nearby Stinsford and Max Gate (below) for more Hardy associations.

Max Gate (Alington Ave, A351 1m E) Among the places associated with Thomas Hardy (who lived in Dorchester for most of his life), this is the house he designed and lived in from 1885 to his death in 1928, and where he wrote *Tess* and *Jude the Obscure*. You can see only the dining and drawing rooms (the study has been moved to the County Museum), but the gardens are fascinating, not least because they inspired so much of Hardy's poetry. Shop, disabled access; open pm Sun, Mon and Weds 2 Apr–29 Sept; (01305) 262538; £2.40; NT. The Trumpet Major food pub is very handy.

148. A medieval town by the house Sir Walter Raleigh built

Sherborne is attractive to wander through, given a feeling of unchanging solidity by the handsome stone medieval abbey buildings that mix in with later ones of the public school here, and by many other fine old buildings in and nr the main street. The **abbey** itself is a glorious golden stone building with a beautifully vaulted nave; at the Dissolution the townspeople raised the money to buy it, and it's been the parish church ever since. The West Window is beautiful, as is the Laurence Whistler engraved glass reredos in the Lady Chapel, and for 20p you can illuminate the fan vaulting of the roof; (01935) 815191; free. The unspoilt Digby Tap (handy for the abbey but no food Sun), cheery Cross Keys (Cheap St – where the market is) and very foody Skippers (Horsecastles) are useful for lunch. Several craft shops include a working saddlery (Cheap St).

Sherborne Castle (just E) This striking old house, which has been in the same family for almost 400 years, was built by Sir Walter Raleigh in 1594. Its wonderful period furnishings are the highlight, though there are also interesting paintings and porcelain. Outside are gardens designed by Capability Brown, and beautiful parkland with an enormous lake. Meals, snacks, shop, limited disabled access; open Apr–Oct exc Mon (exc bank hols) and Fri; castle cl Sat am; (01935) 813182; £6 castle and gardens, £3.20 grounds only.

149. An imposing stately home and one of King Arthur's camps

Kingston Lacy House (B3082 NW of Wimborne) Impressive 17th-c mansion later remodelled by Charles Barry, with grand Italian marble staircase and superb Venetian ceilings; outstanding paintings such as the 'Judgement of Solomon' by Sebastiano del Piombo, and others by Titian, Rubens and Van Dyck. The enormous grounds have landscaped gardens and a herd of red Devon cattle in the park. Lovely snowdrops in Feb and early Mar. There's easily enough here to fill a good day out. Meals, snacks, shop, disabled access to park and gardens; open Apr–Oct, house cl am and Mon–Tues; (01202) 883402; £6.80, £3.50 grounds only; NT. The Anchor at Shapwick is fairly handy for a good lunch (not Mon).

The once formidable **Badbury Rings** (also just off B3082) is an Iron Age hill fort associated by some with King Arthur. It's a good strolling ground with an impressive range of wild flowers – and if you feel more energetic, a Roman road lets you strike out for miles N.

150. Devon's most ancient building

Bickleigh Castle (Bickleigh) Charming moated and fortified manor house, still very much a family home; the 11th-c chapel is said to be Devon's oldest complete building. Also medieval hall, armoury and guard room, Tudor bedroom, 17th-c farmhouse, and exhibitions on maritime history and the Civil War. All done with great enthusiasm, and with a fair bit to amuse children. A restaurant is open for evening meals (Thurs–Sat, booking essential), limited disabled access; open pm Weds and Sun Easter–Sept; (01884) 855363; *£4. The Fishermans Cot is a beautifully placed riverside dining pub.

151. Civil War derring do

The quiet dairy-farming town of **Torrington**, on a ridge above the River Torridge, has some attractive buildings inc 14th-c Taddiport Chapel (for a former leper colony), the imposing Palmer House, and a rather grand church built to replace the original blown up in the Civil War. There are good views from the neatly mown hill above the river, and other nearby strolls on the preserved commons surrounding the town. The Black Horse is useful for lunch.

Torrington 1646 (South St car park) This lively heritage centre brings to life one of the lesser-known battles of the English Civil War, fought here in February 1646. Four or five actors, all in period clothes, and rarely stepping out of character, work hard to get children involved. The scene-setting first part is a fairly traditional exhibition of Civil War history, where you can try on a helmet or find out from touch-screens whether you'd have been a Cavalier or a Roundhead. A video shows a large-scale recon-struction of the battle by the Sealed Knot. Small groups are ushered in and told to imagine they're back in the 17th c; the guide disappears and is replaced by a 17th-c local, keen to usher you away from the battle to safety. He'll take you through various reconstructions and situations, until you get to the church. Outside, army stragglers will try to sell you their armour and weapons; they'll show you how to charge into battle, let you examine their swords, and may introduce you to period games. Finally you're shown around a reconstructed 17th-c garden. Teas, snacks, picnic area, shop, disabled access; cl Sun outside school hols, best to check winter opening times; (01805) 626146; £6, £4.50 children.

152. Historic Exeter

Though large parts of the centre were devastated by World War II bombing, some choice streets and buildings survive, with picturesque partly Tudor narrow lanes leading from the mainly pedestrianised High St into the serene tree-shaded cathedral close. In the centre, modern shops are integrated into the old layout very discreetly. With many smaller churches, decent book and other shops, pubs and so forth nearby, this is a very pleasant part for browsing around, and there's a pleasantly easy-going atmosphere. Particularly attractive streets include Southernhay at the end of the close, and Stepcote Hill, a picturesque detour from Fore St. The Quay, beyond the streams of fast traffic on the ring road (there are quiet underpasses), has become lively and entertaining, with handsomely restored buildings, resurgent cafés and pubs (the Prospect and Port Royal are worth knowing), and craft shops and the like; the Old Quay House has a visitor centre with audio-visual show; (01392) 265213). Civilised pubs and wine bars with decent food include the sumptuous Imperial (New North Rd), Ship (14th-c, Martins Lane) and Well House (The Close – cathedral view and Roman well). There are **boat trips** down the ship canal to Turf Locks; or you can walk down, passing the Double Locks (a favourite pub) and ending at the Turf Hotel looking out over the estuary. A range of daily free guided tours leave the Royal Clarence Hotel (Cathedral Cl) throughout the day (phone (01392) 265203 for details, or pick up a programme from the Tourist Information Centre, Paris St).

Exeter Cathedral England's finest example of Decorated Gothic architecture, with its magnificent nave soaring to the vaulted roof, and intricately carved choir stalls; the 13th-c misericords are thought to be the oldest set in the country. It also boasts the longest unbroken Gothic vaulting in Europe, superbly atmospheric.

Lots of colourfully embroidered cushions, chronologically illustrating English and local history. The façade has three tiers of sculpted figures, inc the Apostles. Meals, snacks, shop, disabled access; guided tours 11am and 2.30pm (plus 12.30 July–Aug) wkdys, 11 Sat, 4 Sun Apr–Oct, or by appointment; £3 suggested donation.

153. Devon's most haunted castle

Berry Pomeroy Castle (Berry Pomeroy, off A385 just E of Totnes; keep on past village) Reputedly Devon's most haunted castle, hidden away on a crag over a quiet wooded valley. Appropriately spooky medieval gatehouse and walls around the ruins of an imposing and unexpected Tudor mansion, with an interesting 15th-c fresco inside; a new audio tour will tell you more about the castle and its inhabitants. The lawns in front are ideal for a picnic. Snacks; cl Nov–Easter; (01803) 866618; *£2.80; EH. The red sandstone 15th-c village **church** is worth a look on the way; odd monument in Seymour Chapel. The road through here from Ashburton via Littlehempston and on to Stoke Gabriel is a nice drive.

154. Historic Dartmouth

This charming waterside small town has many exceptional buildings, esp around the inner harbour. Though so popular, it's kept its own strong character, and stays very much alive through the winter. Cobbled Bayards Cove, with old fort and steep wooded hills behind, is particularly photogenic, as is pedestrianised Foss St. Markets Tues, Fri: Old Market is picturesque. The Royal Naval College is a striking building. Interesting shops, plenty of waterside seats, lots of action on the river. Parking in summer can be trying: best to use good park-and-ride on B3207 Halwell Rd.

Dartmouth Castle (slightly SE of town, off B3205) Classic late 15th-c battlemented fortress, virtually intact, with cannon and later gun batteries (a video display shows it firing), and great views out into the Channel. Snacks, shop; cl winter lunchtimes, and all day Mon and Tues Nov–Mar, 24–26 Dec, 1 Jan; (01803) 833588; £3.20; EH. In summer a little ferry leaves the South Embankment for here every 15 mins or so. Otherwise it's an enjoyable and fairly gentle 20-min walk from Dartmouth itself, though the immediate hinterland is unremarkable.

155. Plymouth preserved

Barbican Carefully restored since the war, a series of narrow twisty streets of old buildings W of working Sutton Harbour; photogenic – and evocative even in wet weather. New St is its oldest core. The Dolphin pub has original Beryl Cook paintings.

Crownhill Fort (Crownhill Fort Rd, just N) The biggest and least altered of Plymouth's Victorian forts, though from the road it looks little more than a wooded hill. Used by the Army right up to 1986, it's been well restored by the Landmark Trust, with barrack rooms, underground tunnels, secret passageways, and lookout towers to explore; children can run around quite freely, and there's an adventure playground. You can stay here in a Victorian officer's flat (all year), and have the run of the place after dark. Snacks, shop, limited disabled access (lots of steep steps); cl Nov–Mar, but hours vary so phone to check; (01752) 793754; £4.75.

Elizabethan House (32 New St) Splendid timber-framed Tudor sea-captain's house with period furniture. Shop; cl Mons and Tues, and Oct–Easter; (01752) 304380; £1.10. There's an Elizabethan garden just down the road at number 39.

156. Two contrasting ancient sites in Torquay

Kents Cavern Showcaves (Ilsham Rd, Wellswood) The oldest directly dated archaeological site in Britain; continuing excavations often make scientists reconsider their theories about prehistoric life. Good guided tours really bring out the history of the caves, and colourful stalagmites and stalactites add to the eerie atmosphere. In summer they do spooky evening tours (booking essential). Very well presented, and definitely worth an hour or so if you're in the area. Special visits at Christmas. Summer meals, snacks, shop, disabled access (with prior notice); cl 25 Dec; (01803) 215136; £5.70, £6.30 evening tours.

Torre Abbey (Kings Drive) As we went to press, plans for an extensive £7 million four-year restoration of the abbey and gardens hadn't yet been confirmed (they include a new entrance, better disabled access, and a new interactive family art gallery), so phone to check opening times. Some of the earlier parts of the abbey remain, inc the medieval barn, gatehouse, undercrofts and ruined Norman tower, but they've been eclipsed by the later house with its 18th- and 19th-c period rooms. The main feature is Devon's largest art gallery, and there's an Agatha Christie room full of possessions of the locally born author; also garden and palm house. Snacks, shop; probably open Easter–June; (01803) 293593; £3.

157. Elizabethan Totnes

Totnes is busy in summer, but still keeps most of its charm then, particularly early in the morning. The picturesque Elizabethan area known as **The Narrows** is very atmospheric, esp along the High St down to the arch at the top of Fore St, with quaint pillared arcades (on Tues mornings May–Sept there's a little Elizabethan and craft market). There's a working harbour, and you can walk some way downstream on either side of the River Dart. Behind the church of St Mary's (which has a super rood screen), several rooms in the 11th-c **guildhall** may be open (wkdys mid-Oct–Easter); it was originally part of a Benedictine priory. Perhaps unexpectedly, Totnes has quite a New Age flavour; there's even a flotation tank to wash away city stresses. The Kingsbridge Inn (Leechwell St) has enjoyable food.

Totnes Castle Part Norman, part 14th-c, these classic circular remains were lucky enough to avoid any battles, so the keep is pretty much intact. There's a tree-shaded inner lawn, and lovely views of the town and down to the river. Snacks, shop; cl Nov–Mar; (01803) 864406; £1.80.

158. Cornwall's 15th-c gem

Cotehele (1m W of Calstock by footpath, 6m by road) Tucked away in a network of twisting roads high above the Tamar, this rambling granite house has hardly changed since being built in the late 15th c; there's no electricity, so the dark rooms – with fine furniture, armour and tapestries – have an authentically medieval atmosphere. Outside are lovely terraced gardens, a medieval dovecote, restored watermill, and miles of peaceful woodland walks. Down at Cotehele Quay a National Maritime Museum outpost shows the quay's history, and the last of the Tamar ketch-rigged barges has been restored here; there's a little art gallery too. Meals, snacks (tearoom in pleasant riverside setting with good cream teas), shop, some disabled access; house cl Fri and Nov–Mar, mill as house (but cl am and open Fri July–Aug), garden open daily all year; (01579) 351346; £6.40, £3.60 garden and mill only; NT. Pleasant walks along the Tamar from the charming village. The unusual Who'd Have Thought It at St Dominick is good for lunch.

159. A remote Iron Age village

Chysauster Ancient Village (off B3311 N of Gulval, where the Coldstreamer is a well run dining pub) Highly evocative Iron Age site, perched on a windy hillside: remains of eight courtyard houses grouped beside what might be Britain's oldest village street give an idea of Celtic life almost 2,000 years ago. The site is also notable for its large untreated meadow, popular with wild birds, and, depending on the season, bright with bluebells, heather or unusual orchids. Snacks, shop; cl Nov–Mar; (07831) 757934; £1.80; EH.

160. Falmouth's defence from Henry VIII to World War II

Pendennis Castle (1m SE of Falmouth) Superb views from this well preserved fort, one of Henry VIII's chain of coastal defences; displays of firearms and uniforms in the museum, a hands-on discovery centre and World War II guardroom with cells. Meals (Apr–Oct), snacks, shop, some disabled access; cl 24–26 Dec, 1 Jan; £4; EH.

161. Cornwall's island castle

St Michael's Mount (Marazion) There's something particularly awe-inspiring about this medieval castle, rising majestically from the sea. On gloomy or stormy days the picturesque silhouette seems even more dramatic. The little island is reached by ferry (it doesn't go in bad weather), or at low tide on foot along a causeway; the walk up to the castle, still the home of the family which acquired it in 1660, is quite steep. Fine Chippendale furniture, plaster reliefs, armour and paintings. Summer meals, snacks, shop; open (tide and weather permitting) wkdys and some wknds Apr–Oct, and Mon, Weds and Fri only Nov–Mar, phone to check; (01736) 710507; *£5; NT (members have to pay at wknds). The extensively redeveloped Godolphin Arms has popular food.

162. The tin miner's life

Geevor Tin Mine (Boscaswell, Pendeen) You get a good idea of what mining was really like at this nicely undeveloped tin mine (readers tell us the changing rooms are especially evocative), which was working until 1990; you can explore the mine's surface, a guided tour takes you underground, and there's a small museum. Meals, snacks, shop, limited disabled access; cl Sat Easter–Oct (exc on Sat near bank hols), plus Sun Nov–Easter; (01736) 788662; £6. The Radjel has good value food.

163. Tintagel

Tintagel Castle Forgetting the myths and legends, these dramatic 12th- and 13th-c ruins have a spectacular setting and unrivalled views. A good start is from Rocky Valley, a craggy valley leading from the B3263 to the sea. Try to come out of season, when the crowds are fewer and the mist and crashing waves add a touch of mystery. There's quite a lot of climbing involved, and the often steep steps among the crags can be slippery in wet weather. As for King Arthur, latest theories suggest he was a Shropshire lad, but a small exhibition makes the most of the Cornish case, inc the recently found Arthnou stone, a 1,400-year-old inscribed slate naming the hero. Shop; cl 24–26 Dec and 1 Jan; (01840) 770328; £3; EH. In summer, a Land-Rover can ferry you to the site from the village (a tourist trap since the 19th c) at regular intervals throughout the day. The Old Malthouse is a useful food stop, and the parish **church** is worth a look.

HISTORIC PLACES TO STAY

Cornwall

CRACKINGTON HAVEN Manor Farm *Crackington Haven, Bude, Cornwall EX23 0JW (01840) 230304* **£60***; 4 pretty rms. Lovely Domesday-listed, no smoking manor surrounded by 25 acres of farmland and carefully landscaped gardens; antiques in four lounges, a log fire, a house-party atmosphere, big breakfasts, and a delicious 4-course dinner at 7pm; cl 25 Dec; no children

RUAN HIGH LANES Crugsillick Manor *Ruan High Lanes, Truro, Cornwall TR2 5LJ (01872) 501214* **£80**, plus special breaks; 3 rms. One of the loveliest houses in Cornwall, this Queen Anne manor is extended from a pre-Elizabethan farmhouse and surrounded by a big quiet garden with wooded valley views; log fire in drawing room with Napoleonic ceiling, candlelit dinners in 17th-c dining room using home-grown produce where possible, fine breakfasts, and charming owners; self-catering cottages in grounds – excellent disabled access, and children welcome (but must be over 12 in main house); house cl Christmas (self-catering open then); dogs anywhere in cottages, not in bedrooms in house

SALTASH Erth Barton *Elmgate, Saltash, Cornwall PL12 4QY (01752) 842127* **£70**; 3 rms. Lovely old manor house with its own chapel, peaceful rooms with lots of books, pictures and big fireplaces, good enjoyable food, bird-watching in the surrounding estuaries, and riding (you can bring your own horse); children over 12; dogs welcome anywhere

Exeter & East Devon

GITTISHAM Combe House *Gittisham, Honiton, Devon EX14 0AD (01404) 540400* **£138**, plus winter breaks; 15 individually decorated pretty rms with lovely views. Peaceful Elizabethan country hotel in gardens with 700-year-old cedar of Lebanon, and walks around the 3,000-acre estate; elegant day rooms with antiques, pictures and fresh flowers, a happy relaxed atmosphere, very good food using some home-grown produce, and fine wines (the cellar is popular for wine tastings); can use the house for special occasions and meetings; dogs welcome in bedrooms

SIDFORD Blue Ball *Sidford, Sidmouth, Devon EX10 9QL (01395) 514062* **£70**; 6 rms, most with own bthrm, and with nice touches like free newspapers, fruit and fresh flowers. Welcoming thatched 14th-c inn run by the same family since 1912, with lovely winter log fire in low partly panelled lounge bar, heavy beams, lots of bric-a-brac, no smoking snug, very friendly service, and decent food inc hearty breakfasts

Devon

South Devon & Dartmoor

CHAGFORD Easton Court *Sandy Park, Chagford, Newton Abbot, Devon TQ13 8JN (01647) 433469* **£140** inc dinner, plus special breaks; 8 redecorated rms. Creeper-clad, thatched and newly refurbished 15th-c house with beams, inglenook fireplace, granite walls, and big library (literary connections inc Evelyn Waugh writing *Brideshead Revisited* here), cosy bar, charming sitting room, good breakfasts, delicious evening meals in candlelit restaurant; cl Jan; children over 12; dogs welcome in bedrooms

DREWSTEIGNTON Silkhouse *Drewsteignton, Exeter, Devon EX6 6RF (01647) 231267* **£60**; 2 rms. Quietly set, rambling 16th-c longhouse named by the Huguenots who wove silk here; low beams, fine paintings, antiques and richly coloured fabrics and paintwork, a relaxed atmosphere, imaginative food in low-ceilinged dining room, and a really lovely garden with ponds and streams, lots of wildlife, and all-weather tennis court; horses welcome; no children; dogs welcome

LEWDOWN Lewtrenchard Manor *Lewdown, Okehampton, Devon EX20 4PN (01566) 783256* **£175**, plus special breaks; 9 well equipped rms with fresh flowers and period furniture. Lovely Elizabethan manor house in garden with fine dovecot and surrounded by peaceful estate with shooting, fishing and croquet; dark panelling, ornate ceilings, antiques, fresh flowers, and log fires, a friendly welcome, relaxed atmosphere, and candlelit restaurant with very good imaginative food; children over 8; partial disabled access; dogs welcome in bedrooms

SOUTH ZEAL Oxenham Arms *South Zeal, Okehampton, Devon EX20 2JT (01837) 840244* **£60**, plus special breaks; 8 rms. Grandly atmospheric old inn dating back to 12th c and first licensed in 1477 (a neolithic standing stone still forms part of the wall in the TV room); elegant beamed and panelled bar with chatty relaxed atmosphere and open fire, a wide choice of enjoyable food and wines, and charming ex-monastery small garden; dogs welcome away from dining room

Dorset

ABBOTSBURY Abbey House *Church Street, Abbotsbury, Weymouth, Dorset DT3 4JJ (01305) 871330* **£70***; 5 pretty rms. Partly 15th-c house (said to have been the Abbey infirmary) with 17th- and 18th-c additions, and set in gardens which slope down to the mill pond, behind which stands the impressive Abbey Tithe Barn, the largest in England; in the corner of the garden stands the only surviving Benedictine water mill in this country; comfortable, homely sitting room, reasonably priced and enticing lunches and teas in attractive country-style dining room, and friendly, efficient service

CORFE CASTLE Mortons House *45 East Street, Corfe Castle, Wareham, Dorset BH20 5EE (01929) 480988* **£118**; 17 individual rms inc 2 suites. Fine Elizabethan manor house in walled garden, with an oak-panelled drawing room, log fire, nice prints, and carved wooden friezes, the original stone fireplace in the entrance hall, very friendly, helpful staff and owners, delicious modern evening meals, and plenty to do nearby; no smoking; children over 5 in restaurant

Gloucestershire

ASHLEWORTH Ashleworth Court *Ashleworth, Gloucester, Gloucestershire GL19 4JA (01452) 700241* **£50***; 3 rms, shared bthrms. By a small elegant church and NT tithe barn, this striking ancient house is part of a working farm and has a homely kitchen with an Aga, a comfortable sitting room, enjoyable breakfasts served in what was originally part of the Great Hall, and chickens in the back garden; two good pubs in the village; cl Christmas; partial disabled access

BIBURY Bibury Court *Bibury, Cirencester, Gloucestershire GL7 5NT (01285) 740337* **£125**, plus special breaks; 18 individual rms. Lovely peaceful mansion dating from Tudor times, in beautiful gardens, with an informal friendly atmosphere, panelled rooms, antiques, huge log fires, conservatory, a fine choice of breakfasts, and good interesting food; cl Christmas and New Year; disabled access; dogs welcome in bedrooms

CHARINGWORTH Charingworth Manor *Charingworth, Chipping Campden, Gloucestershire GL55 6NS (01386) 593555* **£150**, plus special breaks; 26 lovely rms with thoughtful extras. Early 14th-c manor with Jacobean additions, mullioned windows, antiques, and log fires and heavy oak beams in relaxing sitting room; good modern cooking in charming restaurant, excellent breakfasts, friendly staff, fine grounds and leisure spa with indoor swimming pool, gym, and all-weather tennis court

Herefordshire

KINGTON Penrhos Court *Lyonshall, Kington, Herefordshire HR5 3LH (01544) 230720* **£95**, plus special breaks; 19 elegant rms. Beautifully restored 13th-c hall in six acres, with fine beams and flagstones, a magnificent hall for dining, a huge wood fire, and very good carefully cooked food using seasonal organic home-grown herbs and vegetables; they run regular food and health courses; cl Jan; disabled access

LEDBURY Feathers *25 High St, Ledbury, Herefordshire HR8 1DS (01531) 635266* **£95**, plus special breaks; 19 carefully decorated rms making the most of the old beams and timbers. Very striking, mainly 16th c, black and white hotel with a relaxed atmosphere, log fires, comfortable lounge hall with country antiques, beams and timbers, particularly enjoyable food and friendly service in hop-decked Fuggles bar, a good wine list, and a fine mix of locals and visitors; health and leisure spa with indoor swimming pool; dogs welcome

Somerset

NORTON ST PHILIP George *High St, Norton St Philip, Bath BA3 6LH (01373) 834224* **£80**; 8 comfortable rms of real character in galleried wing. Carefully restored, exceptional building that has been offering hospitality to travellers for nearly 700 years; individual bars with trusses and timbering, fine old stone fireplaces, really heavy beams, 18th-c pictures, oak dressers and settles and so forth, a marvellous restaurant, good food, real ales, decent wines, and organised, friendly service; a stroll over the meadow behind the pub (past the picnic-sets on the narrow grass pub garden) leads to an attractive churchyard around the medieval church whose bells struck Pepys (here on 12 June 1668) as 'mighty tuneable'.

TAUNTON Castle *Castle Green, Taunton, Somerset TA1 1NF* *(01823) 272671* **£180***, plus special breaks; 44 lovely rms. Appealingly modernised partly Norman castle, its front almost smothered in wisteria, with fine old oak furniture, tapestries and paintings in comfortably elegant lounges, really excellent modern English cooking, good breakfasts, a range of good value wines from a thoughtful list, and efficient friendly service; pretty garden; disabled access; dogs welcome in bedrooms

THORNBURY Thornbury Castle *Castle St, Thornbury, Bristol BS35 1HH (01454) 281182* **£185**; 25 opulent rms, some with big Tudor fireplaces or fine oriel windows. Impressive and luxuriously renovated early 16th-c castle with antiques, tapestries, huge fireplaces and mullioned windows in the baronial public rooms, three dining rooms (one in the base of a tower), fine cooking, extensive wine list (inc wine from their own vineyard), thoughtful friendly service, and vast grounds inc the oldest Tudor gardens in England; cl 4 days Jan; partial disabled access; dogs allowed at discretion of manager

Worcestershire

BUCKLAND Buckland Manor *Buckland, Broadway, Worcestershire WR12 7LY (01386) 852626* **£225***; 14 sumptuous rms. Really lovely 13th-c building in 10 acres of beautifully kept gardens, comfortable lounges with magnificent oak panelling, flowers and antiques, and elegant restaurant with fine food using home-grown produce; outdoor swimming pool, riding, tennis, croquet, putting; children over 12

WICKHAMFORD Wickhamford Manor *Manor Rd, Wickhamford, Evesham, Worcestershire WR11 6SA (01386) 830296* **£75***; 3 rms. Striking 16th-c timbered manor, once owned by Queen Elizabeth I and first mentioned in the Domesday Book; set in 20 acres of woodland and pasture with a 12th-c dovecote and lake (created by monks when the abbot lived in a grange here); big log fire in beamed drawing room, good breakfasts in the flagstoned kitchen, and a really warm welcome from the friendly owners; tennis and coarse fishing; cl Christmas and New Year; children over 12 (or babies)

South Wales

LLANFIHANGEL CRUCORNEY Penyclawdd Court *Llanfihangel Crucorney, Abergavenny, Gwent NP7 7LB (01873) 890719* **£80***; 4 period rms with mountain views. Interesting medieval manor house below Bryn Arw mountain in Brecon Beacons, with an Elizabethan knot garden, herb garden, Norman motte and bailey, and yew hedge maze; careful renovation, hidden heating and no electricity in dining room (breakfast by candlelight), as well as flagstones, beams and sloping floors, and a friendly relaxed atmosphere; children over 12

Northern England & North Wales

Including Cumbria, Northumbria, Lancashire, Yorkshire, Lincolnshire, Nottinghamshire, Derbyshire, Staffordshire, Cheshire, Shropshire and North Wales.

◆ ◆ ◆

164. Glorious gardens around a richly furnished mansion

Holker Hall & Gardens (Cark-in-Cartmel) With its opulently built and furnished mansion, first-class gardens, and entertaining motor museum, this busy estate easily has enough to keep most families occupied for the bulk of the day. The house dates back to the early 16th c (and has been in the same family ever since), but the present building is mainly Victorian, constructed after a disastrous fire destroyed much of the original. Despite its beauty, it has an appealingly unstuffy feel, and remains very much a family home. But it still has some splendidly grand features: look out in particular for the stunning staircase, where each baluster has a unique design. Impressive as they are, the rooms are rather eclipsed by what's outside: the glorious 25-acre formal and woodland gardens are among the best in the county, with spectacular water features, a sunken garden, rhododendron and azalea arboretum, and rare plants and shrubs. A potting shed has an exhibition on garden history, and there's a very good nursery. The motor museum – not huge, but very appealingly presented – has a good collection of cars, bikes, tractors, and all sorts of related equipment and memorabilia, from enamel signs through models to petrol pumps. Perhaps most interesting is the display on Donald Campbell's world record-breaking attempts, with a full-size replica of the ill-fated Bluebird. Children enjoy the 125-acre deer park, and are given a Discovery Card when they arrive at the estate to help them explore; there's also an adventure playground for under-12s, and a picnic area. Dogs on a lead are welcome in the park. There's a good Garden Festival towards the end of May; opening times may vary slightly then. Meals, snacks, shop, disabled access; cl Sat, and Nov–Mar; (015395) 58328. An all-in ticket is £8.25 (£4.65 children over 6), or they do just about every other possible ticket combination: house and garden only is £6.50 (£3.95 children), motor museum and garden only £6.90 (£4.20), or a garden only ticket £3.95 (£2.25 children).

165. The literary lions of yesteryear loved this house

Mirehouse (off A591 S of Bassenthwaite) The family that still live in this modest 17th-c house once had excellent literary connections, so the fine rooms have mementoes of Wordsworth, Carlyle and Tennyson among others. They frequently have informal piano recitals (guests are welcome to sit by the fire and listen), and on Weds in Jun, July and Sept they usually have lace-making demonstrations. Interesting garden (bee/butterfly plants) with changing poetry exhibitions in the verandah, as well as peaceful lakeshore grounds, lakeside church, and woods with well thought-out adventure play areas. Lots to do, with a surprising number of activities for children, also a trail, secret drawers, and dolls to play with – they may even be allowed to sound the big dinner gong. Generous Cumbrian home cooking in ex-mill tearoom, disabled access; open Apr–Oct, house Sun and Weds pm, garden daily; (017687) 72287; £4, £2 garden only.

166. Carlisle's medieval past

Carlisle Castle This extensive medieval fortress, rather gaunt and forbidding, is surprisingly well kept considering its violent history. Interesting period furnished rooms, a portcullised gatehouse, lots of staircases and passages, and centuries of prisoners' carved graffiti in the dungeons; good views from the ramparts. Snacks, shop, limited disabled access; cl 24–26 Dec; (01228) 591922; £3.20; EH.

Carlisle Cathedral This unpretentious abbey church, founded in 1122 and severely damaged in the Civil War, has fine stained glass; try to go on a bright morning when the sunlight comes streaming colourfully through the east window. Also medieval carvings inc the Brougham Triptych, painted panels and stonework, and crypt treasury. Meals, snacks, good shop (some tasty local foods), disabled access (exc to restaurant); access may be restricted during services (01228) 535169; free but donations encouraged.

167. Where Wordsworth was brought up

Wordsworth House (Main St, Cockermouth) The poet's happy childhood home in a quietly attractive riverside town, a restored 18th-c town house with fine furniture, pictures by friends and contemporaries, good original panelling, and walled garden above river. Worth a visit in its own right as well as for its Wordsworth associations, and interesting to see how different it is from the places he lived in later on. Meals, snacks, shop, some disabled

access (not to house); cl wknds (exc Sats Jun–Aug or before bank
hols), and Nov–Mar; (01900) 824805; £3.50; NT. The nearby
Trout has good food.

168. Wordsworth's beautiful village

The pretty village of **Grasmere** swarms with visitors in summer,
most of them here to see **Dove Cottage** – still much as
Wordsworth had it in his most creative years (he completed *The
Prelude* here), with sister Dorothy's journals and his extensive
cottage garden. Informative guided tours cope well with the bustle,
but in early morning (opens 9.30) out of season you may get some
space to yourself. The place always was crowded; barely big
enough for two, with the poets' children and friends it often had a
dozen or more people living here. The adjoining **Wordsworth
Museum**, included in the price, has changing exhibitions and
possessions of the poet and his family and friends, as well as a
reconstructed Lakeland kitchen and contemporary art gallery.
Meals, snacks, shop, limited disabled access; cl mid-Jan to mid-Feb,
24–26 Dec; (015394) 35544; £5.50 museum and house, £2.75
museum only. Wordsworth is buried in the graveyard of the
pebbledashed old church, which is better inside than outside. Sarah
Nelson's gingerbread shop by the church is wonderfully old-
fashioned. The Travellers Rest (A591) is our current pick for lunch.
The lake itself, with Rydal Water and Elterwater, is the very heart
of picturesque Lakeland.

169. This family's castle home through eight centuries

Muncaster Castle and Owl Centre (A595, 1m E of Ravenglass)
The same family have lived in the elegant house since 1208, and will
continue to do so as long as a magical glass drinking bowl remains

intact. Extended over the centuries (esp the 19th) from its original tower, it still feels very lived-in, and the rich furnishings and décor include some fine Elizabethan furniture and embroidery. There's an entertaining audio tour, and young children will especially like the underground maze (you can advance only by answering questions about the environment). Muncaster is the HQ of the World Owl Trust, and they have over 180 birds from 50 different species; an interpretation centre has closed circuit TV of nesting owls. There are talks and flying displays at 2.30pm, and you can watch wild herons being fed (every afternoon Mar–Nov, weather permitting). The lovely 77-acre grounds are particularly rich in species rhododendrons and have unusual trees, nature trails, adventure play area and lots of rescued birds of prey. Various special events. Meals, snacks, shops, good plant centre, mostly disabled access; castle open daily (exc Sat) beginning Mar–Oct, garden and owl centre open all year; (01229) 717614; £7.50 for everything, £5.50 for the garden, owl centre and maze.

Ravenglass & Eskdale Railway England's oldest narrow-gauge steam trains, lovingly preserved, with open carriages chugging up seven miles of unspoilt valley to Dalegarth; admirers say it's the most beautiful train journey in England. Cafés each end, and at Ravenglass a small museum and audio-visual display; free. Shop, disabled access (with notice); open daily end Mar–beginning Nov, trains many winter weekends, phone to check; (01229) 717171; £7.80 return. Enjoyable 3-hr summer walk back from Boot (walks booklets from stations).

170. The Windsor of the North

Alnwick Castle This, the second-largest inhabited castle in the country, dates back to the 11th c. Stone soldiers stand guard on the battlements, and inside all is Renaissance grandeur, with a magnificent art collection taking in works by Titian, Van Dyck and Canaletto, and an outstanding Claude. Also a famous collection of Meissen china, Roman remains, refurbished museum with displays on the Duke of Northumberland's own private army and local archaeology, and children's playground. Meals, snacks, shop, some disabled access; open Apr–late Oct; £6.95, joint ticket with garden (which is being excitingly redeveloped) £9.50.

Busy **Alnwick** itself, at the heart of prosperous farming country, has some attractive old streets nr the market square – it was used in the film *Elizabeth*. The hillside church of St Michael and All Angels above the river is a perfect example of a complete Late Gothic building.

171. A stunning clifftop castle

Bamburgh Castle (Bamburgh) Huge square Norman castle on a cliff above the sea, its clock serving as timekeeper for the cricket green in the attractive village below. Despite the forbidding exterior, and a collection of armour from the Tower of London, the inside is very much a lived-in stately home. Snacks, shop; cl Nov to mid-Mar; (01668) 214515; *£5. There's a neo-Gothic shrine to Grace Darling the local shipwreck heroine in the yard of the interesting 13th-c **church**. The Lord Crewe Arms is well placed for lunch.

Grace Darling Museum (Radcliffe Rd) Pictures and mementoes of the local heroine, inc the boat in which Grace and her father rescued nine survivors from the wrecked SS *Forfarshire*. Shop, disabled access; cl Sun am, and Nov–Easter; (01668) 214465; free (donations to RNLI).

172. The past vividly brought to life

North of England Open Air Museum (Beamish, A693) An amazingly ambitious 300-acre museum exhaustively re-creating life in the North of England in the early 1800s and 1900s. There are five main sections: a town with streets, shops, houses and businesses (and a new horse-drawn vehicle collection), a colliery village with mine, chapel, cottages and school, a manor house with formal gardens, orchard and heavy horses, a railway station, and a home farm with animals and exhibitions (ducks and geese wander around for extra authenticity, and local Teeswater sheep graze on the ridge-and-furrow corrugations which were the rule in the English landscape before steam ploughs). Costumed staff really bring the place to life, answering questions and showing off period crafts and skills. What's nice for children is that they can wander around touching everything and joining in most of the activities – learning how to play hoops and hopscotch, for example, or taking part in lessons in the schoolroom. The sweet factory and the dentist offer demonstrations, and a Victorian fairground has rides and a proper Hall of Mirrors (the only bit that has a small extra charge). A re-created engine shed has a magnificent 1822 locomotive, and a full-scale replica of Stephenson's *Locomotion No. 1*, which carries visitors down a ½-mile track (they've now also a full-size replica of another early locomotive, the *Steam Elephant*). Extra activities most wknds, from vintage car rallies to Meccano-building or whippet racing, and in summer there may be brass bands or choirs. Working trams and buses link the different areas, and there's plenty of space for picnics (dogs are allowed on a lead). Meals and snacks (some in a period pub), good shops, some disabled access; cl Mon and Fri Nov–Mar, and 16 Dec–1 Jan; (0191) 370 4000; £12, £4 in winter, when only the town and tramway are open. The Shepherd & Shepherdess not far from the gate is useful for lunch, as is the more individual Beamish Mary (the sign to follow from A693 is a lovely one – 'No Place & Cooperative Villas').

173. A Roman fort plundered to build a Saxon church

Binchester Roman Fort (Binchester) Quite a lot left of this 1st-c 10-acre fort, inc the best-preserved military baths in the country, with an exceptional hypocaust system. Interesting events include days when you may be able to sample Roman food. Shop, disabled access; open cl Oct–Easter; (01388) 663089; £1.60. Nearby Escomb church is interesting, built in the 7th c from stone from the fort. A 3rd-c fort can be seen a few miles S at Piercebridge, and finds from both sites are shown at the Bowes Museum in Barnard Castle – see next entry.

174. The treasure-house of the north

Bowes Museum (Barnard Castle) A beautiful French-style chateau in 20 acres of meticulously kept formal grounds. The 40 rooms are filled with sumptuous fine arts and an outstanding display of paintings of national importance; also local history section, small display of 1950s toys; they hold concerts, events and temporary exhibitons throughout the year. Relatively few people find their way to this knock-out treasure-house, though it's one of the most worthwhile places to visit in the entire country – those readers who do get there love it. Meals, snacks, shop, disabled access; cl 25–26 Dec, 1 Jan; (01833) 690606; £5.

175. Durham, full of history

The ancient core of the town stands on a crag defended by an almost complete loop of the River Wear, with a rewarding riverside path going from Prebends Bridge up to South St (with some of the best views of the cathedral's magnificent pinnacled towers), recrossing the river by Framwellgate bridge. The old part of town has a new £2 charge on vehicles entering its citadel core (daytime exc Sun). It has attractive cobbled alleys and narrow medieval lanes, and fine medieval buildings among the Georgian and later ones, particularly around the 12th-c pedestrians-only Elvet Bridge (comfortably overlooked by the big-windowed Swan & Three Cygnets). There are several medieval churches, and interesting little shops. You can hire rowing boats nr Elvet Bridge, which is also the departure point for launches; (0191) 386 9525. The Millennium City, a £29 million development at the bottom of Claypath, includes a theatre, visitor and tourist information centre, craft workshops, and an IMAX-style giant-screen rundown on the city's past, plus a large public square. Work is starting on redeveloping the adjacent Walkergate area into a new leisure quarter (inc multiplex cinema, lots of bars, cafés and restaurants). Ghostly guided walks leave from outside the Tourist Information Centre at various times throughout the summer – phone to check (0191) 386 1500. The bus service linking station, coach and car parks to the cathedral now runs more frequently. Bistro 21 out at Aykley Heads (off B6532 N) and the Seven Stars just out at Shincliffe are our firm food recommendations, and the Court Inn and Cathedrals café (both Court Lane) are also useful for decent food all day exc Sun.

Durham Cathedral Huge, and probably England's finest, a fiercely beautiful and unusually well preserved Norman building, breathtaking and very masculine inside; it was the first in Britain to use pointed arches. St Cuthbert's shrine is here, and they say that the Lady Chapel owes its odd position at the W end to his hatred of women; every time they tried to build it in the right place his spirit apparently caused the foundations to collapse. Try to spot the unique bronze knocker that seems to have a cheery grin. Rare books and manuscripts in the 15th-c monks' dormitory, and an exhibition on the cathedral's 900-year history. Meals, snacks, shop, disabled access; monks' dormitory open Mon–Sat, Sun pm Apr–Sept (80p), Treasury cl Sun am (£2), tower cl Sun, during services and inclement weather (£2); entry to the cathedral is free, but a donation of £3.50 is suggested. The close behind the cathedral has some handsome old houses (a shame about the cars).

176. Hadrian's Wall

An amazing sight, if you've never seen it before. It's extraordinary to imagine those Roman military engineers, so far from their warm homeland, building this remarkable construction through such inhospitable surroundings. Many of its 73½ miles run along the natural hard rock ridge of the great craggy Whin Sill, making it that much more formidable; the overall sense of grandeur is a definite part of the appeal. The stone Wall itself, with its turret watchtowers, milecastles and more sporadic forts, defines the N side of a narrow frontier zone, bounded on its S side by an equally remarkable ditch between turf ramparts; a military road runs between wall and ditch. It was this whole installation rather than just the Wall which the Romans used to control trade and cross-border travel. The B6318 following the military road is a fine drive, with some of the best views of the Wall. This road also gives walkers easy access to the line of the Wall, with numerous car parks on the way. There's not a lot of point trying to make walks into circuits: all the interest is along the Wall itself, although in places you may prefer to drop down beneath the switchback Whin Sill, which itself can be quite tiring. The views are bleak and exhilarating, with particularly well preserved sections at Walltown

Crags and Cawfield Crags; Cuddys Crag, with glorious views, is very photogenic. Even in fine summer weather the wind can be chilly on the Wall, so go well wrapped up. English Heritage have been cutting back on the publicity for some sites – thousands of marauding tourists have caused more damage than centuries of harsh weather and unstable politics ever managed. However, an environmentally friendly path will let you follow the Wall from beginning to end. In summer a tourist bus runs between Hexham and several of the main sites (and even as far as Carlisle), and you can get on or off at any of the stages along the way; check with the the information centre on (01434) 652220 for times. The best place to eat nr the main sites is the Milecastle Inn on the B6318 NE of Haltwhistle. The top places we pick out below run from west to east, or left to right.

Vindolanda Started well before the Wall itself, this Roman fort and frontier town soon became a base for 500 soldiers. Full-scale reconstructions, lots of well preserved remains, and further excavations in progress (weather permitting Sun–Fri Apr–Aug). The adjacent museum has a fascinating selection of hand-written letters and documents found on the site, inc party invitations, shopping lists and a note that could have been written by many a modern mother: 'I have sent you socks and two pairs of underpants.' Meals, snacks, shop, disabled access to museum but not site; cl Tues–Thurs mid-Nov to mid-Feb; (01434) 344277; £4.

Housesteads Roman Fort and Museum (B6318) The best-known and most visited section of the Wall (and also one of the best-preserved), pretty much slap bang in the middle. It owes its fine state of preservation partly to the fact that while other stretches were being used as a handy source of free recycled quality masonry, this fort was base camp for a powerful group of Border bandits; woe betide anyone who tried to use their fortifications as material for cowsheds or churches. A museum has altars, inscriptions and models, and there are good walks in either direction. Snacks, shop; cl 24–26 Dec, 1 Jan; (01434) 344363; £3; EH.

Chesters Roman Fort (B6318, slightly W of Chollerford) The best-preserved example of a Roman cavalry fort in Britain, in an attractive riverside setting. In the bath house you can see exactly how the underfloor heating system worked, and a museum has sculptures and inscriptions from here and other sites. Summer snacks, shop, some disabled access; cl 24–26 Dec, 1 Jan; (01434) 681379; £3; EH. The Hadrian Hotel at Wall (A6076 S) has good value food.

Segedunum (Buddle St/Station Rd, Wallsend) The remains of this great terminal fort lay buried under Victorian housing until the 1970s, after which they were excavated more thoroughly than just about any other site in the Empire: you can see plenty of the finds. The most striking feature of the complex is the spectacular 35-metre (115-ft) viewing tower, which superimposes virtual reality reconstructions on the actual excavations. Another unique feature is a completely functional reconstructed Roman bath house. Elsewhere are videos, more reconstructions, and plenty of hands-on and touch-screen activities. There are also galleries on mining (there was once a colliery here) and shipbuilding (Swan Hunter are based next door). Children under 6 aren't going to be engaged for long, but older ones can be happily distracted for an hour or two, particularly if they learned about the Romans at school. Snacks, shop, disabled access; cl 25–26 Dec, 1 Jan; (0191) 295 5757; £3.50.

177. Saxon survivals in this great abbey church

Hexham Abbey Founded around 674 by St Wilfrid, once the largest church N of the Alps. The bulk of what is seen today dates from the 12th c, though there are two splendid Saxon survivals –

the superbly atmospheric crypt, and the throne of the Bishop (St Wilfrid's Chair or Frith stool). The choir still descend the unique Night Stairs for services. Summer snacks, shop, disabled access; cl Good Fri; free, but £3 suggested donation.

178. Holy Island

Lindisfarne, an important centre for Christian pilgrims, is linked to the mainland by a causeway which you can drive (or walk) over at low tide. Tide tables are posted at each end, or phone (01289) 330733; it really is worth checking these carefully – the causeway is impassable for around two hours before high tide and four hours after. If you want to visit a particular attraction, make sure that the tide and the opening times match on the day you want to go. There are nature-reserve dunes, fishermen's huts made of upturned former boats, old lime-kilns, a small extended village with tourist cafés and pubs (the Ship has good value food inc local seafood), and good views from the close-grazed grassy crags. The 3m walk around the island's shores is easy but fascinating.

Lindisfarne Priory From here St Aidan and monks from Iona replanted the seeds of Christianity in 7th-c England. These early monks were driven out by Vikings, so it's the extensive remains of a later 12th-c church you can see today; a very peaceful and romantic spot, with graceful red sandstone arches bordered by incongruously neat lawns. Shop, disabled access to visitor centre; cl 24–26 Dec, and 1 Jan; (01289) 389200; £3.

Lindisfarne Castle The rather lonely and austere exterior belies what's within; the 16th-c fortress was restored by Lutyens for the editor of *Country Life* in a suitably monolithic quasi-medieval style. Sumptuous furnishings include a fine collection of antique oak furniture, and there's a walled garden designed by Gertrude Jekyll to protect against the North Sea winds. Cl Fri (exc Good Fri), and

Nov–Mar, but varies according to tides; (01289) 389244; £4.20; NT. It's a mile's walk fom the car park.

179. A grand country house

Dunham Massey Hall, Garden and Park (off B5160 W of Altrincham) Early Georgian manor house extensively remodelled in the early 20th c, with impressive silverware, paintings and furnishings, and restored kitchen, pantry and laundry. The largely unaltered grounds have plenty of deer, formal avenues of trees, and a working Elizabethan saw mill. Concerts and events even in winter when the house is closed. Meals, snacks, shop, disabled access to ground floor of hall; open Sat–Weds Apr–Oct, house cl am; (0161) 941 1025; £5.50 house and garden, £3.50 garden only; NT. The Axe & Cleaver (School Lane) is a roomy nearby family dining pub.

180. A dazzling medieval timbered manor house

Bramhall Hall (Bramhall) One of the finest houses in the area (particularly from the outside), a splendid timber-framed 14th-c hall with rare 16th-c wall paintings and furniture, and extensive parkland; attractively restored in the 19th c. Meals, snacks, shop, disabled access to ground floor; open pm Mon–Sat, and all day Sun and bank hols Good Fri–Sept, pm Tues–Sat, and all day Sun Oct–Dec (exc 25–26 Dec), and pm wknds the rest of the year; (0161) 485 3708; £3.95, small parking charge. The Davenport Arms at Woodford does decent lunches.

181. Where Moll Flanders was filmed

Astley Hall (Astley Park, Chorley) This unusual-looking timber-framed 16th-c house has particularly elaborate carvings and plasterwork, interesting pottery and paintings, and extensive gardens and woodland. It was used in the TV adaptation of *Moll Flanders*. Shop, disabled access to ground floor only; cl am, Mon (exc bank hols), and Mon–Thurs Nov–Mar; (01257) 515555; £2.95, free for Chorley residents. The Farmers Arms at Eccleston over towards Southport is a good value dining pub.

182. Lancaster – a rich past

Friendly and relaxed despite the grandeur of many of its stone buildings; ambling down Lancaster's cobbled streets and alleyways (much is pedestrianised), it's hard to believe this was once a major West Indies shipping port; these days the water traffic is more sedate. Riverside paths have been improved; there's now a 10-mile footpath and cycle route that follows the river from Lancaster to Lune Valley at Caton – along the way are various sculptures and other art works. The Lancastrian (Scale Hall Farm, A589 Morecambe road) has good food, and other places worth knowing for lunch include the Brown Cow (Penny St) and canalside White Cross.

Lancaster Castle Dramatic 12th-c Norman fortress famous for hangings and witch trials, owned by the Queen as Duke of Lancaster. Part of it is still used as a prison, but the dungeons, tower and 18th-c Gothic Revival Shire Hall can all be visited. Shop; cl 2 wks over Christmas and New Year; (01524) 64998; £4.

183. Two Manchester firsts – Britain's oldest public library, and the start of the Suffragette movement

Chetham's Library (Long Millgate, Manchester) Nestled among the modern developments of the Millennium Quarter, this is the oldest public library in Britain, founded in 1653. The attractive building itself dates from the 15th c and was originally a college for priests. Many of the original features remain, inc fellows' dormitories and 17th-c reading tables (still used). Cl 12.30–1.30, wknds, bank hols, Sats in Jun, and 25 Dec–1 Jan; (0161) 834 7961; free.

Pankhurst Centre (62 Nelson St, Chorlton on Medlock) Emmeline Pankhurst launched the Suffragette movement from this Georgian semi, with period-furnished parlour and interestingly planted garden. Meals, snacks, shop, disabled access; cl Sun and bank hols; (0161) 273 5673; free.

184. Fine costumes and fabrics in a 1600s country house

Gawthorpe Hall (Padiham) Early 17th-c country house with fine panelling and moulded ceilings, minstrels' gallery, Jacobean long gallery, and some mid-19th-c alterations. Important collections of costume, embroidery and lace, and paintings from the National Portrait Gallery. Snacks, shop, limited disabled access; house cl am, Mon (exc bank hols), Fri, and Nov–Mar, grounds open all year; (01282) 771004; £3; NT. The hilly cobbled alleys in the town's centre are now a conservation area. The Red Rock (Sabden Rd) has good value food, with fine views from its garden.

185. The soap king's garden village

Port Sunlight Heritage Centre (Port Sunlight) Sets the scene for this most famous of the garden villages built by 19th-c philanthropists, contriving something better than the appalling squalor of northern England's factory towns. Historically important as the precursor of garden cities, garden suburbs and New Towns, it's perfectly preserved, with groups of mock-Tudor cottages, swathes of greenery and parkland: no two groups of houses are alike. Useful village trail leaflets. Shop, good disabled access; cl

Christmas wk; (0151) 644 6466; 70p. The Seven Stars at nearby Thornton Hough is useful for lunch.

186. Intricate and eye-catching black and white timbering

Speke Hall (Speke) Built around a square courtyard, this is one of the most beautiful and richly timbered black and white houses in the country; the inside is mainly Victorian, though there's a vast Tudor Great Hall. Restored Victorian garden. Hard to believe the centre of Liverpool is just six miles away. Meals, snacks, shop, disabled access; house open pm exc Mon and Tues 22 Mar–Oct, plus wknds Nov–8 Dec, garden open exc Mon all year (house and garden open bank hols); (0151) 427 7231; £6, £3 grounds only; NT.

187. Local life a hundred years ago

Wigan Pier (Wallgate, Wigan) Rather different from when Orwell knew it, this is now a dynamic and entertaining wharfside centre demonstrating local life in the early 1900s, with actors performing in a reconstructed mine, pub, school, music hall, houses and even seaside. An ingenious mix of museum and theatre, it's an enormously enjoyable family day out, and you really do get a tangible impression of what life was really like at the turn of the century. A museum takes a nostalgic look at each decade of the 20th c; you can see a Victorian schoolroom, mill steam engine and textile machinery hall, and take a canal boat trip. Meals, snacks, shop, disabled access; cl Fri (exc Good Fri), 25–26 Dec, and 1 Jan; (01942) 323666; £7.50.

188. A classic old-fashioned market town

Richmond is one of Britain's most satisfying small towns, on a spectacular hillside high above the Swale, with steep and pretty streets of old stone buildings, and a splendid broad sloping market square (still cobbled, and perhaps the biggest in the country; market day is Sat). Scollards Hall, built in 1080, is possibly the oldest domestic building in Britain. The very friendly **Richmondshire Museum** is worth a look, with some detailed re-creations inc the vet's surgery from the TV series *All Creatures Great and Small*. Shop, disabled access; cl Nov–Good Fri; (01748) 825611; £1.50. An attractive riverside walk beneath the towering bulk of its castle heads W through Hudswell Woods, with an extension to Whitcliffe Scar, a cliff above the Swale with an exciting path along its top. The army connection with the town is still strong; nearby Catterick Camp is the biggest in the north. The Black Lion in Finkle St is good value, as is the Coffee Bean Café (Market Pl) and the old-fashioned grocer below it.

189. A picture-book castle

Ripley Castle (Ripley, off A61) Beautifully picturesque castle, in the same family for an amazing 26 generations. Most of the current building dates from the 16th c, inc the tower housing a collection of Royalist armour. For some the main attraction is the splendid gardens, the setting for a national collection of hyacinths and (under glass) a fine tropical plant collection; also lakeside walk. Very good meals and snacks, shops inc a superb delicatessen, some disabled access; cl Sept–May exc Tues, Thurs and wknds; (01423) 770152; £5.50, £3 gardens only. The attractive village was rebuilt around a French theme in the 1820s, and consequently has a rather continental feel; the Boars Head Hotel is a fine old place for lunch.

190. Where the bugler still calls nightfall

In **Ripon**, colourful stalls fill the attractive and ancient market square on Thurs; it's largely unspoilt, lined with specialist shops and old inns and hotels. At 9pm each night the Wakeman, a red-coated bugler, blows a buffalo horn here, as one has done for centuries. Going from here down one of the town's engagingly narrow old streets, you're rewarded by a magnificent view of the elegant Early English W front of the cathedral. The Golden Lion just off the market square has good value food. Fountains Abbey is within a walk from here, and Newby Hall and Norton Conyers are also quite close.

    Ripon Cathedral Spectacularly floodlit at night, this is one of the largest half-dozen in the country, and has plenty to see, inc very fine carving indeed in both stone and wood, and a 7th-c crypt – probably the oldest surviving crypt outside Italy. Shop, disabled access; (01765) 603462; £3 suggested donation.

191. Glorious minster church in appealing Georgian town

Beverley is an attractive country town, in a way like a small-scale York, with much the same sort of appeal. It's partly pedestrianised, with many fine Georgian buildings, several antiques shops and the like, but unlike York is still very much an honest market town rather than a tourist place. There's a market on Sat (and a little one on Weds), and the racecourse is central to local life. The Corner House (Norwood) has good food. The B1248 N gives rolling Wolds views.

    Beverley Minster Wonderful 13th/14th-c building, considered by some to be one of the most architecturally interesting in Europe, with elegant buttressing and elaborately pinnacled towers. The W front is richly carved yet extraordinarily harmonious. Inside are several delights, inc the intricately carved Percy tomb canopy, the unusual Saxon *fridstol* (one of only two such seats in the country), and the biggest collection of misericords in Britain. Shop, disabled access; open daily exc 25 Dec and during weddings and funerals, guided tours in summer and by appointment in winter; (01482) 868540; £2 suggested donation.

192. From Elizabethan carving to the Impressionists

Burton Agnes Richly decorated Elizabethan house, with fantastically carved Great Hall, 16th-c antiques, and some splendid Impressionist paintings. A fine walled garden has colourful borders, there's a pets' corner and topiary bushes. Meals, snacks, shop, disabled access to gardens and ground floor only; cl Nov–Mar; (01262) 490324; £4.80. The earlier Norman manor house stands between here and the church. The attractive church at nearby Kilham has a Norman door; the 18th-c Bell in Driffield is pleasant for lunch.

193. Yorkshire's sumptuous palace

Castle Howard (off A64 W of Malton) Magnificent 18th-c palace designed by Sir John Vanbrugh, who up to then had no architectural experience whatsoever, but went on to create Blenheim Palace. The striking 90-metre (300-ft) long façade is topped with a marvellous painted and gilded dome, an unforgettable sight beyond the lake as you approach from the N. Splendid apartments, sculpture gallery and long gallery (58 metres ((192 ft)) long to be exact), magnificent chapel with stained glass by Burne-Jones, and beautiful paintings inc a Holbein portrait of Henry VIII. The grounds are impressive but inviting, inc the domed Temple of the Four Winds by Vanbrugh, a beautiful rose garden with over 2,000 roses, a notable woodland garden, and the family mausoleum designed by Hawksmoor. There's a good unobtrusive adventure playground. Meals, snacks, shop, disabled access; cl Nov to mid-Mar; (01653) 648333; £8. A grand public road runs through the grounds, from Slingsby on the B1257; the vast estate is also threaded by a few public footpaths which gain glimpses of the great house and the landscaped parts of its grounds. The Bay Horse at nearby Terrington has good food.

194. Spectacular ruins of one of England's oldest abbeys

Rievaulx Abbey Elegant and evocative ruins of magnificent and once highly prosperous abbey, among the wooded hills of Rye Dale (the most dramatic views are gained by walking down the dale from the N). The nave, dating from 1135, is one of the earliest built in England. Also among the spectacular three-tiered remains is a fine 13th-c choir; there's a visitor centre, and interesting museum with hands-on displays about the site's history. The graceful colonnades, arches and lancet windows are especially impressive without the crowds, early or late on a wkdy out of season. Snacks, shop, some disabled access; cl 24–26 Dec, 1 Jan; (01439) 798228; £3.60; EH. Besides the many places in Helmsley not far off, the Hare over in Scawton (a pleasant drive) is good for lunch.

195. Count Dracula, Captain Cook and the Synod of Whitby

Whitby was where Count Dracula came ashore; Bram Stoker got the idea for the book in the fishermen's graveyard of the partly Norman church, 199 steps up from the harbour, with lovely woodwork. Not too far from the abbey on Church St is a small but interesting workshop where you can watch jet being crafted into jewellery. Away from the bright waterfront the town is steep and quite attractive, with picturesque old buildings (now often rather smart shops and cafés) and some quaint cobbled alleys in its original core E of the busy harbour, where excellent fresh fish is sold straight from the catch in the early morning. Besides excellent fish and chips from the Magpie café, the Duke of York (Church St, at the bottom of the 199 steps) does decent food all day, though sadly a new bye-law has banished its nice tables outside. In the two wks around the summer solstice the sun both rises and sets above the sea.

Whitby Abbey Impressive set of 13th-c ruins dramatically overlooking the harbour from their windswept clifftop setting. You can see the skeletal remains of the magnificent three-tiered choir and the N transept, and it's an evocative spot for a picnic. An earlier building had been the site of the Synod of Whitby, where the dating of Easter was thrashed out in 664. Also here are a Celtic Christian cemetery, and a recently restored 17th-c stone garden made by descendants of the family who bought the abbey after Henry VIII's dissolution of the monasteries. Though admission price has doubled, we think it's justified by recent improvements under a £5½ million English Heritage conservation and access project. An innovative new visitor centre, housed in the roofless shell of a 17th-c house, has well thought-out displays with plenty of interactive features, videos and an activity centre, and there's a good new audio tour. Snacks, shop, disabled access; cl 24–26 Dec, 1 Jan; (01947) 603568; £3.60; EH.

Captain Cook Memorial Museum (Grape Lane) In the house where the great explorer lived as an apprentice in the shipping trade from 1746; rooms are furnished in period style with models, letters and drawings from Cook's later voyages. Shop, disabled access; cl Nov–Feb; (01947) 601900; £2.80.

196. The walled medieval city of York

York's centre, ringed by medieval city walls, has twisting alleys filled with lovely ancient buildings, interesting shops, and lively cafés, pubs and bars – and all this is virtually traffic-free, wonderful for carefree strolling. It has plenty of remarkably varied things well worth visiting – good for all ages. The magnificent Minster is one of Britain's great sights, the Castle Museum and National Railway Museum are first-class, and Jorvik Viking City is among the country's best heritage centres (though over rather quickly for the price). This is undeniably a tourist city, with crowds at the main attractions; but most people find that all the other visitors actually seem to add to the atmosphere, rather than detract from it. You can do the circuit of the 13th-c city walls and their many towers in a couple of hours or so, mostly on top. One of the best stretches, with good views of the Minster, is between the Monk Bar and Bootham Bar. Besides the Minster, the city has a good few other fine medieval churches, though many are no longer used for services. Most were built during the prosperous 15th and 16th c, and among the finest are Holy Trinity (Goodramgate, which also contains in Our Lady's Row the oldest houses in the city) and St Helen's (St Helen's Sq). All Saints (North St) has some fascinating windows illustrating the last 15 days of the world. There's a good fun guided ghost walk at 7.30pm (exc 24–31 Dec) beginning at the Shambles; (01904) 608700; £3. The York Pass is worth considering if you plan to visit lots of sites in one go (£21 for a day, it covers more than 30 of the city's attractions), and there are Nov–Mar special offers on many of the major attractions, restaurants, and places to stay – phone the tourist information (01904) 621756 or take a look at their website www.visityork.org for more information.

York Minster A glorious example of Gothic architecture, in soft-coloured York stone, this is Britain's largest medieval building, begun in 1220 and taking a staggering 250 years to build. The richly detailed interior contains more original medieval glass than any other church in England – and indeed is reckoned to house half of all that's known in the country. Look out for the great E window which shows Genesis and Revelations in 27 panels, the splendid five sisters window in the N transept, and the beautiful ceilings of the central tower and chapter house. The choir screen has 15 niches containing statues of the kings of England from William the Conqueror to Henry VI. There's a display on the church's turbulent history in the Undercroft, Treasury and crypt. Meals, snacks, shop, disabled access and facilities (touch and hearing centre, Braille guides, guide dogs welcome); cl Sun am, and occasionally for major services; (01904) 557216; £3.50 suggested donation; £3 Undercroft museum, Treasury and crypt. You can climb the tower for good views of the city (£3). Largely traffic free, the Close outside is fairly quiet, but not enclosed, and without the tranquil serenity of say Exeter, Salisbury or Winchester.

Fairfax House (Castlegate) Magnificently restored mid-18th-c town house, probably one of the finest in England, its richly decorated rooms fully furnished in period style. Much of the impressive collection of paintings, pottery, clocks and Georgian furniture was donated by the great-grandson of the confectionery baron Joseph Terry, and there's a re-created mid-18th-c meal; changing exhibitions. Shop, some disabled access by arrangement (steps at front); cl Fri (exc guided tours, 11am and 2pm), Sun am, and 6 Jan–14 Feb; (01904) 655543; £4.50.

Jorvik Viking City (below Coppergate Shopping Centre) A well researched and absorbing re-creation of Viking life: a time capsule carries you back to the year 975, then a viewing car floats you over a muddy road, past street scenes with workshops and alleys, and even up through a two-storey house, all enhanced (if that's the word) with smells from the polluted River Foss, a cess-pit, and the reek of newly tanned leather. A darkened futuristic gallery brings seemingly mounted artefacts slowly to life (using illuminations and mirrors) as they would have appeared in contemporary Jorvik. You're unlikely to spend as much as an hour here, so you have to reckon on the realism rather than the time you spend here making this worth while. It's best to book ahead, to cut the queue; snacks, shop, disabled access; cl 25 Dec; (01904) 643211; £6.95.

197. The Brontës' village

Haworth is admittedly touristy, with plenty of craft shops, antiques shops and tea shoppes catering for all the people drawn here by the Brontës (spelt Brunty before father Patrick went posh). A visit out of season catches it at its best, though at any time the steep cobbled main street has quieter more appealing side alleys. Most of the family are buried in the churchyard, except Anne, interred in Scarborough. For the most evocative views and atmosphere go up to the moors above town, very grand and not much different from when the Brontës knew them – despite the Japanese footpath signs. The Old White Lion (West Lane) and the 17th-c Old Hall (Sun St) are good value for lunch. The A6033 is an interesting drive to Hebden Bridge, and there's a fine old moors road via Stanbury (with its nice Old Silent pub) over to the Colne Valley in Lancashire.

Parsonage Museum The Brontës' former home has some 80,000 visitors a year (it was something of a tourist attraction even while Charlotte still lived here). The house is very carefully preserved, with period furnishings, very good changing exhibitions, and displays of the siblings' books, manuscripts and possessions inc the sisters' writing table. Shop; cl 24–27 Dec, 2–31 Jan; (01535) 642323; £4.80.

Keighley & Worth Valley Railway Actually begins just N at

Keighley (where you can connect with BR trains) but is based here. Run by enthusiastic volunteers, the line was built to serve the valley's mills, and passes through the heart of Brontë country. The prettiest station is Oakworth (familiar to many from the film *The Railway Children*). Snacks, shop (open daily exc 25 Dec), some disabled access; steam trains (good buffet car) run wknds all year, Tues–Thurs last 2 wks Jun, daily July–early Sept, and most school hols; (01535) 645214 for timetable; £6 return.

198. 17th-c grandeur and miles of deer park

Belton House Splendid Restoration-period mansion with wonderful carvings, ornate plasterwork, and sumptuous furnishings, paintings and ceramics, as well as a 1,000-acre deer park (picturesque public road through here on the E side), orangery and formal Italian garden. Meals, snacks, shop, limited disabled access to house (best to phone); open Weds–Sun and bank hol Mons April–Oct; (01476) 566116; £5.60; NT. The Brownlow Arms in picturesque Hough-on-the-Hill is a good restaurant.

199. Tour this stately home's grounds in the ranger's Land-Rover

Grimsthorpe Castle A patchwork of styles from its medieval tower and Tudor quadrangle to the baroque N front by Vanbrugh; the state rooms and galleries have especially fine furnishings. Outside are formal gardens and parkland with lake (you can take a tour with the ranger in his Land-Rover), and red deer tame enough for children to feed, also play and picnic areas. Meals, snacks, shop, some disabled access; open Sun and Thurs Apr–Sept, plus Thurs–Sun in Aug, castle cl am; (01778) 591205; £6.50 all-in, £3 park only. The Black Horse is a good dining pub.

200. Lincoln's crowning hilltop

The cathedral and castle, both very striking, share **Lincoln**'s central hilltop, with enough old buildings around them to keep a sense of unity. There's a lot to appeal up here, and in Steep Hill and Strait St ancient buildings run steeply down to the 15th-c Stonebow Gate at the top of the High St. The Time Travel Pass (from participating attractions, or the Tourist Information Centre on Castle Hill, giving unlimited access for a week) lets you visit the cathedral, castle, Museum of Lincolnshire Life, Ellis Mill, medieval Bishop's Palace and the Usher Gallery for £20. Guided tours leave from the tourist information in Castle Sq 11am, 2.15pm wknds (daily July–Aug); phone (01522) 873213; £3. The **Greyfriars Exhibition Centre** (Broadgate) is in a lovely 13th-c Franciscan building (open Weds–Sat (exc 1–2pm) and Tues July–Aug; (01522) 530401; free). The Wig & Mitre and Browns Pie Shop, both on Steep Hill, and Lincolnshire Poacher (Bunkers Hill) are good for lunch, and behind the castle the unpretentious Victoria (Union Rd) is good value. Brayford Pool, the heart of the Waterfront Quarter, has boat trips, a multi-screen cinema, and lots of places to eat (bargain food at the riverside Royal William IV, for instance). There are some good views from the A607 to Grantham.

Lincoln Cathedral Many people reckon that this is England's finest. The original building was largely destroyed in an 1185 earthquake, but the magnificent W front survived, and after nearly a century of rebuilding it was complete by 1280. The triple towers rise spectacularly above the nearby rooftops, and are beautifully lit at night. Inside, the carvings and stained glass are stupendous, and the architecture gracefully harmonious. Meals, snacks, shop, disabled access; (01522) 544544; £3.50. The impressive ruins of the once formidable medieval Bishop's Palace are close by,

Lincoln Castle In beautiful surroundings on a formidable earthwork, this was originally built in 1068 for William the Conqueror, but only two towers and two impressive gateways date from then. One of only four remaining originals of Magna Carta is on display, and there are super views from the ramparts. A 19th-c prison has suitably gruesome exhibits; its chapel is unusually designed so that none of the congregation could see each other. Special events such as medieval re-enactments, and open-air theatre (phone for details), and they do free guided tours. Meals, snacks, shop, limited disabled access; cl 24–26, 31 Dec, 1 Jan; (01522) 511068; £2.50.

201. A classic windmill

Trader Mill (Sibsey, A16 N of Boston) A splendidly restored six-sailed tower windmill with fine views from the top. Refurbished tearooms, shop, some disabled access; usually open 2nd and 4th wknds and bank hol Mons Apr–Sept; (01205) 750036; *£2; EH. The village's second windmill is now a private house.

202. England's most attractive town?

That was John Betjeman's verdict on **Stamford**, and many would agree. Within the medieval walls are no fewer than 500 listed buildings, inc a good number of attractive medieval **churches** – particularly All Saints in the centre, St George's with excellent 15th-c stained glass, and St Mary's nearby. There are riverside strolls and quite a few craft and antiques shops. The George, one of the town's grandest buildings with some parts going back to Saxon times, is excellent for lunch (and has food all day), and the much more modest Daniel Lambert (St Leonard's St) is also good.

Burghley House A 20-min walk from Stamford's centre leads to this splendid mansion, built by William Cecil and still the home of his family. The exterior is Tudor at its most solidly showy, but the state rooms inside are largely baroque, with wonderful frescoes by Antonio Verrio – the Heaven Room is astonishing. The peaceful grounds, where the Burghley Horse Trials are held, were landscaped by Capability Brown; there's a sculpture garden, and readers enjoy strolls in the deer park. Meals, snacks, shop, disabled access; cl Nov–Mar; (01780) 752451; £7.10.

203. A towering Tudor castle

Tattershall Castle 15th-c red brick castle with magnificent 30-metre (100-ft) turreted keep, with fine heraldic chimneypieces and stained-glass windows on each of the four storeys; there's a double moat, waterfowl and peacocks, and children can try on medieval costumes. Snacks, shop, disabled access to ground floor; cl Jan–Feb, Thurs, Fri Apr–Oct and Mon–Fri Nov–Dec, and Mar; (01526) 342543; £3.20; NT. The airy 15th-c **church** is also attractive, and just off the A153 towards Sleaford, on the left before you reach Tattershall Bridge, is a preserved steam engine which worked at keeping this area of fens drained for nearly a century. The Abbey Lodge Hotel (B1192 towards Woodhall) has good food.

204. Cave homes from the Ice Age

Creswell Crags Visitor Centre Stone Age man lived in the caves and rock shelters of this limestone gorge right by the Nottinghamshire/Derbyshire border. Even on days when there aren't cave tours it's an intriguing prehistoric site, with a good visitor centre, reconstructions of Ice Age family life, and other displays and activities. In summer and school holidays a tour for children leaves at 11.30, best to check for other cave tour dates.

You can't go into the caves wearing sandals or open shoes. Picnic area, shop, disabled access; cl Nov–Jan exc Sun; (01909) 720378; site free, cave tours £2.75. The Mallet & Chisel in nearby Whitwell (Hillside) has cheap food.

205. Byron's romantic home

Newstead Abbey (off A60) Splendid former home of Lord Byron, in gorgeously romantic grounds; many of his possessions can still be seen. Rooms are decorated in a variety of styles from medieval through to Victorian, and there are substantial remains of the original priory. Adventure playground, and dressing up for children. Meals, snacks, summer shop, limited disabled access; house cl am and Oct–Mar; grounds cl last Fri in Nov only; (01623) 455900; £4 house and gardens, £2 gardens only. The Horse & Groom in the attractive nearby village of Linby is a useful stop, as is the Griffins Head at Papplewick (B683/B6011).

206. Nottingham's castle and caverns

Castle Museum and Art Gallery Up on the summit, this dates from the 17th c, but the gateway is from an earlier 13th-c fortress. It now houses an appealing museum, with a history of the site and the underground passages. Meals, snacks, shop, disabled access; cl 24–26 Dec and 1 Jan; (0115) 915 3700; £2 wknds and bank hols.

    Cave tours The rock on which old Nottingham stood is honeycombed with hundreds of galleries, cellars and passageways. Tours (which are quite strenuous) usually leave the castle at 11, 2 and 3 Mon–Thurs and Sat, and 2 and 3 Fri, there may be additional tours in the summer, and in case of occasional rock falls it's best to call (0115) 915 3700 first; £2. The attractive Olde Trip to Jerusalem (Brewhouse Yard) has a fascinating bar tunnelled many centuries ago right into the rock face.

Wollaton Hall (Wollaton Park, 3m W) Splendidly ornate Tudor house with the city's natural history collection. The delightful 500-acre grounds have two adventure playgrounds, a sensory garden, and picnic areas. Snacks, shop, disabled access to the ground floor only; cl 24–26 and 1 Jan; (0115) 915 3900; £2 wknds and bank hols, free at other times; £2 car parking for the day. The **Industrial Museum** (Courtyard Buildings) looks at lace-making and other local industries, and has working steam-powered machines (steamings last Sun of month); cl Nov–Mar; (0115) 915 3910; £1.50 wknds, £2 joint ticket with Wollaton Hall, also free wkdys).

207. The cathedral, the cooking apple and the workhouse

Southwell Minster Magnificent 12th-c cathedral, a fine sight from miles around (especially at night when it's floodlit), and glorious to walk through. Fine leaf carvings in the chapter house, and lovely choir screen; Evensong is sung daily during term time, and it's worth catching one of the regular concerts. There's also a smart visitor centre. This attractive old town of Southwell, small and quiet, is the home of the Bramley apple, developed by Henry Merryweather in the 19th c. The original tree survives in a private garden at 75 Church St, and another prospers at his descendant's garden centre on Halam Rd, where there's a small exhibition on the subject. The Bramley Apple just down from the cathedral has decent food.

Workhouse (Upton Rd) The National Trust's only workhouse, and one of the best-preserved, it has rapidly become a hit since opening in 2002 (booking strongly recommended at peak times). Vividly conjuring up the stern gloom of how the 19th-c poor were treated, it's laid out in three wings, for men, women and children: the long rows of closely placed beds allowed no privacy, and death was often the only release from disease and punishment. Shop, limited disabled access; open pm daily exc Tues and Weds 2 Apr– 2 Nov; (01636) 817250; *£4.20.

208. Plain and untouched, a typical 1920s home

Mr Straw's House (7 Blyth Grove, Worksop) One of the NT's most unusual properties, an ordinary 1920s semi, left untouched by two brothers who inherited it when their parents died. Even the calendar remains unturned. A fascinating time-capsule, it's open for prebooked timed tickets only – by limiting numbers the National Trust ensure that you can get a really good feeling of what it was like to live here; cl Nov–Mar and Sat, Sun; (01909) 482380; £4.20. The Mallard at the station ½m away is an apt refreshment stop. The town museum has a display on the Pilgrim Fathers (cl Sun and Thurs and Sat pm; free), and the priory church is worth a look for the elaborate scrollwork on its 12th-c yew door.

209. A particularly intriguing stately home

Calke Abbey One of the most rewarding NT properties in Britain, an unusual baroque mansion still in pretty much the same state as when the last baronet died here in 1924. You might expect the splendidly decorated rooms with their fascinating displays (inc an extensive natural history collection), but it's quite a surprise to find the more dilapidated corridors and areas where family possessions were just bundled together in heaps. This gives you a better appreciation of how the abbey was a much-loved family home – and of how things forgotten in the attic can quickly become social history. Also extensive parkland and walled gardens.

Meals, snacks, shop, disabled access to ground floor; cl am Thurs, Fri, and Nov–Mar; (01332) 863822; £5.60, £2.80 garden only – there's a £2.70 vehicle charge on entering the park, refundable on entry to the house (which has a timed ticket system on busy days); NT. The nearby Saracens Head (Heath End Lane) has great value snacks.

210. Huge caverns and historic Blue John mines

Castleton is very much geared to visitors, and filled with walkers and cavers in summer; plenty of cafés, and shops selling expensive worked pieces of the Blue John fluorspar that's found only in the nearby mine workings. The village's attractive dark stone buildings (one of the most impressive now a youth hostel) are dominated by the ruins of **Peveril Castle**, built high above in the 11th c – magnificent views. Shop, snacks; cl Mon and Tues in Nov–Mar, 24–26 Dec and 1 Jan; (01433) 620613; £2.40; EH. There's decent food at the Castle Hotel, Rose Cottage and George, and in the pretty nearby village of Hope the Cheshire Cheese is good.

    Peak Cavern Right in the village, this is the biggest natural cavern in the country and really does seem huge – the entrance hall is so large it used to house an entire village; no significant stalactites or stalagmites. From there it's a ½-mile walk along subterranean passageways to the Great Cave, 45 by 27 metres (150 ft wide, 90 ft long). By the time you reach the Devil's Staircase you'll be nearly 140 metres (450 ft) underground. Rope-making demonstrations. Snacks, shop; cl wkdys Nov–Mar; (01433) 620285; £5.25.

211. Perhaps Britain's most rewarding stately home

Chatsworth (off B6012) is a wonderful estate on the banks of the River Derwent, with almost as much appeal for children as it has for adults. The first-class adventure playground is perhaps the highlight for younger visitors, and a working farmyard has plenty of opportunities to get close to cows, sheep, pigs and horses. The house itself has been home to the Duke of Devonshire's family for nearly 450 years. Sumptuously furnished, the 26 rooms on display show off a superb collection of fine arts, with memorable paintings by Rembrandt and Van Dyck, and a set of nine Regency bedrooms is also usually open for a small extra charge. Private guided tours are available by prior arrangement (extra charge). The gardens cover 100 acres; brass bands play on summer Sunday afternoons. The surrounding park was landscaped by Capability Brown, and covers 1,000 acres; well marked walks and trails. Good meals and snacks, shop, garden centre, disabled access to garden only; open Apr–21 Dec; (01246) 582204; £8 house and garden, £4.50 garden only, and a further £3.60 for the farm and adventure playground. Entry to the park is free (open all year). Car parking is £1. Also in the grounds, at Stud Farm, 1½ miles towards Pilsley, is one of England's best farm shops (they also have a branch in Pimlico, London). The Devonshire Arms at Beeley has decent food all day.

212. Vintage trams in a vintage village

Crich Tramway Village (Matlock Rd, Crich) When you enter this enthusiastically run place, you're given an old penny (or half-penny for children), which you use to pay for unlimited rides on the lovingly restored vintage trams that run up and down a one-mile period street and beyond, through lovely parts of the Derwent Valley (familiar to viewers of *Peak Practice*). A comprehensive exhibition has more trams, from all over the British Isles and further afield. There are plenty of play areas: a big one outside, with bridges, ropes and balancing poles, and a tram-themed one inside with a section for under-5s. Nice walks through the surrounding woodland, and regular special events – it's particularly good fun in the run-up to Christmas. They've a new workshop viewing gallery (where you can watch the trams being restored). New pub and restaurant, picnic areas, disabled access (one tram has been adapted for wheelchairs, and they have a guide book in Braille); cl wkdys in Mar and Tues–Fri Nov–22 Dec (exc 2nd wk in Dec), best to check; (0870) 758 7267; £7. The Cliff Inn nearby has great views.

213. A village with a dark past

When the Great Plague struck the attractive secluded village of **Eyam,** sick villagers confined themselves here for fear of infecting people outside. Plaques record who died where, and stones on the village edge mark where money was disinfected. The Miners Arms is very good for lunch. Just up the B6521 at Upper Padley, **Padley Chapel** is an interesting 15th-c revival, effectively restored in 1933.

Eyam Hall Sturdy-looking 17th-c manor house, still very much a family home, with furniture, portraits and tapestries, fine Jacobean staircase and impressive flagstoned hall; there's a small craft centre in the stables. Meals, snacks, shop, some disabled access; house open Weds–Thurs, Sun and bank hol Mon June–Aug, craft centre open daily exc Mon, and over Christmas and New Year; (01433) 631976; £4.25 – timed ticket system.

214. A medieval manor, frozen in time

Haddon Hall One of the most perfectly preserved medieval manor houses in England, still with its 12th-c painted chapel, 14th-c kitchen, and banqueting hall with minstrels' gallery. Perhaps because they're furnished with the original furniture and tapestries, some rooms can seem rather bare; a bright spot is Rex Whistler's painting of the house in the silver-panelled long gallery. It's a particularly pretty location in summer when the long terraced rose gardens are in full bloom. Several films and TV adaptations have had scenes shot here in recent years. Meals, snacks, shop; cl Mon–Weds in Oct, and all Nov–Mar; (01629) 812855; £5.90. The Lathkil Hotel up in Over Haddon is good for lunch, and nearby roads have attractive views.

215. A pinnacle of the Elizabethan age

Hardwick Hall The marriages of the redoubtable Bess of Hardwick couldn't necessarily be described as happy but she certainly did very well out of them, the fourth leaving her enough money to build this triumphant Elizabethan prodigy house. The beautifully symmetrical towers are crowned with the monogram ES, and there's an amazing expanse of glass (her sight was dimming). Also fine tapestries and needlework, large park, and gardens laid out in walled courtyard. They're restoring the huge and ancient Gideon tapestries which run the length of the 50-metre (167-ft) Long Gallery, a silk canopy, and the garden walls; a gazebo houses an exhibition on garden history; guided walks to stone mason's yard (Weds and Thurs at 11.30, 1.30 and 3). Meals, snacks, shop, disabled access to ground floor only; open pm Apr–Oct, garden cl Tues, house cl Mon, Tues and Fri (exc bank hols), hall cl am; £2 vehicle charge to enter the grounds; £6.40 house and garden, £3.40 garden only; NT. Not far from this 'new' house is the shell of Hardwick Old Hall, Bess's birthplace; (01246) 850431; £3. A joint ticket is available for both houses (£8.50). Also on the estate is a restored watermill (adult £2.10; NT). The park is attractive for walks, and nearby Hardwick Inn, also NT-owned, is good for lunch.

216. A perfect Adam house

Kedleston Hall This 18th-c Palladian mansion is thought by many to be the finest example of Robert Adam's work – it's certainly the least altered. Interesting objets d'art, original furnishings, good collection of paintings, and a museum of items collected by Lord Curzon when he was Viceroy of India. Adam designed a charming boathouse and bridge in the park outside, which also has extensive formal gardens with marvellous rhododendrons, and long woodland walks. Meals, snacks, shop, disabled access; open pm Sat–Weds Apr–Oct, grounds also open am, and wknds Nov–Dec; (01332) 842191; £5.10, £2.30 grounds only; NT. The Joiners Arms in Quarndon does good value weekday lunches.

217. An inspiration for P G Wodehouse

Weston Park (Weston-under-Lizard, A5) This striking 17th-c house has a good range of features for all age groups, and the family ticket is quite exceptional value: five people can spend a day here and still have change from a tenner. Run by an educational charity, it's very well organised, and the staff are knowledgeable and friendly. Each of the richly decorated rooms has its own dedicated guide, as good with the family gossip as they are with the facts about the furnishings and art. You generally get to see nine of the main rooms, of which the highlight is the very elegant dining room, with its excellent collection of works by Van Dyck. The library, home to over 3,000 books, also impresses, and there are plenty of other notable paintings, including works by Rubens, Gainsborough and Constable. They've recently started showing off the family silver, and may in summer open a few of the first-floor bedrooms. There's a small toy museum, and letters and mementoes of Disraeli, who was a frequent 19th-c visitor; he claimed to detest country houses, but described Weston as 'a place that always pleased me'. One of the gifts he brought was a yellow parrot, which for years was thought to be male, until it suddenly produced two eggs, and promptly died; parrot and eggs are still proudly on display. Landscaped by Capability Brown, the grounds are huge, with a deer park, restored 18th-c terrace garden, brightly planted broderie garden, and interesting trees and shrubs; in the last century it took 37 gardeners to look after it all. The best way to explore is with one of their fairly detailed walking trails, which you can pick up free from the visitor centre. Children are well catered for: there's a good adventure playground in the woodland, and a pets corner with the usual animals to fuss. The miniature railway has a small extra charge. The inspiration for P G Wodehouse's Blandings Castle, the estate still maintains a tradition for hosting influential events, in recent months providing the setting for an international peace conference, and the music festival V2002. During events like this it may be closed to visitors, so best to ring before visiting. Meals, snacks, shop, disabled access; usually open weekends Easter–early September, and daily in July and August, though see above; (01952) 852100; entry to the park and gardens is £2.50 (£1.50 children), with the house a further £2 (£1 children), but you'll very quickly make savings with the family ticket, £7.50 for two adults and up to three children.

218. 18th-c town with a graceful cathedral

Lichfield's attractive centre is largely pedestrianised, with many 18th-c and older buildings among the more modern shops (and antiques shops). The **cathedral**, with its three graceful spires and close with lovely half-timbered buildings around it, is magnificent inside, and its W front is memorable, esp at dusk or in the dark when shadows seem to bring the profusion of statues to life.

Wonderful illuminated 8th-c gospels in the chapter house; cl during services and concerts; (01543) 306240; suggested donation £3. On Sat May–Sept you can see two bleak 16th-c cells under the Guildhall (Bore St); (01543) 264972; 40p. The Queens Head (Queen St) does good value lunches.

Samuel Johnson Birthplace Museum (Breadmarket St) Dr Johnson was born here in 1709; the house is now furnished in period, with many mementoes of him. Shop; cl am Oct–Mar, 25–26 Dec, 1 Jan; (01543) 264972; *£2.20 – and a nice celebratory gesture, free entry on Sat nearest to Dr Johnson's birthday, 18 Sept.

219. Lord Lichfield's family seat

Shugborough Hall & County Museum (Shugborough, A513) Imposing ancestral home of the Earls of Lichfield, begun in the late 17th c and enlarged in the 18th; magnificent state rooms, restored working kitchens, interesting puppet collection, and exhibition of the present Earl's photography. The park has a variety of unusual neo-classical monuments, working rare-breeds farm, and restored corn mill. Meals, snacks, shop, disabled access; grounds cl Christmas–Mar, everything else cl Mon and Oct–Feb (exc Suns in Oct and special events); (01889) 881388; £2 entry to estate, £6 house and museum, £4.50 house, £4.50 farm; NT. Their all-in ticket £8 is best value on one of their special event days, when there are more activities (such as hands-on Victorian cookery displays) for no extra cost. The canalside Wolseley Arms towards Rugeley is a handy food stop.

220. Life for 18th-c cotton workers

Quarry Bank Mill & Styal Estate (Styal) A real favourite with readers, this is one of the best and most extensive places in the country to get to grips with the Industrial Revolution, and as you can easily spend most of a day here, it's also good value for money. The 18th-c cotton mill that's the centrepiece is still operational, so there's always plenty going on, with lively displays and demonstrations of cotton production spread over five floors, bringing vividly to life the factory conditions for mill-workers and their bosses. The most dramatic sight is the 50-ton water wheel, the most powerful in Europe; it still turns every afternoon, very much the best time to visit if you have only half a day free, as that's when the steam engines are working too. Children have plenty to stimulate their interest: the Power gallery has multimedia displays illustrating how water and later steam were used to power the mill, there's a good film and lots of interactive exhibits (one on the restoration of the 1840 beam engine in the original engine house), and they have a very full programme of activities such as rope-making and dip-dyeing, particularly in the summer holidays (most are included in the ticket price, though you will need to pay extra – and book in advance – for their occasional more elaborate events such as scarecrow-making). Our favourite part isn't in the Mill at all – it's the Apprentice House in the village outside, where enthusiastic guides in period dress explain the lifestyle and 12-hour working days faced by the young pauper children who worked here. By the start of the 19th c, 90 children were living here – half the mill's workforce. Children love discovering how grim their lives could be back then, and are positively encouraged to pump water from the well, test out the straw-filled beds, and stir the porridge in the kitchen. There are timed tickets in operation here, so it makes sense to come here at the start of a visit if you can (though note the opening times, below). The garden has some rare fruit and vegetables. The surrounding village is nice to stroll around, with its carefully preserved workers' cottages, chapels and shop, and there are good woodland and waterside walks in the park, with plenty of space for picnics by the river. Meals, snacks, shop, disabled access; mill cl Mon Oct–Mar, Apprentice House and garden usually cl Mon all year (exc in summer hols), and Tues–Fri am in term time; (01625) 527468; an all-in ticket is £6.50 (£3.70 children), with a family ticket for £16.50; a mill-only ticket is £5 (£3.40 children), with the family ticket £14.50; free to NT members. Parking in the estate car park is £2.50, with £1.50 of that refundable against entry to the mill.

221. Roman and medieval Chester

A great place for a visit, **Chester** was the site of an important fort in Roman times, and later plentiful river traffic kept it rich; nowadays, it's a cheerful bustling place with interesting shops, and lots of places to eat and drink. The old centre is ringed by a medieval **town wall** that's more complete than any other in Britain. You can walk the whole way round, enjoying marvellous views; there are usually summer exhibitions, and music festivals for you to visit along the way. Partly because of the limit set by the wall, the centre of town is easy to get around on foot, not too big, and with the main streets pretty much free of cars (there may be a few buses), although in summer the sheer number of tourists and shoppers can still make them appear congested. Guided walks leave the Chester visitor centre on Vicars Lane at 10.30am daily, and also 2.15pm May–Oct; £3.50. If you're driving in, you'll be shunted round to one of the big car parks, and you may have to queue a while to get a space, so it's best to use the park and ride on the major approach roads. Chester's racecourse, the Roodee, is the oldest in Britain; it still has fashionable races Mar–Sept, with lively family events in Aug (01244) 304600. The quaint Albion (Park St) and canalside Old Harkers Arms (Russell St) both have good food.

Chester Cathedral Not unlike an ordinary church at first glance, this is far more impressive inside, with some marvellous medieval carving in and above the choir stalls, and some fine vaulting. Many of the former abbey buildings survived the Reformation, so the precincts still include peaceful arcaded flagstoned cloisters, a medieval chapter house, and older Norman parts inc a refectory – brought back into use as an excellent café (which even has a resident pianist Tues, Fri lunchtimes). Handel first rehearsed *Messiah* here in 1742, and they show a copy of his marked score. All the carved bosses have been gilded, and a model of the cathedral has a Braille text. Shop, disabled access; cl for Sun am services (up to 12.30pm); (01244) 324756; donation suggestion. There are quiet cobbled Georgian lanes around Abbey Sq, behind the cathedral a little way down Northgate.

222. The Forsyte Saga at home

Lyme Park (Disley) You might recognise this wonderful country estate, outside the pleasant hillside village of Disley, from the recent TV series *The Forsyte Saga*. The Hall at its centre is a magnificent blend of Elizabethan, Georgian and Regency architecture and styles. Tours are unguided, so you can take your time looking at the intricate carvings, and lovely tapestries, paintings and furniture. There's a particularly grand staircase, and a fine collection of English clocks. Around the house are 17 acres of Victorian gardens with orangery, sunken Dutch garden and wilderness garden, and a sprawling ancient park with a newly restored hunting tower, herds of red deer and nature trails inc one suitable for wheelchairs. Pleasant walk down to the canal. Meals, snacks, shop, disabled access (to part of the house only); house open pm Fri–Tues Apr–Oct, garden open Apr–Oct, plus wknds Nov; the park is open all year; (01663) 766492; £3.50 per car to go in the park, then £5.50 house and garden, £2.50 garden only; NT. The White Horse is a useful food stop (with OAP lunch days).

223. A great collector's unique classical mansion

Tabley House (Tabley, off A5033) The only Palladian house in the North-West, with a splendid collection of paintings. Sir John Fleming Leicester (whose family lived at Tabley for over 700 years) was the first great collector of British art, and though plans to turn his home into a National Gallery came to nothing, most of the works he assembled are still here, inc pictures by Turner, Reynolds, Henry Thompson and James Ward. Snacks, shop, very good disabled access (though they prefer notice); open Apr–Oct, Thurs–Sun pm and bank hols; (01565) 750151; £4. The Smoker at Plumley is good for lunch.

224. The birthplace of industry

Ironbridge This steep town, with intriguing hillside paths and narrow lanes, was the birthplace of the Industrial Revolution: it was Abraham Darby's use here of coke instead of charcoal for smelting which made mass-production of iron possible. Well set among the woods and grassy slopes of the Severn Gorge, it was known as Coalbrookdale until the Darbys built the restored **iron bridge** across the river that today gives the town its name. As their industry took off they produced the world's first iron rails, boats, trains and wheels, and for quite some time the valley, so quiet now, was the biggest iron-making area in the world. Attractively placed by the riverside, the Meadow, Robin Hood and particularly the Malthouse are all good lunch stops. The Boat at Jackfield and Shakespeare at Coalport are handy for Maws craft centre and the Coalport Museum. There's a pleasant terraced walk between the river and the Golden Ball (Wesley Rd, off Madeley Hill). For a fuller restaurant meal, the Coracle in the square is nice.

Ironbridge Gorge Museum (Ironbridge) It's fair to say there's now no way you could ever hope to see all ten of this outstanding collection of linked attractions in one day, but luckily you don't need to: the all-in Passport ticket (one of the best value admission deals we've come across, offering a single visit to each) lasts indefinitely, so it's easy to spread them over several visits, which can be hours, days or even years apart. The various parts of this 'museum' – not in one place, but scattered over six miles along the Gorge – are based around the sites that give this area its claim to be the birthplace of the Industrial Revolution.

For most visitors the undoubted highlight is still the reconstructed Victorian village at **Blists Hill**, a fascinating 50-acre site that's the biggest, and many would say the best, open-air museum of its kind. Every aspect of 19th-c life is here, from shops, houses, bank, and steam-operated pit, to the school, pub, pig sties and summer fairground. Costumed staff add authenticity, and there are lots of extra activities at weekends and in the holidays – including the occasional period wedding. They nicely illustrate seasonal events, from May Day to Hallowe'en and Christmas, but at any time there's lots for children here. Dogs on a lead are allowed in this part of the museum only.

On bank holiday Sun and Mon the various museums are usually linked by a bus, otherwise it's best to drive (or walk if you're keen); you'll need to use Pay and Display car parks at the Museum of the Gorge and the Iron Bridge itself. Useful leaflets (and the website, www.ironbridge.org.uk) have suggested itineraries for visits of three hours, a day and longer. You can buy individual tickets for the parts you're most interested in (Blists Hill is £8, Enginuity £4.95), but it really does make sense to get the Passport. Meals, snacks, shop, disabled access; cl 24–25 Dec, 1 Jan, and some parts cl Nov–Mar – best to ring first then; (01952) 432166; a full Passport ticket, including Enginuity, is £12.95 for adults, £8.25 for children over 5; a family ticket, covering two adults and up to five children, is excellent value at £40 (remember it's valid for as long as it takes you to use it). You can get a Passport ticket that leaves out Enginuity (the new interactive design and technology centre), which may suit older visitors better: £10.50 adults, £6.50 children (£32.50 for families).

225. Near Ironbridge, an appealing Elizabethan house

Benthall Hall (just NW of Broseley) Well liked by readers, an Elizabethan sandstone house with fine oak woodwork and panelling, decorative plasterwork, interesting garden, and 17th-c church (services 3.15 pm 3rd Sun in month). Some disabled access; open pm Weds, Sun and bank hols, cl Oct–Mar; (01952) 882159; £3.60, £2.30 garden only; NT. The Pheasant (Church St) is a good country dining pub.

226. 18th-c grandeur

Attingham Park (Atcham) Splendidly grand late 18th-c house on the site of an old Roman town, with an imposing three-storey colonnaded portico. The extensive picture gallery was designed by Nash, who made imaginative use of early curved cast iron and glass for the ceiling. A new visitor room has interactive activities; attractive mature gardens, deer park and children's adventure playground in the walled garden. Snacks, shop, disabled access by prior arrangement; grounds open daily (exc 25 Dec), house open pm, cl Weds and Thurs and Oct–late Mar; (01743) 708123; £4.60 house and grounds, £2.20 grounds only; NT. The Mytton & Mermaid opposite the entrance is a useful food stop.

227. Charles II and the Civil War

Boscobel House (Boscobel) Interesting old house renowned for sheltering Charles II after the Battle of Worcester, with an unusually well preserved 17th-c garden and cobbled courtyard, and 19th-c décor giving a romanticised view of his escape. Good guided tour. Meals, snacks, shop, disabled access to gardens only; cl Dec–Mar and wkdys during Dec; (01902) 850244; £4.40. The **Royal oak** here is said by some to have been the hiding place of the king, by others to be a descendant, and by still others to be just a fine old tree. The Bell in Tong has decent food.

White Ladies Priory (just SW) Ruins of Augustinian nunnery destroyed in the Civil War; free; EH.

228. An old town of real character

On the Severn, **Bridgnorth** is an old market town that's picturesque without being touristy. It's divided into the High Town and Low Town, with steps between the two – though it's easier (and more fun) to take the hair-raising **Cliff Railway** (70p return). At the bottom of the cliff are some small caves that people lived in till 1856 (they're not open, but labelled). As well as some handsome red brick, High Town has lots of fine timbered buildings, such as the odd town hall built on a sandstone-arched base that straddles the road in the High St. The **castle** was largely destroyed in the Civil War, but part of the keep remains, left at a scary tilt by the constant bombardment; the grounds are now a park with good views – the best are from Castle Esplanade. The unusual **church** on nearby East Castle St was designed by Thomas Telford. **North Gate Museum** looks at local history (open Fri–Sun Easter–Oct, bank hols and school hols exc Thurs). The best pubs for food here are the Bear (Northgate) and Punch Bowl (B4364 W; good carvery, great views).

229. A beautiful town, packed with fine buildings

Ludlow was laid out in the 12th c, and its original grid plan is still obvious today. The best road in is via Wigmore and Leinthall Starkes – lovely views as you approach. Dotted around are 500 listed buildings, with particularly good examples down Broad St, a charming mixture of Tudor and Georgian architecture. Book well in advance if you're planning to visit during the festival in the last wk Jun/first wk July. The most famous building is the lavishly carved and timbered Feathers Hotel on the Bull Ring; some parts inside are almost as striking. The Broadgate, the only one of the town's 13th-c gates to have survived, is interesting. Quite a few antiques shops, and no shortage of good restaurants; the Unicorn is the nicest pub for lunch.

Ludlow Castle Dating from around 1086, this splendid fortress has lots of original parts inc the Norman keep, and the chapel with its unusual circular nave. The towers and battlements on their wooded crag over the River Teme have wonderful views, and a properly 'castle-ish' feel. Shakespeare plays are performed here during the end Jun/beginning July festival, also various events throughout the year. Shop; cl 25 Dec, and wkdys Jan; (01584) 873355; *£3.50.

230. Finding Shrewsbury's treasures

Shrewsbury is rich in striking architecture, both Tudor timbering and Georgian brick and numerous buildings reflect the medieval wool fortunes, inc the old market hall; adjacent are fine half-timbered houses worth looking at from outside. The walk up Castle St is worth while, passing the original Grammar School building and the half-timbered Council House Court. Nearby the church of **St Mary** has one of the tallest spires in England and is known for its beautiful stained glass, some dating back to the 14th c. The unusual Greek Revival St Chad's Church (St Chad's Terrace) caused great controversy when it was built in 1792 because of its round nave (even the pews are circular). Shrewsbury Abbey (Abbey Foregate) is well known through the novels of Ellis Peters. Besides the church (partly 11th c) very little of the Abbey buildings survives. A guided walk of the town leaves the Tourist Information Centre daily at 2.30 May–Oct exc Sun in Oct and Sat only Nov–April (£2.50), or you can pick up a trail leaflet (99p) which will take you round some of the more interesting buildings. The original town is almost entirely ringed by a loop of the Severn which has quiet waterside paths and parks, and you can hire boats along some stretches or take a river cruise (hourly in summer from Victoria Quay by the Welsh Bridge). Our two main food recommendations are the Armoury (Victoria Quay) and Poppy's (Milk St), and other useful stops are the no smoking Three Fishes (Fish St), riverside Boat House (New St/Quarry Park), Coach & Horses (Swan Hill; brews its own beer) and Cromwells (Dogpole). The restaurant in 12th-c St Julian's church (St Alkmunds Sq) is nice, especially for vegetarians.

Shrewsbury Castle 12th c, guarding the narrow neck of land between the river's loop. It was refurbished by Thomas Telford in 1790 when the romantic Laura's Tower was built, though still has parts of the earlier building. Shop, some disabled access; cl late Dec to mid-Feb, Sun–Tues Oct–late Dec and mid-Feb to Apr, and Mon–Tues (exc bank hols) in May; (01743) 358516; £2. The attractive grounds (cl late Dec–early Jan) are free.

231. A medieval castle, always lived in

Powis Castle (A483, 1m S of Welshpool) In magnificent gardens with splendid 18th-c terraces, this dramatic-looking castle was built in the 13th c, but far from falling into decay like so many others, has developed into a grand house. It's been constantly occupied since its construction, once by the son of Clive of India – there are displays about his father's life. Meals, snacks, shop; cl Mon, Tues (exc July–Aug), and Nov–beg Apr (castle and museum cl am); (01938) 551944 information line, (01938) 551920 property office; *£8, £5.50 garden only; NT.

232. A distinctive Welsh town

Machynlleth has a wide main street with a tall, dark and handsome 19th-c clock tower and a very relaxed feel. There's quite a lot to see here and nearby, and the White Lion and Wynnstay Arms do enjoyable lunches.

Parliament House Local history museum in 15th-c building, with a particular emphasis on the 1404 rebellion of Owain Glyndwr (it's on the spot where he held parliament); great events planned for the 600th anniversary next year. Brass rubbing centre, shop, disabled access; cl 12.30–1.30pm, Sun (exc bank hols), and all Oct–Easter; (01654) 702827; free.

233. Anglesey's most historic and attractive town

Beaumaris Castle (Beaumaris) One of the most impressive and complete of those built by Edward I, despite the struggle over it with Owain Glyndwr in the early 1400s, and the plundering of its lead, timber and stone in later ages. Beautifully symmetrical, it took from 1295 to 1312 to build (though the money ran out before it could be finished). Shop, good disabled access; cl 24–26 Dec, 1 Jan; (01248) 810361; £3; Cadw. The Olde Bulls Head (dating partly from 1472) and Sailors Return are good for lunch.

Beaumaris Gaol Paints a vivid picture of the harshness of the 19th-c prison system, particularly in the dark, poky cells. Shop, very limited disabled access; cl end Sept–Easter exc by appointment, (01248) 810921; £2.75, £3.50 joint ticket with Courthouse.

234. A medieval fortress town with Roman origins

Surviving lengths of **Caernarfon**'s 13th-c town walls still crowd in its quaintly narrow streets (quaint, that is, unless you're trying to drive through them). The town harbour is busy with yachts in summer. The Hole in the Wall and Palace Vaults have good value food.

Caernarfon Castle With its nine polygonal towers and walls of colour-banded stone, this was planned by Edward I as a Royal residence and seat of government for North Wales. Edward's son was born here and presented to the people, setting the precedent for future Princes of Wales. Exhibitions include the regimental museum of the Royal Welch Fusiliers, and an impressive audio-visual display. Shop; usually cl 24–26 Dec, 1 Jan; (01286) 677617; £4.50. In the square outside, around the statue of former PM David Lloyd George, there's a busy Sat market.

Segontium Roman Fort & Museum (A4085) Roman fort dating from AD 78; excavations have exposed various rebuildings during its three centuries of importance, and a museum shows some of the finds. There's a tradition that Constantine the Great was born here (and the walls of the nearby castle used to be thought to be modelled partly on the walls of Constantinople). Shop; cl Sun am, 24–26 Dec, 1 Jan; (01286) 675625; free; Cadw.

235. Conwy, Edward I's military masterpiece

This cheerful old town is dominated by its castle, the key part of the town's elaborate defensive system – 21 (originally 22) towers linked by walls some 9 metres (30 ft) high, still the most complete town wall in Wales, with craggy old town gates. You can walk along some parts, looking down over the narrow little streets that still follow their medieval layout. The Castle Hotel is a civilised place for lunch.

Conwy Castle One of the best-known in Wales, and one of the most important examples of military architecture in the whole of Europe. Built for Edward I in 1283–89, it's very well preserved, still looking exactly as a medieval fortress should – despite the ravages of the Civil War and beyond. There's an exhibition on Edward and the other castles he built. The top of the turrets offer fine panoramic views; the most dramatic views of the castle itself are from the other side of the estuary. Shop; cl 24–26 Dec, 1 Jan; (01492) 592358; £3.50; Cadw.

236. A trio of unusual churches

Derwen church (off A494 a few miles N of Corwen) Interesting medieval building with an elaborately carved rood screen and loft, some old wall paintings, and an excellent Celtic cross in the churchyard. The Crown in Corwen has good value food.

Llangar old parish church (B4401 S) Built in the 13th c, with remarkable paintings of the seven deadly sins; it's visited from Rug chapel (and covered by the same ticket).

Rug chapel (1m N) 17th-c, not inspiring from the outside, but inside is a riot of colour, almost every available piece of woodwork covered with cheery patterns and paintwork. Cl Mon (exc bank hol wknds), Tues, Oct–Mar; nearby Llangar church is open 2–3pm on the same days; (029) 2082 6185; £2; Cadw.

237. Another of Edward I's mighty castles

Harlech Castle Splendid-looking structure built in 1283–89 by Edward I, its rugged glory the massive twin-towered gatehouse. It was starved into capitulation by Owain Glyndwr in 1404, and later dogged defence inspired the song 'Men of Harlech'. Before the sea retreated there was a sheer drop into the water on one side, but it now stands above dunes, with wonderful views of Snowdonia from the battlements. Shop; cl 24–26 Dec, 1 Jan; (01766) 780552; £3; Cadw. The riverside Victoria at Llanbedr does decent food. Some of the most sensationally remote scenery in Wales stretches inland from here, where a few tortuous roads wind past hill farms towards the splendidly isolated lake of **Llyn Cwm Bychan**.

238. Upstairs and downstairs in a splendid 17th-c house

Erddig (well signed S of Wrexham) Superb late 17th-c house, especially interesting for the way you can explore the life of the gentry and their servants equally as thoroughly; the gallery of servants' portraits is very touching. Enlarged and improved in the early 18th c, the house is filled with splendid original furnishings, inc a magnificent state bed in Chinese silk, and a butler's pantry with silver collection. Restored outbuildings include a laundry, bakehouse, estate smithy and sawmill, and the surrounding parkland is very pleasant to stroll through. It's one of the most attractive places to visit in all of Wales. Meals, snacks, shop, some disabled access; cl Thurs, Fri (open Good Fri), and Nov–Mar, house also cl am; (01978) 355314; *£6.60, *£3.40 garden and outbuildings; NT. The Cross Foxes at Overton Bridge, a few miles S, has good food.

HISTORIC PLACES TO STAY

Cheshire

CHESTER Castle House *23 Castle St, Chester CH1 2DS (01244) 350354* **£50***, plus special breaks; 5 comfortable rms, 3 with own bthrm. Small carefully preserved 16th-c guest house in the middle of the city, with helpful friendly owners, and fine breakfasts; dogs welcome in bedrooms

MACCLESFIELD Sutton Hall Hotel *Bullocks Lane, Sutton, Macclesfield, Cheshire SK11 0HE (01260) 253211* **£90**; 9 marvellous rms. Welcoming and secluded historic baronial hall, full of character, with stylish rooms, high black beams, stone fireplaces, suits of armour and so forth, friendly service, and good food; can arrange clay shooting/golf/fishing; dogs welcome in bedrooms

POTT SHRIGLEY Shrigley Hall *Shrigley Park, Pott Shrigley, Macclesfield, Cheshire SK10 5SB (01625) 575757* **£120**, plus special breaks; 150 smart well equipped rms, some with country views. In over 260 acres of parkland, this impressive country house has a splendid entrance hall with several elegant rooms leading off, enjoyable food in the orangery and restaurant, and good service from friendly staff; championship golf course, fishing, tennis, and leisure centre in former church building; plenty to do nearby; disabled access; dogs welcome in bedrooms

SANDBACH Old Hall *High St, Sandbach, Cheshire CW11 1AL (01270) 761221* **£70**, plus special breaks; 12 comfortable rms. Fine Jacobean timbered hotel with lots of original panelling and fireplaces, relaxing refurbished lounge, friendly welcome, and popular, newly refurbished restaurant; disabled access; dogs welcome

Cumbria

BASSENTHWAITE LAKE Armathwaite Hall Hotel *Bassenthwaite Lake, Keswick, Cumbria CA12 4RE (017687) 76551* **£180***; 42 rms. Turreted 17th-c mansion in 400 acres of deerpark and woodland; handsome public rooms with lovely fireplaces, fine panelling, antiques, paintings and fresh flowers, good French and English cooking, a super wine list, and helpful staff; snooker room, croquet, pitch-and-putt, tennis court, indoor swimming pool, gym and beauty salon, fishing and riding, archery and clay pigeon shooting, and jogging and mountain-bike tracks; disabled access

Derbyshire

BAKEWELL Hassop Hall *Hassop, Bakewell, Derbyshire DE45 1NS (01629) 640488* **£98.90**, plus winter breaks; 13 gracious rms. Mentioned in the Domesday Book, in lovely parkland surrounded by fine scenery, this handsome hotel has antiques and oil paintings, an elegant drawing room, oak-panelled bar, good food and friendly service; tennis; no accommodation 3 nights over Christmas; partial disabled access; dogs welcome in bedrooms

MATLOCK Riber Hall *Matlock, Derbyshire DE4 5JU (01629) 582795* **£136**, plus special breaks; 14 lovely beamed rms with antiques, chocolates, and baskets of fruit. Elizabethan manor house in pretty grounds surrounded by peaceful countryside, with antiques-filled heavily beamed rooms, fresh flowers, two elegant dining rooms with enjoyable food and fine wines, and tennis and clay pigeon shooting; children over 10; dogs welcome in bedrooms

SHIRLEY Shirley Hall Farm *Shirley, Ashbourne, Derbyshire DE6 3AS (01335) 360346* **£52**; 3 rms. Timbered and part-moated farmhouse on family-run dairy and arable farm, with homely sitting room, and good breakfasts with home-made bread, jam and marmalade, and local organic sausages; private coarse fishing and lots of walks; nearby pub for evening meals; self-catering cottages

Lincolnshire

STAMFORD George *71 St Martins, Stamford, Lincolnshire PE9 2LB (01780) 750700* **£105**, plus special breaks; 47 individually decorated rms. Ancient former coaching inn with a quietly civilised atmosphere, sturdy timbers, broad flagstones, heavy beams and massive stonework, and open log fires; good food in Garden Lounge, restaurant and courtyard (in summer), an excellent range of drinks inc very good value Italian wines, and welcoming staff; well kept walled garden and sunken croquet lawn; disabled access; dogs welcome in bedrooms

Northumbria

CAMBO Shieldhall *Wallington, Morpeth, Northumberland NE61 4AQ (01830) 540387* **£60**; 4 well equipped suites, each with its own entrance. 18th-c stone house and carefully converted farm buildings around a courtyard, with antiques and other interesting furnishings (Mr Robinson-Gay is a fine cabinet-maker), a library, bar, and cosy lounge with French windows opening on to the neatly kept big garden; enjoyable freshly produced food in candlelit beamed dining room; cl Christmas and New Year; children over 12

Shropshire

KNOCKIN Top Farmhouse *Knockin, Oswestry, Shropshire SY10 8HN (01691) 682582* **£48***; 3 pretty rms. Most attractive Grade I listed black and white timbered house dating back to the 16th c, with friendly owners, lots of timbers and beams, a log fire in the restful comfortable drawing room, good breakfasts in the large dining room, and an appealing garden; grand piano; children over 12; dogs welcome away from dining room

SHREWSBURY Fitz Manor *Fitz, Bowmere Heath, Shrewsbury, Shropshire SY4 3AS (01743) 850295* **£60***; 3 rms, shared bthrm. Lovely black and white timbered 15th-c manor house with oak panelling and log fire in comfortable sitting room, a big dining room with antiques, paintings and parquet flooring, good evening meals, big breakfasts, and friendly owners; outdoor heated swimming pool

WESTON Citadel *Weston, Shrewsbury, Shropshire SY4 5JY* (01630) 685204 **£90**; 3 rms in twin turrets. Fine castellated house overlooking Hawkstone Park, with country-house atmosphere, baby grand piano and unusual strapwork ceiling in the elegant sitting room, full-sized table in snooker room, enjoyable food (bring your own wine) in no smoking dining room, and welcoming owners; cl Christmas and Easter; children over 12

West & South Yorkshire
MONK FRYSTON Monk Fryston Hall *Main St, Monk Fryston, Leeds, West Yorkshire LS25 5DU* (01977) 682369 **£109**, plus wknd and special breaks; 30 comfortable, recently refurbished rms. Benedictine manor house in 30 acres of secluded gardens with lake and woodland, an oak-panelled lounge and bar with log fires, antiques, paintings and fresh flowers, good honest food, and friendly helpful staff; disabled access; dogs welcome away from restaurant

North Wales
TALSARNAU Maes-y-Neuadd *Talsarnau, Gwynedd LL47 6YA* (01766) 780200 **£143*** inc 4-course dinner, plus special breaks; 16 luxurious rms. Looking out across Snowdonia, this attractive extended 14th-c mansion stands in eight acres of landscaped hillside; flowers, plants, antiques and open fires, peaceful atmosphere, very good food (herbs and vegetables from their own garden), friendly cats, and charming staff; disabled access; dogs welcome in bedrooms

Scotland

Including South, West, East and North Scotland

◆ ◆ ◆

239. A majestic island castle and garden

The rewarding **Isle of Arran** is just under an hour by ferry from Ardrossan, a popular public-transport day trip from Glasgow, with summer ferries from Claonaig on Kintyre too; (01475) 650100 for ferry enquiries. It has a marvellous variety of scenery from subtropical gardens to mountain deer forest. Brodick, the main settlement, has several places to hire bikes. The Kingsley on Brodick esplanade has decent home cooking, and the Brodick Bar (Alma Rd) is simple good value. On the opposite side of the island nr Machrie are several intriguing Bronze Age stone circles. Arran has a good circular walk up and down Goatfell, prominent for miles around, and you can follow the shore right around the N tip, the Cock of Arran. Up near here the waterside Catacol Hotel has decent food. There's a good walk on the W coast, from Blackwaterfoot to the King's Cave, which supposedly sheltered Robert the Bruce.

Brodick Castle and Garden Fine old castle, in lovely surroundings between the sea, hills and majestic mountain of Goatfell. Partly 13th-c, and extended in 1652 and 1844, it's very fierce-looking from the outside, but comfortably grand inside – even a little homely in places. Magnificent formal gardens, the highlight being the woodland garden started in 1923 by the Duchess of Montrose, inc many lovely rare and tender rhododendrons. Adventure playground, plants for sale, meals, snacks, shop, limited disabled access; castle cl Nov–Mar, garden and country park open all year; (01770) 302202; £7; NTS.

240. One of Britain's most glorious stately homes

Culzean Castle (Culzean – pronounced 'Cullane') The 18th-c mansion is one of great presence and brilliance, and the grounds (nearly a square mile) are among the finest in Britain, lushly planted and richly ornamental, with woods, lake, an abundance of paths, bracing clifftop and shoreline walks, and an 18th-c walled garden. The house was splendidly refashioned by Robert Adam, and has been well restored to show off his work to full effect. Meals, snacks, shop, disabled access; house open Apr–Oct, and possibly some winter wknds, park open all year; (01655) 884455; £9; NTS. You can stay in rather smart self-contained apartments on the top floor.

241. Edinburgh, Queen of the North

Edinburgh is one of Britain's most rewarding cities for visitors; there are lots of interesting places within a pleasant walk of each other. It's dominated by the ancient silhouettes of Edinburgh Castle on its castle cliff and of the long erratic line of tall, thin Old Town buildings stretched along beside it. Up here narrow streets and alleys with steep steps between them and courtyard closes leading off the **Royal Mile** have a real flavour of the distant past, with a good many interesting ancient buildings inc antiquarian bookshops and other interesting specialist shops. When the authorities decided to redevelop the city in the 18th c, they did it not by knocking down the medieval buildings, but instead by creating an entirely new part of the city. The resulting New Town is a masterpiece of spacious Georgian town planning, stretching out handsomely below the steep crag of Castle Rock and its medieval skyline. Walking tours in the evenings are often led by students, and the literary pub tour is particularly good fun; (0131) 226 6665; £7. New Town highlights are Charlotte Square, Moray Place, Ainslie Place and Randolph Crescent. The regular bus services have good value daily and weekly passes, and it is worth getting used to the public transport (the city council has plans, unpopular with residents, for a car toll). As in most cities, there's a hop-on hop-off tour bus, and the ticket gives discounts to some of the places to visit. The August Festival has great music and dance and a fun Fringe. If you plan to visit the Festival, make sure you've got accommodation sorted out well in advance. Edinburgh's pubs and bars are a special delight; among the best for atmosphere are the Bow Bar (Victoria St), Bannermans Bar (Cowgate), Bennets Bar (Leven St), Café Royal and Guildford Arms (both W Register St), Cumberland (Cumberland St), Athletic Arms (Angle Park Terrace/Kilmarnock Rd) and Kays Bar (Jamaica St W). For food, we recommend the Abbotsford, Kenilworth and Milnes (all Rose St), Dome (George St), Starbank (Laverockbank Rd), Braidwoods (West Port) and both Fishers and Ship on the Shore (The Shore, Leith). The corner lobby bar of the Balmoral Hotel is a relaxing spot at the hub of the town. For a fuller meal, the city has a remarkable number of good value bistro-style restaurants. There are lots of good shops dotted around town, especially on or near Princes St – its tall, mainly Georgian buildings lining just the one side, giving an expansive view across the sunken gardens to the castle. Parallel George St has some superior shops, while Rose St, an alley between the two, has plenty of pubs and cafés. More bars around the Grassmarket and Lawnmarket, in the Old Town.

Edinburgh Castle A place of great magnetism, it's been a fortress since at least the 7th c, and excavations show there's been a settlement here for 4,000 years. The oldest building today is the beautiful St Margaret's Chapel, thought to have been built in the 12th c and little changed since. Other highlights include the apartments of Mary, Queen of Scots, Mons Meg (the 15th-c Belgian cannon with which James II cowed the Black Douglases), the Scottish Crown Jewels (centuries older than the English ones), and for romantics the Stone of Destiny or Scottish coronation stone. Glorious views from the battlements, over the Firth of Forth to Fife beyond. You can wander around on your own, but the official guides are a great bonus – they leave from the drawbridge, several times a day. Meals, snacks, shop, mostly disabled access; cl 25–26 Dec; (0131) 225 9846; £8.50 (inc audio tour); HS. If you're around at lunchtime, look (and listen) for the firing of the One o' Clock Gun from the parapet.

Palace of Holyroodhouse (Canongate) Imposing yet human-scale palace with its origins in the Abbey of Holyrood, founded by David I. Later the court of Mary Queen of Scots, it was used by Bonnie Prince Charlie during his occupation of Edinburgh, and is still a Royal residence for part of the year. The oldest surviving part is James IV's tower, with Queen Mary's rooms on the second floor, where a plaque on the floor marks where her secretary Rizzio was murdered in front of her. The throne room and state rooms have period furniture, tapestries and paintings from the Royal collection. Much more inviting than many English palaces. Shop, limited disabled access by prior arrangement; cl Good Fri, 25–26 Dec, and occasional other dates (if the Queen is in residence, for example) – best to check on (0131) 556 7371; £6.50.

Royal Mile Between castle and palace at the heart of the Old Town stretches this largely medieval street, around which you'll find all sorts of interesting or historic houses and features, and quaint lanes leading off in all directions. The next four places (down to John Knox House) are listed in order, as you go down the Mile towards Holyrood. Usefully, it's punctuated with cafés and bars in which to stop and work out your next move, starting with the old-world Ensign Ewart on the left as you leave the castle.

Lady Stair's House (Lady Stair's Cl, off Lawnmarket) Named after its 18th-c occupant, this partly 1622 building houses the **Writers Museum**, a collection of manuscripts and objects associated with Robert Burns, Walter Scott and R L Stevenson. Shop; cl Sun exc pm during Festival, 25–26 Dec, 1–2 Jan; (0131) 529 4901; free.

St Giles Cathedral (High St) Scotland's High Kirk, the city's most impressive ecclesiastical building, mainly 15th c, but dating from around 1120. Topped with an ornate crown-like tower, it has monuments to famous Scots from Knox (minister here until his death) to R L Stevenson; cl am Sun, 26 Dec, 1–2 Jan; guided tours; free (donations welcome).

Parliament House (Parliament Sq) Just behind the cathedral, this was the seat of Scottish government until the Union of 1707, and now houses the supreme law courts of Scotland. Don't miss the fine hammerbeam roof in the hall. Snacks, some disabled access; cl wknds and public holidays; (0131) 225 2595; free.

John Knox House (High St) The oldest house on the Royal Mile, where the great reformer is supposed to have died. Now looking every bit of its 500 years, it still has its original timber galleries, oak panelling and splendid painted ceiling. Snacks, shop, disabled access to ground floor; cl Sun (exc July–Aug), 25–26 Dec, possibly closing from March 2003 for refurbishment, so best to check; (0131) 556 9579; *£2.25.

Scott Memorial (Princes St) After the castle, probably Edinburgh's most memorable landmark remarkably ornate, with its handsome if mucky exterior (they've kept the dirt, as cleaning seemed more damaging). The crypt of the very handsome Gothic-revival St John's episcopal church on Princes St has interesting vegetarian and vegan food.

242. Scotland's biggest inhabited house

Floors Castle (Im NW of Kelso) Magnificent building designed by William Adam in 1721, and much embellished in the next century. It's reputed to be Scotland's biggest inhabited house, with a window for every day of the year. Splendid collection of tapestries and french furniture, and wonderful walled garden (best July–Sept). Good home-made meals and snacks, shop, disabled access; cl end Oct–Easter; (01573) 223333; £5.50.

243. Where Mary, Queen of Scots was born

Linlithgow Palace The birthplace of Mary, Queen of Scots, a magnificently sombre lochside ruin. You can still see the chapel, great hall and a quadrangle with an impressive fountain. Shop, limited disabled access, cl 25–26 Dec and 1–2 Jan; (01506) 842896; £2.80; HS. In the town a pleasant old tavern, the Four Marys, is named for her maids-in-waiting Mary Carmichael, Mary Hamilton, Mary Beaton and Mary Seaton, and contains relevant memorabilia.

House of the Binns (3m E, off A904) The home of the Dalyell family since 1612, with some splendid plaster ceilings and a fine collection of furniture and porcelain. Limited disabled access; cl am, all day Fri, and Oct–end Apr; (01506) 834255; £5; NTS.

244. The heart of Robert the Bruce, and Rob Roy's sporran

Melrose Abbey The ruins are among the finest in the country – best in moonlight, as Sir Walter Scott said (though he admitted he never saw them thus himself). Look out for the wonderful stonework on the 14th-c nave (and the pig playing the bagpipes).

Archaeological investigations now leave little doubt that this was the burial place of Robert the Bruce's heart. Shop; limited disabled access; cl Sun am Oct–Mar, 25–26 Dec, 1–2 Jan; (01896) 822562; £3.30; HS.

Abbotsford House (B6360 3m W) Set grandly on the River Tweed, this was the home of Sir Walter Scott until his death in 1832. You can still see his mammoth 9,000-volume library, and several of the historical oddities he liked to collect, like Rob Roy's sporran. Snacks, shop, disabled access; cl Sun am (Mar–May and Oct), plus Nov to mid-Mar; (01896) 752043; £4.

245. Factory work in past centuries

New Lanark (off A73) Now a UNESCO World Heritage site, this is Scotland's best example of an industrial village (founded in 1785), with plenty to keep families amused for a good chunk of the day. Many of the old millworkers' buildings (showing living conditions of the 1820s and 1930s) have been interestingly converted to modern accommodation, so it's very much a living village rather than a museum. The village store has an exhibition about Robert Owen's original store, and his house contains an exhibition on his work; there's also a hotel in a renovated 18th-c cotton mill (01555) 667200. The village can be busy at wknds; try to visit during the week if you can. There's a time travel ride at the visitor centre. Meals, snacks, shop, disabled access; cl before 11am, 25 Dec, 1 Jan; £4.95. In Lanark itself the Crown (Hope St) has a decent restaurant.

246. Scotland's oldest and most romantic house

Traquair House (Traquair, B709) No fewer than 27 English and Scottish kings have stayed here. The Bear Gates have remained closed since 1745 when Bonnie Prince Charlie passed through them for the last time – they won't open again unless the Stewarts regain their place on the throne. An 18th-c brewery still produces tasty beers (£4 for tastings, phone to book), and there's a brewery museum (and shop). Traquair is particularly popular with our contributors, and with a maze, new adventure playground, and antiques and craft shops as well as the house and gardens, there's plenty to see. Meals, snacks, shop, some disabled access; cl Jan–Mar and Nov–Dec (exc for pre-booked parties); (01896) 830323; £5.60, £2.50 grounds only.

247. A communal township

Auchindrain Township Museum (Auchindrain, A83) The only communal tenancy township to have remained on its ancient site much in its original form. All the buildings have been excellently restored and simply furnished in period style, so you get a real feeling of stepping back into the past. Shop; cl Oct–Mar; (01499) 500235; *£3.80.

248. A house of great influence

Hill House (Upper Colquhoun St, Helensburgh) In an area short of many great houses, this is a wonderful example of the work of Charles Rennie Mackintosh, the architect who laid the foundations for uncluttered modern design; there's an exhibition on his life, and the gardens have been restored to reflect features common to the architect's designs. Teas, shop; cl am, and all day Nov–Mar; (01436) 673900; *£7; NTS – it's one of their busier properties.

249. Two of Stirling's gems

Strategically placed on the Firth of Forth, **Stirling** has just been granted city status.

Stirling Castle Provides magnificent views from its lofty hilltop site. It became very popular with the Royal Family in the 15th and 16th c, and most of the buildings date from that period. It's great fun to visit, from the flame-lit medieval kitchen to the splendid Chapel Royal built by James VI (and I of England), and the Great Hall of James V's Renaissance palace. A huge new hammerbeam roof has been crafted here from 350 oak trees, and the restoration of the castle's lavish early 16th-c furnishings continues with on-site tapestry weaving. Snacks, shop; cl 25–26 Dec; (01786) 450000; £7, £2 parking; HS. There's a good visitor centre in a restored building next door, and Whistlebinkies (St Mary's Wynd), formerly part of the ancient castle stables, has decent food.

250. A great house with a private army

Blair Castle (Blair Atholl, off A9) Nestling among forests and heather-clad hills, this is Scotland's most-visited privately owned house, dating back to the 13th c, though largely renovated in the 18th. You can see 30 rooms, and there's an 18th-c walled garden. A display charts the history of the Atholl Highlanders – the Duke of Atholl's unique private army that turns out here for its annual parade in May. A piper outside most days in summer adds to the atmosphere. Meals, snacks, shop, disabled access to ground floor only; cl end Oct–beginning Apr (limited winter opening hours); (01796) 481207; *£6.50, £2 for grounds only. The Atholl Arms has good value food all day.

251. A picture-book castle

Craigievar Castle (Craigievar, A980) Perhaps the most fairytale-romantic of the area's castles, this picturesque early 17th-c multiple tower dotted with erratically shaped windows soars to a mushrooming of corbels, turrets and crow-stepped gables. Inside, a warren of narrow staircases climbs through a rich series of ornately beamed and plastered rooms. The NTS are worried that too many people come here, so if you do decide to visit (and it is worth while), try to avoid busy times – it's not a place to absorb coach parties comfortably. Castle open pm only Apr–Sept, grounds open all year; (013398) 83635; £6.50; NTS.

252. Grand mansion and ruined fortress

Haddo House (Tarves, off B999) Wonderfully grand yet still very much a family home; designed by William Adam, and refurbished in the 1880s in the Adam Revival style, with fine furniture and art throughout. The chapel (regular services) has stained glass by Burne-Jones; both the house and adjacent hall host concerts and events throughout the year, (01651) 851770 for details. House open July–Aug only, shop cl Nov–Mar (01651) 851440; £7; NTS. Charming terrace garden leads into 200-acre country park with waymarked trails, wildlife hides, visitor centre and events; (011651) 851489; free; Aberdeenshire Council. Tearooms serving light lunches and snacks; two shops with estate produce, crafts, gifts and souvenirs; children's play areas. The Redgarth down in Oldmeldrum has decent food and gorgeous views to Bennachie.

253. Two formidable castles

Delgatie Castle (Turriff) Dating from 1050 – but like most Scottish castles rebuilt in the 16th c when the invention of siege guns demanded greater fortification – some walls are up to 4 metres (14 ft) or more thick. There are fine 16th-c painted ceilings, an unusual turnpike stair built into a wall, and a bedchamber where Mary, Queen of Scots spent three nights; displays on the Clan Hay. Excellent tearoom, shop; cl Nov–Mar; (01888) 563479; £3. You can stay here too.

Fyvie Castle (off A947) Each of the five towers of this magnificent castle was built in a different century by the family that lived here throughout; the oldest parts date back to the 13th c, and the whole building is one of the most fantastic examples of Scottish baronial architecture. Collections of armour and tapestry, and paintings by Raeburn, Romney and Gainsborough. Snacks, shop; cl am and Thurs, Fri mid-season, cl Nov–Easter; (01651) 891266; £7; NTS. The Towie Tavern does good food.

254. Scotland's defeat, and Macbeth too

Culloden Battlefield (B9006) The bleak site of the gruesome massacre in which the 25-year-old Duke of Cumberland destroyed the Highland army of Bonnie Prince Charlie. On the moor a cairn marks this last bloody battle fought on mainland Britain. You can see the Graves of the Clans and the Wells of the Dead, as well as the Old Leanach Cottage around which the battle was fought, refurbished in period style. Meals, snacks, shop, disabled access; visitor centre cl 24–26 Dec, and first 2 wks in Jan; (01463) 790607; £5; NTS. The Snow Goose (E of A9/A96) does good food.

Cawdor Castle (B9090, Cawdor) Home of the Thanes of Cawdor since the 14th c. Look out for the tree inside a tower and the freshwater well inside the house, as well as the more usual fine tapestries, furnishings and paintings (inc Dali's odd interpretation of the Macbeth tale). The grounds have several pretty gardens, craft and wool shops, nature trails, and a 9-hole golf course. Meals, snacks, shop, disabled access to ground floor only; cl mid-Oct to end Apr; (01667) 404615; £6.30, £3.20 grounds only. The nearby Cawdor Tavern is good for lunch.

255. Sea views from one of Scotland's grandest homes

Dunrobin Castle (Golspie, A9) Splendid castle – a gleaming elegantly turreted structure with views out to sea and gardens modelled on those at Versailles. The family home of the Earls and Dukes of Sutherland for longer than anyone can remember, the site was named after Earl Robin in the 13th c; he was responsible for the original square keep. Drastically renovated and enlarged to cope with a hugely bigger family in the 19th c, it has fine collections of furnishings and art, and a unique collection of Pictish stones; falconry. Snacks, shop; cl Sun am, and 16 Oct–31 Mar, gardens open all year; (01408) 633177; £6.25. The Sutherland Arms has reasonably priced food.

256. The castle home of the Lord of the Isles

Dunvegan Castle (Isle of Skye) On the sea loch of Dunvegan, home of the Chiefs of Macleod for 800 years; no other Scottish castle has been inhabited by the same family for so long. Among its relics is a lock of Bonnie Prince Charlie's hair. Staying here inspired Walter Scott's *Lord of the Isles*. Good meals and snacks at the Macleod's Table family restaurant. Shops; open daily, cl 25–26 Dec, 1–2 Jan ; (01470) 521206; £6, £4 gardens only.

After Lewis, **Skye** is the biggest of the islands off the Scottish coast, now linked to the mainland by a bridge, though the easier access doesn't seem to have spoilt the island's special air of romance. The coasts have plenty of opportunities for gentle pottering, and for finding quiet coves and bays, particulary on the W coast, where for instance Tarskavaig, or the good Stein Inn in the N, are lovely spots to watch the sun go down. The jagged teeth of the Cuillins mountain range to the SE of the centre are unforgettable. Places doing decent food include the Fig Tree at Broadford, Misty Isle at Dunvegan, Sligachan Inn (A850/A863 in the middle of the island), Flodigarry Hotel nr Staffin (stunning views from this turreted mansion with Flora MacDonald connections), Ardvasar Hotel, Struan Grill at Struan and the waterside Old Inn at Carbost (handy for the Talisker distillery, which can be visited; (01478) 614306).

HISTORIC PLACES TO STAY

South Scotland

BEATTOCK Auchen Castle *Beattock, Moffat, Dumfriesshire DG10 9SH (01683) 300407* **£95**; 25 pleasantly decorated rms, most with own bthrms, some in Lodge. Smart but friendly country-house hotel in lovely quiet spot with a trout loch and spectacular hill views, good food, and peaceful comfortable bar; dogs welcome in bedrooms

CLARENCEFIELD Comlongon Castle *Clarencefield, Dumfries DG1 4NA (01387) 870283* **£110**; 12 rms. Magnificent 15th-c castle keep with 18th-c mansion house adjoining – suits of armour and a huge fireplace in oak-panelled great hall, good food in Jacobean dining room, and a relaxing drawing room; dungeons, battlements, archers' quarters and haunted long gallery; cl first 2 wks Jan

QUOTHQUAN Shieldhill *Quothquan, Biggar, Lanarkshire ML12*

6NA *(01899) 220035* **£160**, plus special breaks; 16 pretty rms. Partly 12th-c castle in fine setting with comfortable oak-panelled lounge, open fires, library, particularly good food in no smoking restaurant, and warm friendly service; disabled access

UPHALL Houstoun House *Uphall, Broxburn, West Lothian EH52 6JS (01506) 853831* **£125**, plus wknd breaks; 72 comfortable rms, quite a few in extension. 17th-c house divided into three distinct buildings: fine food in three panelled dining rooms, vaulted bars (one with a fire nearly all year), quiet lounge, lovely grounds, and leisure complex with swimming pool, sauna, gym, tennis courts and Italian bistro; disabled access

West Scotland

BALLACHULISH Ballachulish House *Ballachulish, Argyll PA39 4JX (01855) 811266* **£120***, plus special breaks; 8 rms with views. Remote 17th-c house with a friendly atmosphere, elegant rooms, log fires, honesty bar, hearty helpings of good food using local fish and beef, and walled garden, croquet lawn; children over 10

TARBERT Stonefield Castle *Stonefield, Tarbert, Argyll PA29 6YJ (01880) 820836* **£170** inc dinner, plus special breaks; 33 rms. With wonderful views and surrounding wooded grounds, this Scottish baronial mansion has comfortable public rooms and decent restaurant food; snooker room; dogs welcome in bedrooms

East Scotland

BALLATER Auld Kirk *31 Braemar Rd, Ballater, Aberdeenshire AB35 5RQ (01339) 755762* **£60**, plus winter breaks; 7 attractive rms, inc 2 family rms. 19th-c church converted to a hotel in 1990, still with bell tower, stained glass and exposed rafters; original pillared pine ceiling in newly refurbished restaurant, other public rooms with homely décor; cl 25–27 Dec, 1–4 Jan; dogs welcome in bedrooms

BALQUHIDDER Monachyle Mhor *Balquhidder, Lochearnhead, Perthshire FK19 8PQ (01877) 384622* **£85***; 10 rms with fine views overlooking Voil and Doine lochs, some newly redecorated. Remote 18th-c farmhouse/hotel six miles W of Balquhidder on 2,000-acre estate with prettily furnished rooms and good food using own game, cured meats and herbs; private fishing and stalking for guests; children over 12; cl Jan

EAST HAUGH East Haugh House *East Haugh, Pitlochry, Tayside PH16 5TE (01796) 473121* **£100*** inc dinner, plus special breaks; 12 rms, 5 in converted bothy, some with four-posters and one with open fire. Turreted stone house with lots of character, delightful conservatory bar, house-party atmosphere and very good food inc local seafood and game in season cooked by chef/proprietor; excellent shooting, stalking and salmon and trout fishing on surrounding local estates; cl 20–27 Dec; disabled access to one room; dogs welcome in bedrooms

FINTRY Culcreuch Castle *Fintry, Glasgow G63 0LW (01360) 860228* **£124***, plus special breaks; 13 individually decorated rms with lovely views. Central Scotland's oldest inhabited castle, nearly 700 years old, in beautiful 1,600-acre parkland and surrounding hills and moors, with log fires and antiques in the public rooms, good freshly prepared food in candlelit panelled dining room, and a friendly relaxed atmosphere, play area; 8 modern Scandinavian holiday lodges, too; disabled access; dogs by arrangement

North Scotland

GARVE Inchbae Lodge *Garve, Ross-shire IV23 2PH (01997) 455269* **£70***, plus special breaks; 15 rms, some in chalet. Former hunting lodge in lovely Highland setting with comfortable homely lounges, winter log fires, small bar (liked by locals), and good fixed-price evening meals using fresh local produce; lots of wildlife, marvellous walks; cl Christmas; disabled access; dogs welcome

GLENELG Glenelg Inn *Kirkton, Glenelg, Kyle, Ross-shire IV40 8JR* (01599) 522273 **£120*** inc dinner, plus special breaks; 6 individually decorated and comfortable rms, all with fine views. Overlooking Skye across its own beach, this carefully refurbished homely hotel has a relaxed bar, comfortable sofas and blazing fires, friendly staff and locals, good food using local venison, local hill-bred lamb and lots of wonderfully fresh fish and seafood, and quite a few whiskies; the drive to the inn involves spectacular views from the steep road (and the pretty drive to Glen Beag broch is nice); open in winter if pre-booked; disabled access; dogs welcome away from dining room

ISLE ORNSAY Kinloch Lodge *Isle Ornsay, Isle of Skye IV43 8QY* (01471) 833214 **£150**, plus winter breaks; 14 rms. Surrounded by rugged mountain scenery at the head of Loch Na Dal, this charming white stone hotel has a relaxed atmosphere in its comfortable and attractive drawing rooms, antiques, portraits, flowers, log fires, and good imaginative food; cookery demonstrations; children by arrangement; cl 22–27 Dec; dogs welcome in bedrooms

POOLEWE Pool House *Poolewe, Achnasheen, Ross-shire IV22 2LE* (01445) 781272 **£240**; 5 beautifully themed suites with remarkable Edwardian and Victorian baths 2½ metres (over 8 ft) tall inc canopied showers. On the shore by the River Ewe, this early 18th-c hotel, remodelled in the 19th c by the founder of Inverewe Gardens and recently refurbished, has original panelling, fine doors and friezes uncovered; restful drawing room with open fire, fine antiques and sea views, delicious food with an emphasis on local seafood; plenty of walks and wildlife; cl Jan–Feb, parts of Dec

SKEABOST Skeabost Country House *Skeabost Bridge, Portree, Isle of Skye IV51 9NR* (01470) 532202 **£105***, plus special breaks; 19 rms, 4 in annexe in Garden House. Smart and friendly little hotel in 29 acres of landscaped grounds on the shores of Loch

Snizort; 9-hole 18-tee golf course and 8 miles of salmon and trout fishing; log fires, comfortable day rooms, friendly, helpful staff, and good, enjoyable food; disabled access; dogs by arrangement

TORRIDON Loch Torridon Hotel *Torridon, Achnasheen, Ross-shire IV22 2EY (01445) 791242* **£132***, plus special breaks; 20 comfortable rms. Built in 1887 as a shooting lodge in 58 acres at the foot of Ben Damph by Upper Loch Torridon, this turreted stone house has unusual ornate ceilings and panelling, log fires and innovative cooking; they also run the Ben Damph Lodge nearby; cl Jan; children over 10 in dining room; disabled access; dogs welcome in bedrooms

MAPS

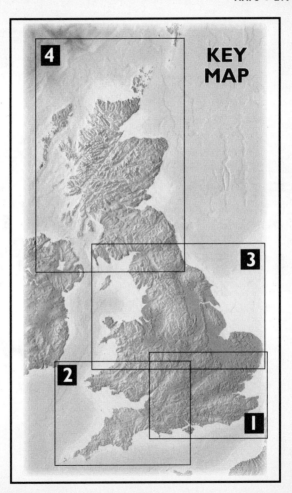

KEY
MAP

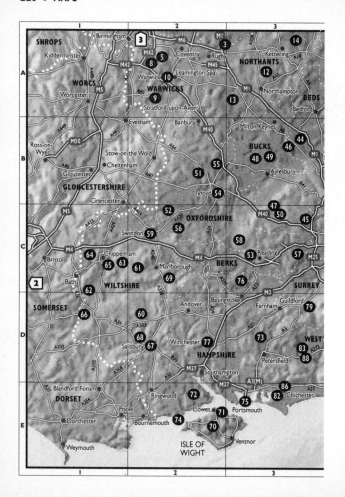

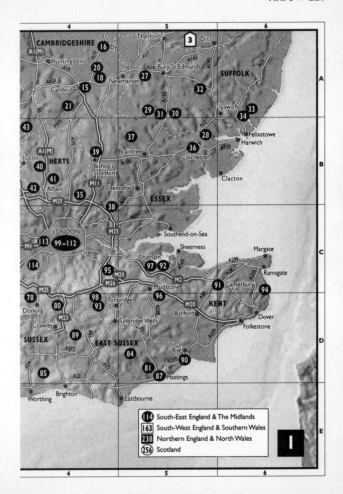

South-East England & The Midlands
South-West England & Southern Wales
Northern England & North Wales
Scotland

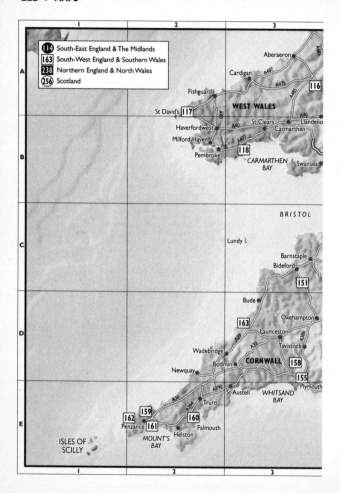

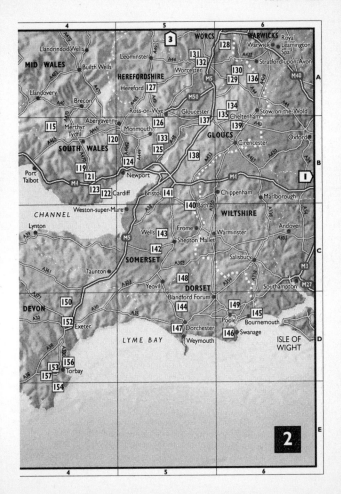

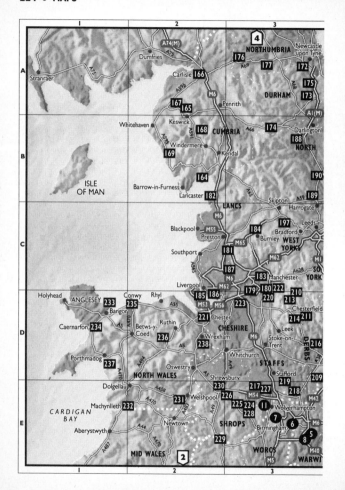

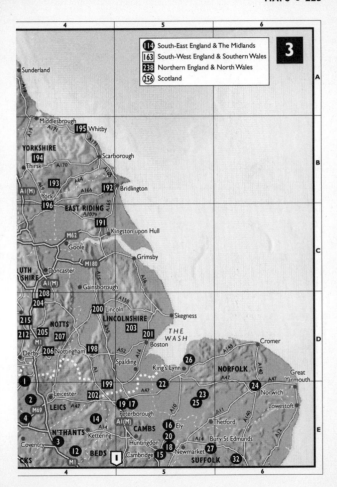

3

- **114** South-East England & The Midlands
- **163** South-West England & Southern Wales
- **238** Northern England & North Wales
- **256** Scotland

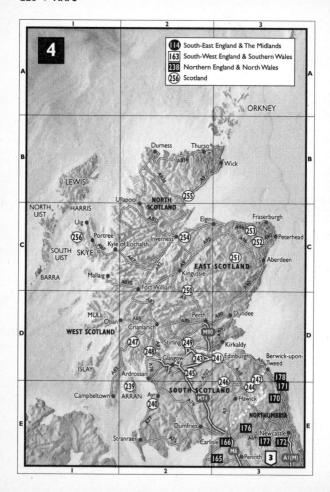

4

114 South-East England & The Midlands
163 South-West England & Southern Wales
238 Northern England & North Wales
256 Scotland

ORKNEY

Durness Thurso
A836 Wick
255

LEWIS

Ullapool **NORTH SCOTLAND**

NORTH UIST HARRIS
Uig Elgin Fraserburgh
256 Portree A96 253
Kyle of Lochalsh Inverness 254 Peterhead
SOUTH SKYE 252
UIST 251 Aberdeen
EAST SCOTLAND
BARRA Mallaig Kingussie
Fort William 250

MULL Perth Dundee
Oban Crianlarich
WEST SCOTLAND M90
247 Stirling 249 Kirkaldy
248 Glasgow 243 241 Edinburgh Berwick-upon-Tweed
245 178
ISLAY Ardrossan 246 242 171
239 244 170
Campbeltown ARRAN Ayr **SOUTH SCOTLAND** Hawick
240 M74 **NORTHUMBRIA**

176 E
Dumfries Newcastle
Stranraer 166 177 172
Carlisle A69
165 M6 3 A1(M)
Penrith

All Ebury titles are available in good bookshops or via mail order

TO ORDER
(please tick)

Pocket Good Guide to Great Food Pubs	£5.99
Pocket Good Guide to Great Family Days Out	£5.99
Pocket Good Guide to The Best Dog Friendly Pubs, Hotels and B&Bs	£5.99
The Good Pub Guide	£14.99
The Good Britain Guide	£14.99
The Good Hotel Guide to UK and Ireland	£15.99
The Good Hotel Guide to Continental Europe	£16.99

PAYMENT MAY BE MADE USING ACCESS, VISA, MASTERCARD, DINERS CLUB, SWITCH AND AMEX OR CHEQUE, EUROCHEQUE AND POSTAL ORDER (STERLING ONLY)

CARD NUMBER:

EXPIRY DATE:............   SWITCH ISSUE NO:.................

SIGNATURE:...

PLASE ALLOW £2.50 FOR POST AND PACKAGING FOR THE FIRST BOOK AND £1.00 THEREAFTER

ORDER TOTAL: £   (INC P&P)

ALL ORDERS TO:

EBURY PRESS, BOOKS BY POST, TBS LIMITED, COLCHESTER ROAD, FRATING GREEN, COLCHESTER, ESSEX CO7 7DW, UK

TELEHONE: 01206 256 000
FAX: 01206 255 914

NAME:

ADDRESS:

Please allow 28 days for delivery. Please tick box if you do not wish to receive any additional information

Prices and availability subject to change without notice.